CONTRACT KILLER

Also by William Hoffman

David: Report on a Rockefeller
Unholy Matrimony
French Quarter Killers
Blood Warning
The Dungeon Master
Deadly Weekend
Hearing the Noise
Fantasy
Texas: A Year with the Boys
Paul Mellon: Portrait of an Oil Baron
The Stockholder
Texas Thunder

and with Lake Headley

The Court-Martial of Clayton Lonetree
Loud and Clear

CONTRACT KILLER

The Explosive Story of the Mafia's Most Notorious Hit Man Donald "Tony the Greek" Frankos

as told to

WILLIAM HOFFMAN AND
LAKE HEADLEY

THUNDER'S MOUTH PRESS
NEW YORK

First edition
First printing, 1992
Published by
Thunder's Mouth Press
54 Greene Street, Suite 4S
New York, NY 10013

LIBRARY OF CONGRESS CATALOGING IN PUBLICATION DATA
Hoffman, William, 1937-
Contract killer : the explosive story of the Mafia's most
notorious hit man—Donald "Tony the Greek" Frankos / William Hoffman,
Lake Headley. — 1st ed.
p. cm.
Includes index.
ISBN 1-56025-045-3 :
1. Frankos, Donald. 2. Murderers—United States—Biography.
3. Mafia—United States. I. Headley, Lake. II. Title.
HV6248.F672H64 1992
364.1'523'092—dc20 92-18539 CIP
[B]

Designed by Fritz Metsch
Set in Bembo
Manufactured in the United States of America

Distributed by Publishers Group West
4065 Hollis Street
Emeryville, CA 94608
(800) 788-3123

To Alice Pohl, who was by my side through the bad times and the good.

—D.F.

To my son Lake III. Without him I never would have survived this past year nor have seen this book completed. His constant care gave me the strength to go forward. —L.H.

To Judy Hoffman, who never stopped believing in this book, and to Neil Ortenberg, whose uncommon courage made its publication possible.

—W.H.

Acknowledgments

William Helmer of *Playboy* provided strength and encouragement during my long stretches in solitary. Neil Ortenberg of Thunder's Mouth Press had the courage to publish my story. I'm grateful to attorney Mary Jo White, who tried to provide protection against the "Dream Merchants" the Justice Department sent to debrief me. Also deserving of thanks are Judy Hoffman; Alicia, Micah, and Ethan Lewis; Joe Hoffman; Peter, Andrew, Dawn, Mary, and P.J. Pohl; Karen Noahr Lamont; Lake Headley III; Yvette Delkos; my great-uncle James Frangos; Georgia Frangos; Alice S. Frangos; my niece Gina Monogious; and my stepmother, Hope Sacoulas Frangos, who tried with all of her heart. —D.F.

The counsel and encouragement of attorney and friend Michael V. Stuhff helped bring this book about. Terri Lee Headley cared enough to do the shopping, cooking, and cleaning, and looked after all of us. My days were brightened by my son Rod, his wife Tammy, and my grandson Matthew. Margie, Kathy, and Michael Stirling provided needed and greatly appreciated support. My son Anthony visited frequently and gave us warmth, comfort, and much-needed laughter.

Finally, to the hundreds of friends who said "I love you" at just the right time. —L.H.

Bill Stack, Jerry and Jane Shields, Mike and Fred Stuhff, and Bill and Thelma Taylor provided critical support. Donald Freed steered me in the perfect direction. John and Anita Reeves, as always, were there when we most needed them. Charles, Betty, and Rudy Ced, and Bill Dear, read the book-in-progress. Special thanks go to Marty Reisman, editor par excellence, William II, Terri, and John Hoffman; to Kasha and her mother Lisa; to Jim Gosdin, Birdie Segrest and Jason Sorrell; and to Julio Escalante and my grandchild-to-be, James Patrick. Attorney David Lubell was a tower of strength. Marian Cole brought the first hint of good news I'd received in a long time. Reuben Burton kept the car running. Finally, to Lake Headley, so the whole world knows: I love you, my friend.

—W.H.

Contents

Cast of Characters

Abbamonte, Oreste ("Ernie Boy"): Drug dealer and Gambino family associate. Sentenced in "Pleasant Avenue Connection" case in 1976 to eight years for heroin trafficking.

Agron, Salvador ("The Cape Man"): Sentenced to death for the 1959 slaying of two youths in a West Side New York playground. Agron's sentence was commuted to life imprisonment, and he was released on parole in 1979. Died after a short illness at Bronx Hospital on April 22, 1986, at the age of forty-two.

Ali-Ben ("The Turk"): Hit man who worked primarily for the Albanian mob. Participant in Pierre Hotel robbery. Shot to death by Donald Frankos.

Amuso, Vittorio (Victor, Vic): Boss of Lucchese crime family. Convicted June 15, 1992, on fifty-four charges in a racketeering trial, including nine murders. Originally charged with other reputed mobsters in 1990 with corruptly controlling New York City's window-installation industry, Amuso disappeared shortly before the windows indictment was filed. He was captured in July 1991, in Scranton, Pennsylvania.

Anastasia, Albert (Albert Anastasio): Head of Murder, Inc., the enforcement division of the national crime syndicate, which was responsible for hundreds of killings. Known in the media as the "Lord High Executioner." Served ten months in jail for tax evasion. Was shot to death on October 25, 1957, while having his hair cut at the barbershop of the Park Sheraton Hotel on Seventh Avenue and 55th Street in Manhattan.

Anastasio, Anthony ("Tough Tony"): Brother of Albert

Anastasia. One of the most powerful leaders of the International Longshoremen's Association. Controlled docks in New York City. Died of natural causes in 1963.

BARNES, LEROY ("NICKY"): First major black organized-crime leader. Main narcotics distributor to black ghetto areas, particularly Harlem. Sentenced to life imprisonment in 1978 for heroin trafficking.

BILELLO, RICHIE: Convicted murderer. Suspected informant. The first prisoner to be convicted of crimes during the Attica riots. Stabbed to death by Donald Frankos at the Clinton Correctional Facility at Dannemora on October 28, 1974.

BLOETH, FRANCIS (FRANK): Sentenced to death for killing three people in Long Island in July 1959. Eventually paroled, Bloeth became a model citizen.

BONGIOVI, BOBBY: Also known as Bobby Darrow. Former bodyguard for Joe Gallo. Convicted in 1973 of murdering Broadway Pub night manager Sam Wuyak and sentenced to life.

BRIGUGLIO, SALVATORE ("SALLY BUGS"): Convicted in 1973 of counterfeiting. Suspect in the Jimmy Hoffa disappearance. Rumored informant. Shot to death on March 21, 1978, on New York's Mulberry Street.

BRUNO, ANGELO ("THE GENTLE DON"): Organized-crime boss in Philadelphia. Shot to death sitting in a car outside his South Philadephia home on March 21, 1980.

CASTELLANO, PAUL (PAULIE): Boss of the Gambino Family. Shot to death on December 16, 1985, in front of Sparks Steak House in New York City.

CLARK, RAMSEY: Former U.S. Attorney General. Lawyer and friend of Joe Sullivan.

COHEN, ALAN: Assistant U.S. Attorney. Part of team that convicted Xhevedet Lika.

COLOMBO, JOSEPH (JOE): Head of Colombo crime family. Founded the Italian-American Civil Rights League. Shot on June 28, 1971, during an Italian-American Unity Day rally in Manhattan's Columbus Circle, he remained in a "vegetable" state for almost seven years, dying on May 22, 1978.

COMFORT, BOBBY: Sensational jewel thief. Convicted of robbing the Pierre Hotel. Died of cancer.

COONAN, JACKIE: Brother of Jimmy Coonan and member of the Westies, the ultraviolent West Side Irish gang. Died of AIDS on April 24, 1988.

COONAN, JIMMY: Leader of the Westies. Convicted in 1986 of murder and racketeering under the federal Racketeer Influenced and Corrupt Organization Act (RICO) and sentenced to seventy-five years in prison without parole.

D'AMBROSIO, SALLY ("SALLY D"): Organized-crime figure. Believed murdered in December 1979 at 8648 Eighteenth Avenue in Brooklyn—a Colombo social club.

DELLAVALLE, JOHN ("BUSTER"): Drug dealer. Bodyguard and hit man for Joe Gallo. Murdered by Donald Frankos.

DI BIASI, CARMINE ("SONNY PINTO"): Hit man for mob boss Joe Colombo. Sentenced to death for the murder of Michael Errichiello in 1951, but conviction was reversed on a technicality and he was acquitted on retrial. Named by Joe Luparelli as the killer of Joe Gallo. Current whereabouts unknown—rumored to be dead.

DIAPOULOS, PETE ("PETE THE GREEK"): Former bodyguard of Joe Gallo. Was with Gallo the night he was killed and received only conviction from events (for illegal firearms possession). Author, with Steve Linakis, of *The Sixth Family,* about Joe Gallo. Retired to Greece.

DUSABLON, HANK: Convicted murderer. Sentenced to death with partner Emanuel Samperi for the murders of Martin Himmelstein and Cesar Largo, he survived death row when the death penalty was outlawed in New York.

FEATHERSTONE, FRANCIS ("MICKEY"): Former member of the Westies. Admitted murderer, loan shark, extortionist, and drug dealer. Turned FBI informant; now in Witness Protection Program.

FRANKOS, DONALD ("TONY THE GREEK"): Contract killer. Convicted in 1983 of murdering Clarence Jones and sentenced to twenty-five years to life.

Galante, Carmine: Boss of Bonanno crime family. Shot to death at Joe and Mary's Restaurant in Brooklyn on July 12, 1979.

Gallina, Gino: Former Manhattan assistant district attorney. Mob lawyer. Was in process of testifying before a grand jury on four top Genovese family gangsters when he was shot to death in New York's Greenwich Village in November 1977.

Gallo, Joey ("Crazy Joe"): Profaci hit man who rose to become head of the Gallo gang, a division of the Colombo family. With his brothers, controlled the rackets in East New York. His wars with Profaci were the basis for Jimmy Breslin's *The Gang That Couldn't Shoot Straight.* In early 1972 Gallo became popular among the social set and began work on an autobiography. Shot to death at Umberto's Clam House on Mulberry Street in Manhattan's Little Italy on April 7, 1972—his forty-third birthday.

Gallo, Larry: Brother of Joey Gallo. Profaci hit man who later controlled (with his brothers Joe and Albert) the rackets in East New York. Died of cancer in 1968.

Gambino, Carlo: Boss of Gambino family. Died in October 1976, of a heart attack.

Gambino, Philly: Nephew of Carlo Gambino. Colombo soldier involved in the killing of Joey Gallo.

Garafola, Gary: Organized crime figure. Manager of light-heavyweight contender Frankie DePaula, whom he later murdered. Killed in New Jersey.

Genovese, Vito: Boss of the Genovese family. One of Lucky Luciano's lieutenants and a major narcotics dealer. Convicted in 1959 of narcotics conspiracy and sentenced to fifteen years in jail. Died of a heart attack in jail in 1969.

Giacalone, Anthony ("Tony Jack"): Detroit mafia captain. Jimmy Hoffa's "rabbi" (chief confidant). Suspect in Hoffa disappearance. Took Fifth Amendment before Detroit grand jury investigating case. Later received ten-year sentence for tax evasion.

Gigante, Vincent ("Chin"): Reputed boss of the Genovese

family. Alleged gunman in murder attempt on Frank Costello on May 2, 1957. Convicted of narcotics conspiracy in 1959. Indicted for racketeering in July 1991, but found mentally unfit to stand trial by psychiatrists. Currently under "house arrest" in New York City (wears electronic monitoring device).

GOTTI, JOHN: Boss of the Gambino family. Convicted in May 22, 1973 killing of James McBratney. Convicted April 2, 1992, of racketeering and murder. Sentenced to life in prison without parole. Case under appeal.

GREEN, AL: Brother-in-law of Ali-Ben. Participant in Pierre Hotel robbery. Shot to death by Donald Frankos.

HOFFA, JIMMY: President of the Teamsters from 1957 to 1967, when he was sent to jail for improper use of Teamster pension funds and for attempting to bribe a juror. Freed in 1972 with a presidential order of commutation from Richard Nixon. Disappeared on July 30, 1975.

IANIELLO, MATTHEW ("MATTY THE HORSE"): Genovese family capo. Convicted in 1986 of racketeering.

JOHNSON, THOMAS: Convicted killer of Malcolm X.

JOHNSON, WILFRED ("WILLIE BOY"): One of John Gotti's most trusted friends, but turned FBI informant. Shot to death on August 29, 1988, in the Flatlands section of Brooklyn.

JOHNSON, JEROME: Shot Joseph Colombo during Italian-American Unity Day rally in Manhattan's Columbus Circle on June 28, 1971. Was immediately shot dead.

JONES, CLARENCE: Former basketball star turned drug dealer. Shot to death outside his Bronx apartment on September 12, 1981.

KELLY, RED: Notorious street enforcer. Dead.

KERSCH, JOE: Codefendant with Donald Frankos in Clarence Jones murder case (both were convicted). Committed suicide in jail in 1991.

KONIGSBERG, HAROLD ("KAYO"): Genovese crime family enforcer. Convicted extortionist. Sentenced to life for murdering Anthony Castellito, but conviction was later overturned.

LIKA, XHEVEDET ("JOE"): Albanian drug lord. Convicted in

1985 of heading a major heroin ring and sentenced to life in prison without parole.

Luparelli, Joe: Former bodyguard and chauffeur of Joe Yacovelli. Turned himself in to FBI and revealed story of Joe Gallo killing. Despite a grand-jury investigation and several indictments, no convictions were made of those named by Luparelli as killers.

Marquez, "Spanish Raymond": Convicted gambler and numbers syndicate operator. Drug dealer. Ran numbers in Harlem.

Moia, Louie: Murderer, drug runner, and rumored FBI informant. Murdered by group including Donald Frankos.

Moseley, Winston: Stabbed Kitty Genovese to death in New York on March 13, 1964, in full view of thirty-eight neighbors who neither came to her aid nor called the police. Sentenced to death; sentence commuted to life imprisonment.

Nalo, Sorecho ("Sammy the Arab"): Convicted robber of the Pierre Hotel. Shot to death in Queens, New York, on October 25, 1988.

Nauwens, Jim: Criminal investigator, Office of the U.S. Attorney, Southern District.

Neary, Robert: Assistant district attorney, Westchester County.

O'Brien, Chuckie: Often referred to as Jimmy Hoffa's "adopted son," although he was not (after his father died when he was a young boy, O'Brien was supported by Hoffa). Suspect in Hoffa disappearance. Took the Fifth Amendment before Detroit grand jury investigating case.

Pagano, Joe Sr.: Genovese crime family captain. Dead.

Persico, Carmine ("The Snake," "Junior"): Boss of Colombo crime family (which he ran even when he was in jail). Convicted in 1986 of racketeering and sentenced to 100 years in prison.

Profaci, Joseph (Joe): Boss of Profaci crime family for more than thirty years. Died of cancer on June 6, 1962.

Provenzano, Nunzio: Brother of Anthony Provenzano. Genovese family member and Teamster official. Dead.

Provenzano, Anthony ("Tony Pro"): Former president of

Teamster Local 560 in New Jersey. Convicted in 1978 of the murder of Anthony Castellito. Convicted in 1979 of racketeering. Suspect in Hoffa disappearance. Took Fifth Amendment before Detroit grand jury investigating case. Died in jail on December 12, 1988.

RASTELLI, PHILIP ("RUSTY"): Boss of Bonanno crime family. His wife was shot to death in 1962 after informing on Rastelli to federal agents. Convicted in 1986 of racketeering. Dead.

ROSENBERG, "JERRY THE JEW": Convicted of killing New York police detectives officers Luke Fallon and John Finnegan on May 18, 1962, and sentenced to death (sentence later commuted to life in prison). Became one of the greatest jailhouse lawyers of all time. Subject of biography and made-for-television movie.

RUGGIERO, ANGELO: Gotti associate. Died of cancer.

SALERNO, ANTHONY ("FAT TONY"): Boss of Genovese crime family. Convicted of racketeering in 1987 and 1988 and sentenced to one hundred and seventy years in jail respectively. Died in prison on July 27, 1992, at age eighty, of complications from a stroke.

SAMPERI, EMANUEL: Convicted murderer. Sentenced to death with partner Hank Dusablon for the murders of Martin Himmelstein and Cesar Largo, he survived death row when the death penalty was outlawed in New York.

SISCA, ALPHONSE ("FUNZI"): In charge of Gotti's drug operations. Convicted of heroin trafficking in 1988 and sentenced to forty years.

SQUITIERI, ARNOLD ("ZEKE," "THE GIMP"): Gotti associate. Convicted of heroin trafficking in 1988 and sentenced to forty-five years.

SULLIVAN, JOE ("MAD DOG"): Contract killer. Only person ever to escape from Attica. Serving seventy-five-to-life term for murder.

SULLIVAN, JOHN: West Side Irish mobster and contract killer for Fat Tony Salerno. Retired.

SUTTON, WILLIE: Famous bank robber rumored to have stolen almost a million dollars. Captured in 1952, he was paroled in 1969 and wrote his memoirs. Died in 1982.

TIERI, FRANK ("FUNZI"): Boss of Genovese crime family from 1972 to 1981. In 1980 he became the first person to be convicted of heading an organized crime family. Died of cancer in March 1981.

TRAMUNTI, CARMINE ("MR. GRIBBS"): Boss of Lucchese crime family. Convicted of contempt and perjury. Dead.

VISCONTI, AL: Lucchese soldier and convicted robber. Murdered on orders of Vic Amuso.

WOOD, FREDDIE: Convicted of murdering two people in Queens on June 30, 1960. Executed in electric chair at Sing Sing.

YACOVELLI, JOE ("JOE YAK"): Captain and rumored boss of Colombo crime family. Suspect in Joe Gallo killing; disappeared during grand-jury investigation.

Introduction

THE BOOK'S GENESIS

"HOW WOULD YOU LIKE TO FIND JIMMY HOFFA?" OPENED A February 1989 phone call from Bill Helmer, senior editor of *Playboy* magazine.

Las Vegas private investigator Lake Headley—*Helter Skelter* author/Manson prosecutor Vincent Bugliosi had once called him "the best p.i. in the world"—leaned back in his easy chair, grinned, and waited for a punch line from his friend and occasional employer.

Instead Helmer continued in a serious vein, saying *Playboy* had received calls from a federally protected witness, identifying himself only as D.F., who claimed to know who murdered Hoffa, why, and where the body was buried.

"D.F.," said Helmer, "has a vast array of names, dates, and details that set him far apart from the average caller. We'd like you to check it out, him and his story."

"Where is he?"

"We don't know. He says it would violate Witness Protection regulations to tell us."

There was a short silence.

"But," Helmer concluded, "we hope to find out."

By answering yes when an operator asked, "Will you accept a collect call from D.F. in a federal correctional facility?" the private detective took the first step along a path that led him through the most bizarre, certainly the most important, investigation of his thirty-plus-year career.

Advised by *Playboy* to call Headley, the prisoner, mysteriously known then and for the next few weeks simply as D.F., got right to the point. "I want to get my story out. My story, and the story of this Witness Protection Program. How the feds promise the moon to get information, then end up rewarding their rats with nothing better than a jail cell."

As if sent from central casting to audition for a godfather part, the voice was low and well modulated, heavy with the New York street, raspy, harsh, throaty, and more. Conjuring images of movie gangsters masterfully played by Jimmy Cagney, George Raft, and Marlon Brando, Headley wondered if this guy might be the real thing. He definitely had the sounds down pat.

Headley learned that D.F. had dictated fourteen cassette tapes detailing his life in organized crime and the Witness Protection Program. "I made these tapes because I might be here one day and gone tomorrow. They could take me outside, shoot me, and claim I was trying to escape. I know it's been done before."

After their first lengthy conversation, Headley wanted to learn more, to talk *in person* with the government witness who was "protected" to the extent of total isolation in a desolate part of the country, without visiting privileges for family or friends. Headley contacted D.F.'s lawyer, Julia Heit in New York, who was preparing a motion for a new trial on D.F.'s murder conviction: he had received a twenty-five-to-life sentence for the killing of basketball-star-turned-drug-dealer Clarence Jones. Headley suggested Julia Heit hire him as a defense investigator. It was a technique he had used in the past. If Heit retained him, he could not legally be denied access to his client.

D.F. called at least twice a day for the next several weeks, conversations never lasting less than forty minutes. He gave Headley his name: Donald Gus Frankos. And his location: the Federal Correctional Facility at Sandstone, Minnesota. During their talks Frankos kept mentioning people he had killed, not in a name-dropping fashion, but during the natural flow of his dialogue. The number of victims mounted into the dozens. There seemed to be no end to them.

Julia Heit employed Headley. In addition, Frankos advised his new defense investigator to call Assistant U.S. Attorney Alan Cohen of the Southern District of New York. Cohen, whose life the hit man had probably saved (see Chapter 20), might be able to expedite matters.

Chilly reluctance best described what Headley encountered in Cohen, who evidently had exhausted whatever gratitude he once felt (Frankos had requested favors before, and Cohen always had tried to help). Now, sounding cold and impersonal, this member of the Department of Justice was not receptive to the prospect of the detective mingling with the inmate they each referred to as D.F. "Of course," Cohen said, "you'll have to be thoroughly checked out and cleared before any visit can occur."

Inferring from tone that Cohen pinned heartfelt hope of refusal on the failure of a background check, Headley could not resist mentioning his recent clearances from the U.S. Marine Corps and the State Department to attend the sensitive, super-secret espionage court-martial (except for a sketch artist, the press had been barred) of Sergeant Clayton Lonetree at the Quantico Marine base. The clearance-givers would learn, if they dug deep enough, that the *Nashville Tennesseean* had described Headley as a detective with "impeccable credentials."

Still, the government resisted as long as possible. It took a month of frustrating, seemingly nonstop phone calls to penal-system bureaucrats in New York and Washington, D.C., before Headley received a go-ahead for what he believes is an unprecedented instance of a private investigator or author obtaining face-to-face interviews with a federal witness held in custody.

In early April 1989, at the remote federal prison in Sandstone, Minnesota, Headley was led through a maze of silent corridors and clanging steel doors to a meeting room. Inside he saw a small elaborately carved altar laden with religious literature and numerous intricate paintings—suggesting artistic talent—adorning the gray institutional walls. Clearly, these were projects of people with a lot of time to kill. Left alone, the detective ambled about the room, searching for "bugs"—concealed monitoring devices. He found none.

"Clear the halls!" someone yelled.

A few minutes later the same lusty voice boomed, "Are those halls clear?" A pause, then, "Okay, bring him down!" This hall-clearing episode demonstrated what Frankos had been saying: that he was protected even from chance encounters with other inmates.

Headley tried to picture the self-confessed hit man, but rational images eluded him. Would the person with whom he had conferred so frequently via long distance appear as some grotesque, shackled monster?

The door opened. In stepped a handsome man with graying temples around a balding crown, neatly dressed in sneakers, tan slacks, and a striped polo shirt. He made a brisk approach, stuck out his right hand, and said, "You gotta be Lake. Glad to meet you. I'm Donald Frankos; that is, in here I am. On the street I'm Tony the Greek."

About fifty years old, Frankos had a fighter's build kept in shape despite, or maybe because of, long periods of confinement. Slightly taller than medium height, weight about 165 pounds, the Greek must have been a ladies' man in his youth. Noticing the "artwork" needled into Frankos's arms, Headley remembered Truman Capote's observation that *all* the killers he had interviewed on death rows around the country had multiple tattoos.

Frankos spoke freely and venomously about the Federal Witness Protection Program, the people in it—"rats like myself"—and the people who run it. "All my life I've hated rats," he said. "I can't believe I became one. I wake up in my cell at night and think, *you're a rat, nothing but a lowdown rat.* That bothers me more than any other thing I've ever done in my life. I went for their bullshit. Me, Mr. Street Smart, and I went for it like a stone sucker. I guess I'm sorry for all the guys I killed, but for the most part they were scumbags. Now John Gotti, John's offered three hundred thousand dollars to anyone who hits the Greek. Gotti was my friend. It makes me more sad than scared. My old friends gone, my self-respect gone, my manhood gone. I was the last person anyone thought would rat."

It was true. Those were the exact words former U.S. Attorney General Ramsey Clark used—"the last person anyone thought would rat"—when he learned Frankos had turned.

Headley questioned the Greek for eight hours on this first visit, and eight more the following day. In all, he made six trips to Sandstone, each time staying two days. In addition to the ninety-six hours spent together in Minnesota, the investigator also met with Frankos at a penitentiary in Maine, at Attica, and for a week in Westchester County, New York, during a court hearing to determine if the hit man should be granted a new trial on his murder conviction.

They also communicated by phone virtually every day for more than two years. When not talking to the prisoner, Headley, voted Outstanding P.I. of 1989 by the prestigious International Society of Private Investigators, meticulously checked out his story.

Ultimately, an interview with Frankos, restricted to the Hoffa murder, was featured in the November 1989 issue of *Playboy*, after the magazine's researchers spent seven months verifying his claims. *Playboy* described its efforts as follows: "Early on in our association with Frankos, we submitted key portions of our interview with him to C. R. McQuiston, the acknowledged dean of voice-stress analysis. McQuiston uses a computer to break down voice patterns to determine the truth or falsity of a person's statements. Although he claims a 70 percent accuracy rate, his test is still considered inadmissible evidence in court. In any case, he found Frankos's confessions to be 'free of mendacious stress' on the whole, indicating that Frankos believed the story he was telling. While that was far from positive proof, it was, at least, a start."

Playboy continued: "Frankos' story hinges on his professed associations with two of the most notorious underworld figures of the eighties: Jimmy Coonan and Joe Sullivan. Coonan made his mark as head of the Westies, a violent band of Irish thugs best known for their tendency to dismember murder victims before disposing of them. Sullivan, the only man ever to escape from Attica prison, is a notorious free-lance hit man. . . . Sources ranging from former U.S. Attorney General Ramsey Clark to T. J. English, author of a forthcoming history of the Westies, have confirmed various relationships central to Frankos's story. We also have confirmed Frankos's ties to such underworld figures as John Gotti and Jerry 'The Jew' Rosenberg.

"Other confirming information on Frankos and his associates was obtained in the course of dozens of interviews, including conversations with Assistant U.S. Attorney Mary Lee Warren, prosecutor of Jimmy Coonan, with FBI agent Arthur Ruffels, and with Andrew Rubin and William Korwatch, the prosecutor and the detective, respectively, who secured Frankos' murder conviction for the killing of Clarence Jones. We have also confirmed that the prime conspirators were out of prison at the time of the murder, and that the burial site was under construction, as Frankos says it was."

Author William Hoffman—thirty-six nonfiction books to his credit, a number of them investigative works—first talked to Donald Frankos in May 1989, when the former hit man called, at Headley's suggestion, to discuss the possibility of collaborating on his autobiography. This was the beginning of an estimated 700 telephone conversations between Frankos and Hoffman, a conservative total of 500 hours. Hoffman made many tape recordings, took voluminous notes, and embarked on some twenty investigative trips. Headley traveled even more, logging about 40,000 miles, a highlight occurring when he interviewed Joe "Mad Dog" Sullivan, named by Frankos as the killer of more than 100 people, and described by law enforcement officials as "the most dangerous man in America."

The private investigator talked with the prolific murderer at the maximum-security Sullivan County Correctional Facility in upstate New York, a prison many inmates the authors interviewed were certain had been named for Mad Dog. It wasn't, but Joe Sullivan's enormous notoriety and underworld exploits—"legend" was the word most frequently used to describe him—made the mistake understandable.

Frankos had said many of the "toughest guys" he knew were "gentlemen," and, indeed, that's how Sullivan impressed Headley. He was soft-spoken, without a trace of braggadocio. A decent, regular guy, above average in intelligence, most people not knowing his past would judge.

Joe Sullivan had every reason for being furious with Frankos, who fingered him in the *Playboy* interview as an accessory-after-the-fact in Jimmy Hoffa's murder. But somehow Sullivan's affection for his longtime partner outweighed all other considerations.

"I assume you read the *Playboy* interview," Headley said.

"Yeah. Twenty times, at least."

"What do you think?"

Sullivan hesitated, obviously wrestling with an internal conflict. He and Frankos had been the closest of friends for more than twenty years but, still, his friend had done the unforgivable—he had turned rat. Finally Sullivan looked at Headley and said, "Everything the Greek told was true. It happened just like he said."

It was a neat answer. What Frankos had told, with one exception, *was* essentially true. He just hadn't told the full story.

Headley and Hoffman, working together and separately, attempted to verify everything that could be verified. They talked to cops, federal agents, journalists who specialized in the Mafia, New York City detectives, even Frankos's former cellmates. Confirmation of what he said piled upon confirmation. Clearest of all was that inside prison and out, Frankos had been an unholy terror, a feared and most dangerous man. Amazingly, he knew almost everyone in the New York underworld, and they all knew him.

Frankos relates his life story with merciless dispassion, without a trace of self-pity. He is easy to listen to, an affable, witty conversationalist for those who can blot out his deeds, or haven't viewed him from the wrong end of a knife, gun, or chainsaw. Even some hardened police investigators say they "like" him, "wish him well," though these are a minority. More typical was the New York State Police detective whose eyes turned ice cold when asked to summarize his feelings about the man called Tony the Greek. Before walking abruptly away, the detective spat on the ground and said, "That's one violent fuck."

Surely. Donald Gus Frankos is a multiple felon. His "rap sheet," held at head level and unfurled, stretches to the floor and forms a pile. He has been convicted of menacing, battery, armed robbery, and two murders, though he has committed many more.

Yet Frankos is also a most entertaining storyteller who laces his accounts with dry humor and has a natural knack for narration coupled with phenomenal recall. Still, it's *what* he tells, not how he does it, that sets him apart. He matter-of-factly ticks off the names of the killers in numerous sensational unsolved hits, some of which he was involved with, some not: the murders of Joey Gallo; Albert Anastasia, the head of Murder, Inc.; Philadelphia godfather Angelo Bruno; Gino Gallina; Carmine Galante; Augie Manori; and, of course, Jimmy Hoffa. Police officials, unable to prosecute these homicides, often totally in the dark about the perpetrators' identities, should be avid readers of Frankos's story.

Hoffman continually emphasized that he wanted nothing held back, and Frankos agreed. "I decided to do this," he said, "and I might as well go all the way. That's how I lived my criminal life; it's how I'll tell my story."

It didn't always work that smoothly. Some events were very painful for even him to recall—for example, the murder of Louie Moia (see Chapter 8)—and Frankos needed to be prodded incessantly. "This don't make me look too good," he'd say, as if other murders did.

Despite Frankos's guarantee of not holding back, he saved his most sensational revelations to Hoffman until quite late in the writing of the book. Earlier in their association Frankos had feared the information, which did *not* appear in *Playboy,* would jeopardize an ongoing appeal of his murder conviction—as well as the immunity he'd been granted by the feds on scores of felonies. However, when his appeals had been exhausted and he faced the depressing reality of years in solitary confinement, Frankos decided to keep no more secrets. He shared with Hoffman a frightening account he had told Lake Headley at their very first meeting under the condition that the story be kept confidential and never appear in print. Lake had given Frankos his word, and he kept it to the very end. Lake, sadly, died of Lou Gehrig's Disease before his last wish was granted: to hold the book he'd worked so hard on in his hands.

It should be borne in mind that for years Donald Frankos has been the *federal government's witness*. Witness Protection Program officials believed him long before Headley and Hoffman checked out his astounding revelations and became convinced of their veracity. The result is this narrative of chilling, bloody crimes committed for, and with, some of the nation's most notorious gangsters.

Frankos probably has "ratted himself out," as the saying goes, a fact he understands. He has read this book, word for word, and *he* at least accords it a rave review. It is true, as he says, that no underworld figure has so completely laid bare his soul. Books done with Mafia or organized-crime collaborators are usually long on felonies for which the statute of limitations has run, and short on what he calls the "down and dirty"—murders.

Why would Frankos reveal numerous incidents in his life that portray him as a cold-blooded killer for hire, and even worse? Why would he want these crimes to appear in print?

The answer is that he has spent a lot of time thinking about his "career," which he believes has been remarkable (true, though the public will surely view it from the perspective of horror, not as the grand adventure Frankos remembers), and he does not want this "epic" (his word) to die with him.

The authors have attempted to capture Frankos's true voice, using the killer's own words whenever possible. Readers should be warned: two voices may seem present, causing the tone of the narrative to vary. Frankos usually speaks in the language of an intelligent, well-read individual, which he is. But on occasion, when describing a crime or a particularly horrible prison experience, he reverts to the rawest language of the street. When this happens he transforms in an eyeblink from cheerful next-door neighbor into a man who has killed, killed often, and enjoys remembering out loud.

CONTRACT KILLER

Chapter 1

FAT TONY WANTS HIM DEAD

THE PHONE RANG EARLY ON THIS SUMMER 1973 AFTERNOON, and right away I recognized the gruff voice of John Sullivan, an important Irish mobster and a contract killer for Genovese crime family boss Fat Tony Salerno.

"You free today?" Sullivan asked.

"Yeah," I said.

"Meet me at Wolf's Deli in an hour."

At this time I maintained two residences: an apartment reserved for privacy on 15th Street; and a suite to conduct business at the Hotel Wilson. Sullivan phoning me at the apartment boded an urgency not normally associated with our business together, since we saw each other three or four times a week in the regular course of affairs. I suspected he wanted somebody hit.

I pulled on a fresh pair of slacks, topped them with my favorite gray silk shirt, and decided to walk the forty-two blocks from my apartment to the deli at 57th and Sixth Avenue.

Sullivan waited for me at a corner table, wearing a dark business suit, starched white dress shirt, and maroon silk tie. He'd started his lunch: a corned beef sandwich and a bottle of imported beer.

About 5'10" and blocky, in his late forties, John never smiled, never lightened up. He asked me how I was doing, and whether I wanted something to eat.

"No thanks. I'm trying to lose a few pounds."

"I need you for a job," Sullivan said. He didn't fool around much, a quality to my liking.

"Who?" I asked.

"Buster DellaValle."

"I know Buster."

"Makes no difference."

"Right," I said.

"So you'll do it?"

"Yeah." I took pride in giving definite answers. No maybes or I'll think it over.

This normally would have ended our conversation, except for Sullivan suggesting likely places for the hit, maybe supplying a picture or two of the intended victim (not necessary here), and providing whatever helpful intelligence he had gathered.

Not the case today. John wanted me to know the pressing reason for the murder contract, so I would act accordingly. I soon sat entranced listening to this veteran gangster explain the twisted course of events leading to the decision that Buster DellaValle had to die.

Buster had been a bodyguard, drug dealer, and hit man for Joey Gallo right up to the time Joey had been killed on April 7, 1972, at Umberto's Clam House in Little Italy. Buster bought the heroin he'd sold for Gallo—and later for himself—from Philip John Manfredi and Philip D. Manfredi, first cousins who operated out of Fat Tony Salerno's neighborhood in East Harlem. The Manfredis, each in his early twenties, filled in while their uncle, narcotics kingpin JoJo Manfredi, did time for the feds.

"You know what happened to JoJo's nephews," Sullivan said.

Yes, I did. On the night of August 9, 1972, they had driven their Oldsmobile to a deserted parking lot in the Clasons Point section of the Bronx, where police found their bodies early the next morning. P. D. Manfredi rested in the front seat of the car, shot three times in the head from a distance of less than six inches. P. J. Manfredi, also hit three times, sprawled on the pavement twenty-five feet from the Olds.

I didn't need to see a police reconstruction to know how the murders came down. Someone those kids trusted had sat in the backseat of the vehicle and without warning had opened fire on P. D. Manfredi. Undoubtedly the killer considered him the more dangerous of the two and eliminated him first. P. J. Manfredi had run for his life, but hadn't made it far before a .38 bullet shattered his hand and two more slammed into his back.

"That cocksucker DellaValle whacked them," Sullivan said. The police professed to have no idea of the killer's identity, and they probably told the truth, but John knew who did it.

DellaValle, like other members of Joe Gallo's crew anxious to avenge the death of their beloved boss, had known the Manfredis were close to Fat Tony Salerno, one of the key players in Joey's assassination, and had waited patiently for the right time to strike. He had continued to purchase heroin from the cousins, as if nothing had changed, until he'd won such a degree of trust that they'd let him sit in the back of their car in that isolated Bronx parking lot.

JoJo Manfredi, seeking *his* revenge, had reached out from prison to Fat Tony Salerno, who in turn had called on John Sullivan. It seemed pretty straightforward for a mob contract—DellaValle whacking the Manfredis as vengeance for Gallo's death, and allies of the drug dealers striking back. But then John Sullivan added a twist that cast a whole new light on the situation.

"Junior Persico and Jerry Lang," he said, "have already taken a shot at Buster."

Then why wasn't he dead? Carmine "The Snake" Persico, known as Junior, boss of the Colombo crime family, and Jerry Langella, his underboss, ranked among the most dangerous Mafiosi who ever lived. I'd met Junior Persico, who ran his gang from a prison cell, and knew he hated everything about Joey Gallo. It was Persico's gang of top-of-the-line killers who had waged a bloody war against Joey's crew in the early 1960s, and won.

"You heard about that restaurant," Sullivan said.

The Neapolitan Noodle. A fancy, newly opened place at 320 East 79th Street. Yes, I knew about it, just like every New Yorker and, no, I didn't have an insider's view of what had happened there. On August 11, 1972, less than two days after the Manfredi murders, four legitimate businessmen, standing at the Noodle bar, had been gunned down in a hail of bullets. Two of them, Sheldon Epstein and Max Tekelch, were killed, and the event became the talk of the town. A lone gunman had blazed away with a pistol in each hand, and police brass speculated that these had been mistaken-identity murders. The cops had it right.

The killings inflamed much of the citizenry and became a hot topic for politicians, none more prominent than Mayor John Lindsay. It was one thing for criminals to kill one another, but quite different to murder ordinary people. The usually staid *New York Times*, under the headline "Run Gangsters Out of City, Angry Mayor Tells Police," quoted Lindsay: "The recent murder of innocent citizens—allegedly the result of mistaken identity—by gangland executioners is an outrage which demands that the romanticization of the mob must be stopped and gangsters run out of town."

The Mafia hated this type of publicity, which focused attention on its activities and guaranteed hundreds of harassment arrests. Even police officers the mob had in its pocket, bought and paid for, were forced to bring Mafiosi in, albeit with profuse apologies, for questioning. Many criminals had to alter the rhythm of their extremely lucrative rackets until the heat cooled.

"Junior passed the order from the joint to Jerry Lang," Sullivan said, "and Jerry was at the restaurant to see that everything went right. Instead, everything went fucking wrong."

The hitter, Sullivan explained, was a guy who'd opened fire before adequately identifying his targets. The intended victims—DellaValle and Bobby Bongiovi, a Gallo soldier—had agreed to a meeting at the Neapolitan Noodle with Alphonse Persico, Sr. (Carmine's older brother, known as Allie Boy), Alphonse Persico, Jr. (Carmine's son, known as Little Allie Boy), and Jerry Langella, who as an underboss should have performed better. DellaValle and

Bongiovi had been told to wait at a specific spot at the bar; they never showed up. Those businessmen had sat down in the wrong place.

The police never solved the Manfredi murders, nor those at the Neapolitan Noodle, nor scores of other hits through the years that a single good informant could have put them wise to. Not nearly as many rats existed then. Savvy detectives admit that a knowledgeable snitch is worth a battery of computers and an army of cops.

John Sullivan ordered a slice of cheesecake and a cup of coffee. Whether planning it or committing it, murder made him hungry.

"You gotta be careful with this guy," John said. "He always packs a pistol."

"Right," I said. I had done time with DellaValle at Dannemora and knew him as a dangerous character.

"You might look for him on Lafayette Street. There's a bank there, and two small Greek restaurants. Buster does business out of those restaurants. In the afternoons."

"Okay." I already had plotted how to do it.

"Fat Tony don't want no delays. This Buster situation's been agitating him for a long time. He couldn't move till now because of the pressure over the Noodle."

Sullivan handed me a package. "That's half," he said. When I later opened it at my apartment I found $5,000, which meant, with Sullivan keeping 50 percent for himself, this was a $20,000 contract. Big money for a hit. Often a crime boss paid an independent hitter like me $5,000 total, or less. Some times he wanted it done for nothing, and I obliged—a professional courtesy, so to speak—to open up other avenues of making money.

"The heat's on," Sullivan concluded, getting up from his chair. "Don't make no mistakes."

The next morning in my suite at the Wilson I carefully prepared for the kill. I spread a yellow-tinted makeup on my face and neck, stuffed cotton balls inside my cheeks, and donned a medium Afro wig. I put on a tank-top undershirt, then applied makeup to all the exposed skin of my upper torso. Next I placed a sawed-off shotgun in a large hollowed-out radio I intended to carry. Wearing a faded pair of Levis and dirty high-top sneakers, I was almost ready to hunt for Mr. John "Buster" DellaValle.

First I went to see a friend who owned a vegetable store near 12th Avenue, which served as a repository for a wide variety of hijacked merchandise and stolen goods, especially cases of guns swagged off the docks. When I walked in, my friend didn't recognize me, nor did he stare as if startled by a bizarre apparition. Good. I needed to be disguised, without calling attention to myself. I greeted my friend and told him I once again wanted to use the back of his store to chop up a body, then handed him a thousand dollars, the agreed-upon price. He didn't want to hear a name and I didn't give one.

For six straight days I repeated the same prey-stalking routine: don the disguise; drive the stolen Buick with the phony license plates to Lafayette Street; park a block away from the Greek restaurants; unload the bicycle I'd folded onto the backseat; place the hollowed-out radio on the handlebars; and pedal by Buster's supposed hangouts. He was never there.

I hated having to psyche myself a mile high each day, then crash down. It was like getting ready to play the Super Bowl and learning the other team hadn't shown up.

John Sullivan, furious, came to my place at the Wilson. "What the fuck is the delay, Greek?" he wanted to know.

I got hot. For years I had maintained my independence, anticipating times exactly like this, and I didn't have to answer to Sullivan. "Fuck you," I said. "You don't talk to me that way."

"Fat Tony wants this guy dead."

"Tough shit! Buster ain't where you said he'd be."

"Well, he's gotta be there," John said. "Fat Tony talks about nothin' else."

"Fuck Fat Tony, too," I groused. Ever since I'd started running with mob people, more than a dozen years earlier, I'd recognized that free-lancing held the secret to maintaining sanity, and I insisted they respect my independence. In return, I did hits the Mafia considered too risky, didn't want their soldiers to handle, or had botched miserably in the first place. Like this one, the DellaValle contract. I showed the wiseguys respect when they showed it to me, and didn't worry that *I* might become a hitter's target. I had a rule about that sort of thing: if the killer didn't get me, I'd go after his boss.

"I have to tell Tony what you're doing," Sullivan said, cooling down.

"Tell him I'm working on it. That it's all I'm working on."

"You want a machine gun? I can get you a machine gun. You know, don't you, that whoever's with Buster, they go too."

"Right. No, I don't want a machine gun." Years before I had practiced with one but hadn't felt comfortable with it. Too often the gun misfired, which could mean bye-bye Greek. I would have no second chance with DellaValle.

John finally said, "What the hell, do it your own way. Just *do* it."

I already had everything set up in the Buick: twenty large black garbage bags, surgeon's gloves, chainsaw, and goggles to shield my eyes from flying tissue, blood, and bone chips. I knew there would be a mop and bucket in the vegetable store.

On my second trip to Lafayette Street after John's visit, my luck changed. As I pedaled by the first Greek restaurant, there sat Buster, stationed in a booth with his back against the wall, gazing at the door. I pedaled back to the car and got in, but in my haste I left the bike on the sidewalk propped against a parking meter. I drove directly toward the Greek restaurant, double-parked the car just out of sight of anyone looking through the front window, and stepped onto the street.

That's when I felt a nervous spasm in the pit of my stomach. My hands grew cold, clammy. It always happened this way, when I went after another killer, when I knew it would be his life or mine, no other result possible. I told myself, *you have the advantage, you're the offense*, a true enough appraisal; but a single mistake with the guy who had killed the Manfredi nephews and I'd be as dead as they were.

Then another feeling, only present when I went to kill someone who might kill me: a powerful wish to be back in the protection of my "mother's" arms. The desire then vanished as suddenly as it had appeared. The time had come.

I entered the restaurant and locked my eyes with Buster's for just a second. I looked away, and with the radio on my shoulder walked straight to the men's room. My heart quickened as I checked the sawed-off shotgun. I calculated the distance from where I sat on the toilet to where Buster sat in the booth as thirty feet. Placing the shotgun back into the radio, which I left slightly ajar for quick access to the weapon, I was momentarily startled by my reflection in the mirror. *I* didn't recognize me, so surely Buster hadn't. *You got the offense, Greek. Take him. Calm and fast.*

I came out of the restroom at a normal pace, picking up speed on my way toward DellaValle. *Goddamn!* I thought, *someone's sitting with him!* A guy about sixty-five years old, his back to the front door, previously obscured from my view by the high-back booth. *This old man could be dangerous,* I told myself. I had known hitters in their seventies, unstoppable tough old cobs, much harder to ice than their young counterparts.

But now, charged with excitement and determination, I could not consider turning back. Not even heroin supplied a rush as powerful as the moments before a kill, adrenaline pumping, senses transmitting messages of astounding clarity, and *fear.* I had reached the top of my profession as a contract killer, living a luxury-filled existence, receiving respect from the crime families; and bone-deep I was afraid of losing it all, a guaranteed denouement if only once I hesitated, lost my nerve, or just plain fucked up. Every time I went on a job I had to psyche myself up, whip my mind and guts into an internal frenzy. Always, acute fear provided the motivating, driving force.

I set the radio down on Buster's table, pulled out the shotgun, and pressed it against his head. We weren't even noticed by the few late-lunchers still scattered in the restaurant. Buster himself had watched me approach, but his warning system had failed him.

"You make the slightest move, you fat piece of shit," I told him in a heavy New York wiseguy accent, "and I'll blow your head off your shoulders. Old man," I growled to Buster's companion, "you keep your hands on the table, or my partner will blow your brains out."

I said all this in a low, calm voice. I didn't want a panic that would necessitate doing the killing here; killing in public is always bad. The newspapers would cover a restaurant murder—as they had the killings at the Neapolitan Noodle—forcing the cops to react more energetically than usual. Mayor Lindsay, grandstanding with that "run gangsters out of the city" order (a command impossible to carry out, given the thousands of threads connecting the "upperworld"—judges, politicians, police, prosecutors, businessmen—to the underworld) could make life uncomfortable for Fat Tony and his ilk, and the mobsters would blame me.

"There'll be no problem," I said, "if you do what you're told. All I want is your money and jewelry."

Although his instincts screamed at him that I lied, DellaValle *wanted* to believe me. I never met anyone who accepted that his life was moments away from ending. I saw the calculating going on in Buster's fearful eyes, watched him convince himself that maybe I told the truth.

"Get up slowly and walk out the front door," I said. "I'll be right behind you. Do what I tell you and you live. Make a break for it and you die right here."

I placed the shotgun against my right side, so it was hidden by the radio, and escorted Buster and his companion out to the sidewalk. From the corner of my right eye I could see a waitress looking at me, but I knew she'd never be able to make an identification. Buster and I had been close at Dannemora, and *he* hadn't recognized me.

I paraded the men the few yards to the car. "Keep moving, motherfucker," I told the old man. "My partner will meet you up the block." To hell with Sullivan's warning—"whoever's with Buster, they go too"—this guy was no threat. I hated leaving the bike behind, but had no choice. I wasn't going to drive back to retrieve it.

Opening the Buick's door on the driver's side, I ordered Buster to get in, then slid him over to the passenger side with my body, maintaining constant pressure on his rib cage with the shotgun. I reached over, opened the glove compartment, and removed a set of handcuffs. Seeing them, DellaValle's face turned white. I assured him they were only a precaution.

"Where you taking me?" he asked.

"Someplace quiet. Where I can check what you're carrying."

"I can give you everything I've got right now. No problem."

"I'll do the looking, cocksucker, when I want." It was good to throw in the bad language: it let him know he didn't deal with an amateur. The speech of a professional gangster, including his tone, deliberately sets him apart. Cops have *their* way of talking. So do doctors.

I pushed the shotgun hard into his ribs. "*This* I'll take right now," I said, reaching inside his belt and snatching out a .22. "Now lean forward, you motherfucker, and put your hands behind your back." I handcuffed him, pushed him down onto the floor, and felt my breathing start to return to normal. It was virtually all over now, though I reminded myself to remain alert for the unexpected.

My hands nevertheless trembled as I inserted the key into the ignition, started the car, and drove off toward the west side of Manhattan. We traveled perhaps a half-dozen blocks before it dawned on Buster. "I know you," he said. "From upstate. You're the Greek, aren't you?"

It didn't matter if he knew. "Yeah. I'm the Greek." This terrified him, but also somehow provided hope.

"Donald . . . you're Donald . . . Donald . . . "

"Frankos."

"Right! The Greek Frankos. Tony the Greek. Jesus Christ, Greek, we were friends."

"Business is business, Buster. Just stay calm. I won't hurt you if you do what I say."

I could sense DellaValle thinking this over as I drove. He was recalling what he knew about me, and found none of it encouraging. He had been in my shoes when he'd worked for Joey Gallo—

there could be only one reason I had him stuffed on the floor of a car.

I let myself imagine what he felt, wondered what would go through my mind in the not unlikely event that I got shanghaied on a similar ride. I didn't think I would beg, as I expected Buster would, but who could know?

"What's going on, Greek? What are you up to? Please. Tell me."

"I already told you."

"You're going to kill me, aren't you, Greek?"

"Where do you get that, Buster? I'm going to rob you."

But DellaValle had been around too long, knew my reputation too well, to buy any nonsense about robbery.

"What are they paying you, Greek?"

"Shut up, Buster. Nobody's paying me." I pulled onto the Westside Highway.

"Greek, please. Listen to me. I got a lot of money. Stashed away nice and safe. It's all yours. I'll take you to it. You can have it all. Just let me go. Please, Greek."

I reached down to my right ankle where I kept a .22 Beretta. I placed the gun in my lap so Buster couldn't see it.

He started to cry. Sobbing and shaking, he pleaded for his life.

"I'm not going to kill you," I repeated. If he died expecting to live, just all of a sudden went to sleep, then he'd die happy. Besides, I wanted him to calm down.

He offered me his loan-shark business, his drug business, "tall stacks" of money he had hidden away. "I'll leave town, Greek. Nobody will ever know you didn't do the job, and you'll be a rich man. Be smart, my friend, *tell* them you whacked me and take everything for yourself."

A few guys *had* saved themselves this way: gave up all they had and moved far away. But it was too risky for the individual with the contract; too many things could go wrong. Anyway, the offer had no appeal to me. At this time my reputation as a good fellow, as a stand-up guy, a hitter (and none ranked higher in the eyes of mobsters than a hitter), meant more than anything in the world to me.

At 30th Street I pulled over to the right and stopped. Traffic was light, and the tension in the car was unbearable. Buster defecated all over himself; the sudden, awful stink filled the car.

DellaValle's last words were an apology for shitting in my car. I shot him twice behind the head, and his head bounced back up and almost tore off the dashboard. Then he slumped down, real peaceful, dead.

I pushed Buster's body down closer to the floor, covered it with a blanket I kept in the backseat, and drove the reeking vehicle to 12th Avenue. Too many people were milling about, so I ran the Buick over the curb onto the sidewalk and parked the passenger side against the vegetable-store entrance. The proprietor and I carried DellaValle to the back.

"It's done," I told John Sullivan over the phone.

"Where you at?"

"Swanee's." A code name we used for the produce market.

"I want to see."

While I waited for John to arrive, I stayed busy. I uncuffed and undressed Buster, an unpleasant job; checked his pockets for money; got help hoisting him onto a table; carried the garbage bags, gloves, goggles, surgeon's smock, and chainsaw in from the car; and, finally, reparked the car. I permitted myself a smile, knowing that when I finished no one could ever put Buster back together again—and the cops would have a helluva time identifying him, if by some odd chance they found any of the body.

A knock on the back door. "Who's there?" I asked.

"Me. John."

When I let him in, he took one look at the naked body and almost knocked the wind out of me. He grabbed me, pounding my back, hugging and kissing me. "*Nobody* can do it better than you," he said. "You're a master at killing. You're the best, Greek. Even Trigger Burke in his grave is smiling at your daring."

Trigger Burke was John's hero. An infamous West Side Irish gangster who went unrepenting and swaggering to the electric chair at Sing Sing in 1957, Burke reputedly murdered more than 100 people. The highest compliment John Sullivan could pay was comparison to Trigger Burke, who had been his mentor.

John then noticed the plastic bags and chainsaw. "Fat Tony decided he don't want Buster chopped up," he said. "He wants the world to see him, as a warning to anyone who tries to kill a member of his own crime family."

Technically, I suppose, John Sullivan was right. Joey Gallo's crew (including DellaValle) belonged to the Colombo organization, with which the Manfredis had been associated, though mainly Gallo had warred against the gang Junior Persico now headed. Fat Tony's connection was the cut of the drug profits his Genovese organization received for permitting access to its territory.

John said, "Just cut Buster's arms off at the elbows and tape them to his stomach." The message: if you kill one of your own with your hands, then you lose the hands that once picked up the pistol.

That night we dumped DellaValle's body in a shallow grave in the farming community of Jewett, New York, about 150 miles north of Manhattan in Greene County. It took longer than we expected for someone to discover the body. Hunters stumbled upon it March 7, 1974.

John paid me the second part of the contract, $5,000, the night after the hit, plus I had another $3,000 I'd lifted off Buster.

We went to a belly-dancing joint, stuffed ourselves with Arab food, and drank heavily as we watched the dancers undulate in perfect rhythm with the intense Middle Eastern music.

I thought about Buster buried upstate as I left the nightclub with one of the girls. John followed me outside and gave me one last hearty hug. "Fat Tony slept good last night," he whispered into my ear. "You satisfied his thirst for blood."

"I'm happy for Fat Tony," I said. *And for you too, Greek,* I thought. *Your belly is full and your pockets are stuffed. You've come a long way.*

Chapter 2

UNCLE GUS

MY FATHER, GEORGE ARGIRI FRANGOS (I CHANGED THE SPELLing of my surname to Frankos), was born in 1891 in the town of Kardanyla on Chios, a Greek island nestled a few miles off the coast of Asia Minor in the Aegean Sea. The first of nine children, he left Chios in 1905 as a crewman on a ship owned by his very wealthy godfather, a man named Livanos, and never returned. A big man, 6'4", George sailed the world as a merchant marine, and despite possessing virtually no formal education, he became a ship's assistant engineer. I was told he learned to speak six languages.

Father arrived in the United States in 1919, disembarking in Jersey City. He obtained employment as a boiler-room supervisor with Bristol-Myers in Newark, and secured part-time work as a handyman.

At age forty in 1931, George married my future mother, Irene, thirty-five, also one of nine children. She was a gentle, attractive blonde who had emigrated from Syracuse, a city of more than 100,000 people on the Ionian Sea in southeastern Sicily. They produced three children: my sister Georgia, in 1932; my brother

Jimmy, in 1935; and me, born in Hackensack, New Jersey, on November 10, 1938.

In 1936, my father established a construction company, building single-family homes in Rutherford, New Jersey. But this Great Depression year represented the worst of times for a small business, and he went broke. Financial hardships contributed to my parents' divorce in 1938, while my mother was pregnant with me. My father headed for Louisiana to make a fresh start in the oil industry.

My mother died shortly after I was born, from complications of a difficult delivery, and the three of us—Georgia, Jimmy, and me—were placed in a Hackensack foster home until our father, remarried, picked us up late in 1939. He drove us to Franklin, Louisiana, where, in spite of a tremendous expenditure of labor, his new venture as oil wildcatter had produced only a string of dry holes.

My childhood memory of my father is of a robust head of household we expected would love and protect us forever; but in reality he was in poor health. Following a severe kidney attack, he was hospitalized and told he hadn't long to live. His new wife, a young telephone operator, told him she couldn't take on the responsibility of raising three children alone; so, not wanting us brought up in an orphanage, he turned to his brothers Nick and Constantine. Uncle Nick agreed to adopt Jimmy and raise him in Newark. Uncle Constantine, called Gus, promised to take me and Georgia to live with him and his wife, Hope, in Ambridge, Pennsylvania.

My father passed away in 1943, at age fifty-two, satisfied that his children had good homes. Uncle Gus, twenty-eight, and his seventeen-year-old bride, our Aunt Hope, came to Louisiana and picked us up.

We lived on the second floor of an Ambridge home owned by Aunt Hope's parents, whom I soon called Grandmother and Grandfather. Aunt Hope I addressed as Mother (as I'll refer to her throughout the book). Even though Uncle Gus legally adopted me in 1945—changing my name (as per the Greek custom of the son's middle name being the father's first) from Donald George Frangos to Donald Gus Frangos—I never called him Father.

My new father figure, a foul-tempered block of granite that

nobody could control, worked as an independent contractor repairing and painting bridges in the eastern quarter of the United States. When home between jobs, Gus beat Mother severely and often, a few times even in front of her parents, who stopped trying to intervene after he turned his anger on them.

In 1947 we moved to Beaver Falls, approximately seventeen miles north of Ambridge, and without my grandparents, life grew infinitely worse. One night Mother went to a relative's house for dinner, leaving Georgia and me at home. Uncle Gus put me to bed early, and I awakened to sounds of my sister crying. When I opened the bedroom door to investigate, Georgia, buck naked and hysterical, came running toward me. She threw her arms around my neck, her body jerking with uncontrollable sobs that made what she tried to say a garble, but I knew it meant *Help me!* Before I could clear the sleep from my head, Uncle Gus yanked her away, slapped her across the face, punched me, and said, "You little son of a bitch, you say anything about this to your Aunt Hope and I'll kick you out of the house. You'll freeze out on the streets, starve to death, and nobody in the world will give a damn."

The following morning, Georgia and I walked the 2½ miles to school, Georgia crying all the way there. As we trudged home in the afternoon, she wept with dread. This became our routine. I ached from the suffering my sister endured, and hated being too little to rescue her from Uncle Gus. He felt her up often, had intercourse with her whenever he pleased, and vowed to kill anyone who told.

At night she and I attended classes at the Greek Orthodox church. We learned the ceremonies of our ritual-conscious religion, heard stories of our martyred saints, partook of the Communion sacrament, and studied the Greek language.

Unlike most kids our age, Georgia and I looked forward to attending school. It kept us out of the house, where not a day went by when Uncle Gus was home from painting bridges that he didn't torment or beat us. Many times when Mother tried to curb his violent outbursts, she, too, was beaten.

Gus would not hold a conversation with anybody. He never just chatted with Mother or me, and spoke to my sister only during sexual assaults. If we had to talk to him, he demanded we speak Greek, and smacked whoever let slip an English word. I imagine Gus viewed himself as a long-suffering provider fulfilling his brother's deathbed request to care for his soon-to-be-orphaned brood.

In 1949 we moved to New York City—"more opportunities there," my uncle said—to a three-room cold-water flat on the fifth floor of a run-down apartment building with no elevator on 47th Street between 10th and 11th Avenues. His bridge-repair business in disarray, Gus hired on as a cook at a 49th Street restaurant.

Mother, taking a first tentative step toward independence, found a job with Western Union, and Georgia clerked part-time at Woolworth's. Gus laid down strict rules. His female workforce had to come directly home at quitting time every day, and give him their paychecks on Friday.

This Hell's Kitchen neighborhood was Irish (there were no Greeks except us), with tenement after tenement crowded close to the streets and overflowing with trash. Laundry dried on lines stretched between fire escapes, old ladies chatted through open windows, and kids everywhere played stickball, stoopball, and kick-the-can. Often the boys wore only underwear, the girls short-cut dungarees. The favorite cooling-off pastime was romping through the spray of an open fire hydrant.

I was a very gregarious kid, starved for friendship and always seeking approval from males (maybe because I never received any from Gus). I have remained that way throughout my life. I think this constant quest for companionship helps explain why, later, I became close with such a wide range of gangsters.

At school I had a painful early introduction to a classmate named Jimmy, who would play a considerable role in my adult life. Jimmy delighted in bullying everybody, and one day he punched me hard in the face and stomach. I got off the pavement, not knowing what to do, and gave him an openhanded slap. He just laughed at my ignorance of self-defense.

Jimmy was eleven years old and looked sixteen. He let me hang out around him, which I did just to defy Gus's decree that I should come straight from school and lock myself in the flat. But how could he know what I did? He worked till 8:00 P.M., then drank himself goofy before returning home.

Jimmy's sole ambition was to become a mobster. He showed me his heroes, like Eddie McGrath, who conducted his business from a Horn and Hardart cafeteria on 59th Street. The red-headed McGrath, a burly guy with ties to (Italian boss of bosses) Lucky Luciano, always wore a suit, and Hell's Kitchen residents treated him with great deference. He was a power on the West Side docks, heavily involved in shylocking, numbers, extortion, and murder, and he owned scores of pinball machines, cigarette machines, and cops. He also had close connections to important politicians.

Another of Jimmy's idols was Hughie Mulligan. Weighing 300 pounds, Hughie nonetheless looked immaculate in a pinstripe suit, thin tie, white-on-white shirt, and pearl gray hat, a gold pocket watch dangling from his vest. He called himself a union delegate, but his considerable earnings came from running numbers. Detectives once taped a conversation Mulligan had on the docks. "Look at that over there," he said sadly. "There ain't a white man in the bunch. Not a single fuckin' white man." The crew he referred to consisted of Italians.

McGrath and Mulligan were bosses, but the two men who intrigued me most were Cockeye Dunn and Elmer "Trigger" Burke, both cold-blooded killers, both later executed in Sing Sing's electric chair. Jimmy and I often peered through the grimy window of a 49th Street bar to watch Burke throw back shots of whiskey and wrinkle his face (terribly scarred from teenage acne) into carbon-copy Jimmy Cagney expressions. Built small like Cagney and wearing a zoot suit, he tried in every conceivable way to mimic his movie idol. I learned that Burke's enormous heroism during World War II had caused many to compare him to Audie Murphy. Still, this was no Audie Murphy. The police believe that he murdered more than 100 people during his tremendously violent criminal career.

I actually met Cockeye Dunn, a triggerman who'd once worked for Dutch Schultz. He was sitting in Horn and Hardart with Eddie

McGrath when he spotted Jimmy and me eyeing them. "Come over here, kid," he said to me. He hoisted me up on his lap and gave me a dollar. "Your mother loves you," he said. "Take care of her when you grow up."

Many in Hell's Kitchen viewed these Irish gangsters as Robin Hoods, and certainly the mobsters were more likely than conventional businessmen to help those in the neighborhood pay their rent, grocery, and utility bills. The tough, powerful hoods drove Buicks, Lincolns, and Cadillacs (always black or dark green), seemed quite glamorous, and were apparently able to acquire anything they wanted. On a subconscious level, I am sure, I wanted to be like them. I was certain they would know how to handle Uncle Gus.

Uncle Gus. Age and a change of scenery hadn't mellowed him; in fact, he became more scary. Without provocation he still lashed out at me, Mother, and Georgia with his fists. And he developed another side that was truly sinister: he professed Georgia as his "real love" and, to my terror and embarrassment, cooed and fondled her right in front of my eyes, as though he were a lovesick teenager.

One day Gus unexpectedly declared he was obtaining a seaman's license and would ship out as a steward aboard the SS *Stony Creek*. He said Mother and Georgia could support the family while he sailed to parts unknown.

Hearing this news, we barely contained our delight. The first time the three of us were alone, we celebrated over dishes of ice cream, a rare treat.

I gradually started hanging out with more Irish kids, particularly a boy named Danny McCrossin, who, like Jimmy, had gangster fixations. To catch a glimpse of Hughie Mulligan strutting down the street was enough to make his month and inspire him to commit his own petty crimes. The tall, thin, shy, pigeon-toed McCrossin, just twelve years old, often put aside his hobby of building boats in glass bottles to burglarize a neighborhood apartment.

Gus stayed at sea for six months on his first voyage, returned home for a month of sex with a strangely quiet Georgia, then shoved off again on another long trip.

I worried greatly about my sister. In Ambridge we had been able to talk and confide in each other; but now as she matured into a spectacularly beautiful young woman, Georgia seemed detached and unreachable. Often sitting silently withdrawn, fists clenched between her legs, jerking convulsively, she became an abnormally reclusive teenager, quit school, and only went out to her job at Woolworth's. It broke my heart to see the glazed emptiness of her eyes.

At night Mother frequently talked to me about violence. "You see how much sadness Gus has caused us," she'd say. "Please, don't you be that way, Donald. Learn from the way we lived. The strongest men are the most gentle."

And I was a gentle person. I acted as Mother told me. I hung out with tough kids—there weren't any other kind in Hell's Kitchen—but I didn't fight, didn't break any laws.

Gus came off a ship with the announcement that we were moving to Pittsburgh, Pennsylvania, where he intended to revive his moribund paint-contracting business. In less than two weeks we'd moved into a small house on Charles Street on Pittsburgh's north side.

Of course, Gus resumed his attacks on Georgia, carried out with a combination of sailor-in-heat intensity and fawning puppy love. She lived in such a daze that I wondered if she felt him, saw him, or even heard his childish assurances of endearment.

Defying Gus's orders to come home immediately after school, I went out for football at Allegheny High in my sophomore year. I loved everything about the game, especially the spirit and camaraderie of my teammates, and refused to worry about what would happen if my uncle found out.

He soon did. At practice two weeks before our season opener a guy tackled me below the knees and rolled over my body, ending up on top of my shoulders and breaking my collarbone. I went home determined to bear the pain in silence. But at supper Gus, sensing something was wrong, badgered the story out of me. Driving to the hospital, he held his face in a fixed, unreadable mask, never saying a word. Then when he stopped the car at the emergency-room entrance, he began maniacally beating on the collarbone with his fist. I thought he would never stop, that my chest would shatter from the blows.

Although Gus put a halt to my high-school football career, I managed not to abandon sports entirely. I competed on the swimming team, excelling in the freestyle middle distances, and Gus never learned about it.

During my junior year, Georgia married a Greek named Spiro who had worked as a painter for Gus. Mother arranged it, and there wasn't a thing Gus could do. I was relieved that my sister had broken away from Gus, but her new happiness was short-lived.

Georgia became pregnant, and soon thereafter someone told her husband that she had been repeatedly raped by Gus. Spiro had a lot of trouble dealing with this information. Georgia begged him not to abandon her—that would mean moving back with us—and eventually he agreed to give their marriage a try in New Jersey. They moved to near where my brother Jimmy lived with Uncle Nick.

Georgia had the baby but her marriage didn't improve. Spiro moved to Detroit with the child, and shortly thereafter, Georgia suffered what polite society called a nervous breakdown: she attempted to kill herself. Uncle Nick had her committed to a state mental hospital where she got worse and worse. All told she suffered through some fifty electric shock treatments, which didn't help her condition at all.

Sweet Georgia. Because I never saw her again after she moved to Newark, I might as well complete her story now. In the mid-1960s, after more than ten years, a still-lovesick Gus managed somehow to check her out of the New Jersey mental institution and took her as his wife to Greece. Gus died in the homeland in 1983, whereupon Georgia came back to the United States—still very unwell, terribly disturbed—and passed away in 1988.

After graduating from Allegheny High School in 1956, I thought joining the navy would be a sensible alternative to living under Gus's roof. Expecting Mother to dissuade me, she instead said, "If you do join the service, I'll be divorcing Gus."

I looked at her in surprise. "I've stayed with him this long," she continued, "only because of you and Georgia. God knows, I failed your sister, and it's just torture thinking of her in that institution. I tell myself it would have been worse if I'd left him, because he would have gotten custody of the two of you, but I don't suppose it could have turned out more tragically for Georgia. At least there's you, Donald."

"I'll try, Mother."

"I know you will. You're a good boy."

I walked over to where she sat and held her in my arms. She was thin and frail. "I can't live with Gus any more," she said. "I'm going for a new life, and hope you will too."

In November 1956, Mother, filled with pride, packed a lunch for me, kissed me, said she loved me, and saw me off at the train station, waving good-bye until she became a speck on the platform.

I've often thought about the road not taken. I had to get away from Gus, but there was a means other than the navy. I had been offered a swimming scholarship to the University of Maryland, and almost had accepted it. Why hadn't I? Because I wanted to put more distance, at least an ocean, between myself and my family. I dreamed of the navy taking me to faraway, exotic places, idyllic sun-drenched paradises where I'd loll leave time away on white sand beaches, my brain washed clean of memories of Gus. Maybe I would even get to Greece.

Chapter 3

AWOL IN NEW YORK

AT BOOT CAMP IN BAINBRIDGE, MARYLAND, I BECAME A GUNG ho swabbie with a washboard stomach who loved jumping off the sixty-foot-high diving platform into a storm-simulated pool. But some of basic training I didn't like. My first fight—except for the one-sided losses to Jimmy and Gus—was against a fellow sailor in judo class. When I didn't tear into him, Chief Petty Officer Boyle took me aside and said, "Listen, in this man's navy strength alone won't cut it; you've also got to move in, be aggressive. Frankos, either go against this guy, or flunk. And flunking means you start boot camp all over again." He shoved me toward a brute from Chicago, an ironworker's kid who threw me down on the mat. I got up; he planted me again.

Boyle stopped the action, such as it was, demonstrated a few moves and said, "This guy's gonna cream you if you don't start offering some resistance. You're just a fuckin' sponge, soakin' up punishment."

I started to move my opponent around. I was so quick that, in comparison, he seemed to be nailed to the mat. I put him down time and again, hoping he would just stay there.

Completing boot camp also meant mandatory boxing class, two hours a week. The coach said, "Put the gloves on, ladies, every recruit has to fight."

"I can't do it, sir," I said.

"Why not?"

"I don't want to hurt anyone," I told him honestly. "And I'm afraid of getting hit."

"Well, Little Miss Muffet, you *got* to."

I climbed in the ring and a recruit began punching me from post to post. I did everything wrong, even doubling over at the waist and turning my back to him. When he started banging me in the kidneys I jumped out through the ropes.

"*This* is supposed to scare the Russians?" the coach asked rhetorically. "Get your cowardly ass back in there!"

"I don't want to," I said.

"I'll whip your crybaby ass myself if you don't," he promised.

Blood poured from my nose as I tried to hold off my opponent with feeble slaps, a farce the coach watched for maybe twenty seconds before blowing his whistle. "Frankos, you sorry son of a bitch, you hit like a sissy!"

Muttering and cursing, he showed me how to hold my hands, then signaled us to begin again. I forgot all Mother's admonitions about violence and started to punch. I landed three good shots, and the sailor went down in a pile. As I helped him up, saying I was sorry, the coach rushed in, yelling in my face, "Frankos! Don't ever apologize to a man you're facing in combat!"

After graduating boot camp, I received orders to report to Norfolk, Virginia, as a storekeeper on the USS *Sierra.* I promptly invited Mother to visit me, and when she flew in I gave her a complete tour of the ship. She stayed two days, looking happier than I'd ever seen her. It was not just because of me; she had moved out on Gus and begun divorce proceedings.

From Norfolk I sailed with the Sixth Fleet to the Caribbean. Occasionally we held boxing matches aboard the *Sierra*, and I won all four of my bouts by knockout. Weight wasn't a consideration. I fought both a nimble, shifty lightweight and a heavyweight over

200 pounds. I didn't enjoy the violence, as some did, taking heavy punches to deliver blows of their own, but I reveled in the collateral benefits: sailors wanted to associate with me and listen to me, and even officers showed me respect. A gentle man, as Mother said, might be the most admirable, but he didn't necessarily have a lot of friends.

Nothing about life in the navy made me particularly unhappy, though missing the Mediterranean tour and a chance to visit Greece and Sicily, the homes of my biological parents, was disappointing. Maybe there, I wonder now, I would have absorbed some European culture, even perchance kindled an interest in the Greek classics. But instead of marveling at architectural splendors in Athens, I saw bordello bedrooms in Barbados; mouth-watering visions of fine Sicilian cuisine washed out of my mind as I downed rum and Coke in Port-au-Prince; and trying to appreciate a medieval tapestry in Florence became watching a needle weave intricate designs under my skin in a San Juan tattoo parlor.

On shore leave I became the stereotypical horny sailor. In Havana I went with my buddies to a sideshow owned by Meyer Lansky and saw a guy named Samson satisfy a woman with his sixteen-inch dick. We paid two dollars to witness this spectacle, and two more to watch a girl being screwed by a donkey. A blow job from one of Meyer's girls cost five dollars.

Early in 1958 I transferred to a destroyer, the USS *Cecil,* temporarily docked in Miami. One day on the beach I met a sun-baked lady of about sixty who invited me to her apartment. I soon learned this very well preserved Jewish woman was quite rich. Her apartment featured expensive furnishings and four miniature poodles that nipped at my ankles. Over dinner—"I make the best matzo-ball soup, I cook the tastiest chicken; the secret is the carrots, greens, and white radish"—she announced that the last course would be her. I woke up the next morning before she did and went to the shower. When I opened a bathroom cabinet looking for a razor, the first thing I spotted was money, ten $100 bills. Without thinking, almost reflexively, I grabbed them and left.

To this day I don't know why I opted for such patently self-destructive, dead-end behavior, but for whatever reason, it represented the inauspicious beginning of my criminal career. Maybe I stole the $1,000 because I was fed up with the discipline of first home and then navy, or maybe simply because here was the largest amount of cash I'd ever seen. The navy paid $85 a month, half of which I sent to my mother, who struggled financially without Gus. Anyway, I didn't spend the money I'd stolen, but I flashed it to a few shipmates.

The next afternoon while I was relaxing on the beach, two police officers appeared, looked me over, searched the bag I carried, and found the stolen cash. At the county jail, the Jewish lady identified me as the thief and I was booked for grand larceny.

They put me in a cell called a bullpen with twenty other inmates. One guy came over and said, "You look like a nice piece of meat," and reached for my crotch. I cowered toward a corner. Another hood's telling the guy to leave me alone started a fistfight. All I could think was, *Oh, my God, you're surrounded by a pack of animals.*

Little did I know. I realize now, after a virtual lifetime in some of the worst institutions mankind has designed, living with many of the planet's most violent men, that this Florida hoosegow was no fearsome place, and that those prisoners, merely a collection of nodding-off drunks, small-potatoes shoplifters, and pitiable rejects, posed no real danger.

It didn't seem that way at the time, however.

Six long hours passed before a guard took me to an office where the shore patrol waited. A desk sergeant gave me a waiver and said, "Set foot in Miami in the next five years, pal, and you can count on being sent to prison."

Back on ship, very frightened, I received a summary court-martial and thirty-day sentence, which I began serving when we docked in New York and I got transported to the Brooklyn Navy Yard brig (another facility, populated largely with AWOLS, that bore no resemblance to the mean, savage joints I'd later call home). The best thing there was the food—tasty and plenty of it. Guards marched us—half-stepping with hands on the man in front—for

2½ hours, mornings and afternoons. The rest of the day we stood at parade rest, a body-aching routine. After serving the thirty days, I received two weeks leave and my life took an irreversible turn for the worse.

Footloose in New York City, I visited my old neighborhood—I'd last seen it in 1953—and ran into a few former school chums. One of them, Danny McCrossin, had become a bright, intellectual guy who attended New York University and committed burglaries on the side. We went drinking in Greenwich Village at some joints owned by Mafioso, a fact I didn't know or care about at the time. In the Club Paris,* a club catering to bisexual women and lesbians, I met a beautiful girl named Gerri.

We hit it off right away: I, dazzled by the novelty of it all, and she, intrigued with a fresh-faced teenager from "the sticks."

"Why don't you forget about the navy?" Gerri said. "I have a suite at the Wilfred Hotel.* Stay there and live with me."

A few days of AWOL wouldn't hurt, I told myself. Actually, I imagined a brief exciting fling with the sort of opulent life those street characters from my childhood enjoyed all the time.

On our second night together, Gerri, a bisexual, invited six girlfriends over to the hotel to party. They rolled on floors and beds, doing things I had never imagined. They invited me to join them—"do whatever you like"—but most of the time I just watched.

My new roommate was definitely easy to look at: cropped jet black hair, dark eyes, a sleek figure she draped in expensive tailored clothes. I wasn't surprised when she showed me her portfolio; I assumed that fashion modeling was her total means of support.

Our first few days we spent every minute together. We took long walks around Greenwich Village, ate all our meals in cafés, and lingered in saloons. Nights featured sex, as often as I could perform. On the sixth night her girlfriends came back. This time I paid more attention to their very sensuous, relaxed exchanges—none of

*These names have been changed.

the frantic fumbling I associated with my own limited sexual experiences. Halfway through what seemed an almost choreographed scene, Gerri got up from the sheepskin rug where the women writhed and tangled, took my hand, and brought me into a circle of pleasure that melted my tension into fluid relaxation.

The next day Gerri said, "Donald, why don't you become my pimp?"

"What?" I asked.

She laughed. "Well, you would only have a few duties of a pimp. I have some clients up in the East Sixties, and . . . "

"You're talking about being a whore."

"Yes. I thought you knew. What I want from you is protection. You'd go to my appointments with me, wait outside, and call the number I give you every half hour to see if I'm okay. If I'm not, or if you can't reach me, come up and see what's the matter. That's all there is to it."

"I don't know."

"It will be a breeze for a strong guy like you. The johns I do business with are older men. They'd take one look at you, and no more problems."

She was right. Most of the time she popped in and came out in less than thirty minutes, and nothing was wrong on the two occasions I did have to phone. Gerri earned $100 a call—a high price then, but she had class—from which she gave me $20.

I luxuriated in an atmosphere free of don'ts, wanted it to go on forever. During one of the orgies I watched from the sidelines, I noticed Gerri sniff powder into her nose and fall asleep a little later on the sofa. I asked one of the girls, "What was that all about?"

"Heroin," she said.

"That's a heavy narcotic, isn't it?"

"Oh, you'll love it. It's good. Makes you feel sexy, uninhibited, and you'll have lots of courage."

"Courage?"

"Yes. You'll feel great and not afraid of anything. Here. Try some."

I snorted the powder and became suddenly and violently ill,

barely making it to the bathroom to throw up. My system, strong and healthy, had rejected the drug. Well, not entirely. I went to sleep and woke up the next day feeling like Superman. My self-esteem peaked—what a treacherous narcotic this is!—and I believed I could accomplish anything. I knew other people became hooked on heroin but, just like them, I told myself *I* wouldn't.

Staying skyscraper high, I was ten days AWOL before I gave the navy another thought. "Don't worry," Gerri said. "They won't send out a posse. Just stay and live with me."

I didn't need coaxing to stick with this life. I had money in my pockets, nobody gave me orders, and booze, heroin, and sex promised perpetual happiness. Gerri was right: to hell with the navy.

About a month later, Gerri came in crying and said, "I've been raped. By the doorman at the Club Paris." The man who had grabbed her had done twenty-five years in prison before going to work for the wiseguy owners of the club. Gerri told me he regularly assaulted young lesbian and bisexual prostitutes, women unwilling to report the rapes to police.

"You've got to do something to that goon," Gerri said. "Kill him. Make it known that these creeps can't mess with me."

"Gerri, can't we just let it ride? Don't go near that guy no more. I hear he's Mafia."

"No! I won't let that asshole get away with it. Donald, this is exactly why I wanted you to work with me. If you can't handle it, I'll find someone else."

"Maybe you should. I don't think . . . "

"You're afraid, aren't you? I thought you were a ballsy man, but you're just a boy."

"I'm not a boy. I think it's stupid, that's all. Okay, okay. I won't kill the guy, but I'll sure as hell smack him."

"Well, that's a measly payback for what he did to me, but I'll take it. Tonight."

We went to the apartment of a male friend of hers and borrowed what he called a "blackjack," but what was in reality a sixteen-inch pipe. About 8:00 P.M. Gerri and I strolled to the Club Paris and stopped several feet from the doorman, a short, enormously fat guy who resembled an old-time wrestler: scar tissue on his forehead, broken nose, cauliflower ears.

He didn't take notice of us, probably because Gerri had dressed as a man, which made us look like two guys. "If you have any caring for me," she whispered, "you'll let him have it right now."

I had no way out. The doorman sensed our presence and was turning his head toward us, when I removed the blackjack/pipe from inside my jacket, took a step forward, and swung it hard with both hands, like Mickey Mantle going for the fence. I caught him full force across the front of his face, and the sound was like the sharp explosion of a gunshot. For sure, I hadn't learned how to pipe a guy: this blow would have killed most people. As it was, his head snapped back violently, his legs gave, and he sank to the ground. Blood spurted from the gash above his nose. Gerri urged, "Smack him again!"

Instead I watched in disbelief as he started to clamber groggily to his feet. I had hit him a shot hard enough to kill a steer, and now he looked at me, stupid eyes filled with hate, spit gurgling from his mouth. He made a low, gutteral noise.

"Let's get out of here," I said, and we took off running down the street. I glanced back once and saw the doorman lurching after us; then we turned a corner and disappeared from his sight.

Gerri told the story with relish to our friends, a few of whom advised us to leave the city. "You don't slug a Mafia guy," one pointed out, "and just walk away."

But we had. There seemed no explanation at first, but later, after I got to know all forms of Mafiosi, from dons and their captains to soldiers, everything made sense. No one wanted to avenge that scumbag doorman for reaping what he richly deserved, and he'd been told to let it ride. I couldn't have gotten by with smacking someone higher up, but our man ranked at the bottom of his family's organization chart.

My own stock went up, and Gerri's crowd began viewing me differently. I was a guy who didn't even fear the Mafia. Actually, though I kept quiet about it, I'd felt very uncomfortable slugging that wiseguy. Reflecting on it, I realize now that people aren't born violent. They *learn* violence. I learned it at home, in the navy, and then in the best schools of all, hard-time prisons.

Gerri and I began spending many hours in the Club Paris and at the 82 Club, both owned by the Genovese crime family. At the Club Paris, a made guy checked ID at the door, and a bull dyke hatcheck girl worked the cloakroom. There was a jukebox and sometimes a live band for dancing, and a backroom for mob sit-downs. The macho Mafiosi loved to snicker at the lesbians, but never interfered with the fun. The place, a poor man's version of the later-day Studio 54, comprised a gold mine for enterprising Vito Genovese. The State Liquor Authority forbade granting an alcoholic-beverage license to any establishment catering "to a homosexual clientele," but Genovese had the clout to break that law—and most others—in the name of profit.

Genovese's wife, Anna, a bisexual, owned the 82 Club, an interesting joint because few customers were what they seemed. The most handsome "guys" were girls. The most beautiful "girls" were guys. Hermaphrodites—chicks with dicks—performed on a flourescent-lit stage, and Greenwich Village never witnessed a louder or more enthusiastic audience. The raucous wiseguys whistled and cheered their favorite, the live fist-fucking shows.

Big-busted Anna Genovese, who always wore dark glasses, later ratted on her husband. Although associates expected Vito to whack her, he couldn't bring himself to do it. She was probably the only person he had any feelings for whatsoever.

Several times I saw Vito and his underboss Tony Bender enduring the 82 Club's loud music. The Naples-born Vito, 5'8" and very thin, wore a cashmere coat and spent his time staring at customers through bloodless eyes. I imagined those eyes had seen it all: Genovese was an associate of Meyer Lansky and, except for Charley Lucky (Lucky Luciano), the most powerful mobster in the country. After fleeing the United States to Italy in 1937 to avoid a murder charge, Vito became a close associate of Mussolini, winning the highest civilian medal the dictator could confer. As a favor for Il

Duce, Genovese arranged the murder of newspaper editor Carlo Tresca, Mussolini's most effective critic in the U.S.

It fascinated me watching people approach Genovese's table. He seemed ancient to me—he was sixty, but looked older. He had effeminate mannerisms, his thin fingers often fluttering like a girl's, yet visitors bowed and scraped as if in front of royalty. Later, when I became a student of Mafia history (wiseguys laughed at this passion, but I ranked it more worthwhile than theirs: studying the moves of Jimmy Cagney and Edward G. Robinson, without which they wouldn't have had an identity), I realized it had to be that way. Total submission and obedience, the blind following of orders, most important, *omerta*—the code of silence—were absolute requisites for the operation of any vast criminal conspiracy. So also was a kinglike figure, all-powerful, entitled to unquestioning respect.

At the moment *I* had to be content with respect at the Club Paris, where the bartender and many of the regulars approved of my cracking that doorman's head. Then another incident boosted my image even higher. A drunk came into the saloon and wanted to dance with Gerri. Nothing unusual about this—many straights got their kicks fooling with bisexuals and lesbians. But when Gerri said no, he swore at her and slapped her on the face. The bartender started for him, but I arrived first. I left-hooked him three times, and he spun halfway around before crumbling to the floor on his stomach. Other customers swarmed all over him, punching his face raw, cracking his ribs with chairs, beating him unconscious, and then tossing him into the street. A passerby must have called for help because fifteen minutes later an ambulance arrived and took him away.

I could tell that my instinctive response (from where had it come?) impressed not only the girls but the underworld onlookers. Later, when I began thinking the same way, I realized what had gone through their heads: mark down a guy who acts swiftly and decisively as someone you might use in the future.

I became aware that I *wanted* to impress wiseguys. They had money, power, jewelry, beautiful women, and fancy cars. Mother had taught me to work hard, to get an education, to keep my nose to the wheel—that was her way to success. But I wondered, what had grinding it out the hard (honest) way gotten her? Or Gus? Or my real father, for that matter? Every made guy I saw in the Mafia-owned bars and nightclubs always had a thick roll of cash and plenty of time to spend it.

My bask in glory for beating up the drunk ended abruptly. The next day the Club Paris barkeep told me, "That guy you cold-cocked was an off-duty cop."

I swallowed hard.

"Yeah," he continued, "I hear that when he woke up in the hospital, he was real pissed, wanting to sue, and threatening to bring some friends back with him and bust this place up. You better take it on the lam for awhile, lay low until things cool down."

I "lammed" as far as midtown and my junior-high-school friend Danny McCrossin. Over a few beers I told Danny what had happened and he asked, "Why don't you stop hanging out with those girls? That's no good. You should strike out on your own."

"How? What can I do to make money?"

"Go on a few burglaries with me. My partner has master keys to some hotels here on the West Side."

I thought it over and said okay, taking another small step toward a track on which I soon would run full speed. Every cop knows this truth: a killer doesn't suddenly sprout full-blown. He commits other crimes first.

Danny took me to a lounge in the Fifties and introduced me to Louie the One-Arm Bandit, who could make a right-arm lightning-quick cleanout of a jewelry-store showcase if a clerk turned his back for an instant. Right away I liked the short, skinny, nattily dressed little guy with machine-gun speech and brown eyes that spun like pinballs. Louie handed me my wallet when we got seated in a booth and said, "Pickpocketing is a small-timer's profession." He classified as a small-timer himself, but I didn't know it then, and it wouldn't have mattered if I had. He liked me and quickly judged that a Jew, an Irishman, and a Greek made up the perfect criminal team. "We'll start tomorrow," he said.

We rented separate rooms at the Edison Hotel on 47th Street near Broadway, paying for two nights. The next afternoon, if someone questioned our roam through the corridors, we at least had the excuse of being hotel guests. "Christ almighty," I could say, "I'm on the wrong floor," and appease the curious by producing a legitimate key.

After the maids finished their rounds, we went to work. I took the top third of the hotel, Danny the middle, Louie the bottom. I would knock on a door, prepared to say, "Geez, I thought my buddy had this room," but usually no one answered. The coast clear, I would let myself in with the master key, empty the place of jewelry or money (most valuables were hidden under the mattress), and head to the next room.

We hit two hotels that week without a hitch, and I had $4,000 in my pocket. Then I received word from the bartender at the Club Paris that everything had been fixed with the cop's superiors, and I moved back in with Gerri.

Danny would call Gerri's suite each morning and tell me where to meet him and Louie. This worked out fine for about a month, until a day when Danny's repeated efforts produced no response and he and Louie rode down to the Village to check on me.

"I can't go with you guys," I said, in bed with a high fever. "I think I've got the flu."

"Why didn't you answer the phone?" Louie asked.

"I didn't hear it ring. I must have been in the bathroom when you called."

Louie and Danny didn't like it, but they saw I wasn't up to robbing hotel rooms.

That evening Gerri fussed over me, playing doctor, and came up with the same diagnosis I had made: bad cold. "Take a couple snorts of this," she said. "It might help."

Help? My symptoms disappeared immediately. I had no cold, no fever, a craving for sex and then a twelve-lap run around the block. Sex, though, I found out wasn't practicable, not if I wanted satisfaction. As a heroin user, I had a terrific sexual drive, could do it for hours, but couldn't release myself.

Nevertheless, I felt on top of the world that night when several of Gerri's girlfriends came over. After I mentioned my miraculous recovery to one of them, she laughed and said, "You don't have a cold. You've got a heroin habit and don't even know it."

Sure enough, four or five hours later when the drug wore off, I became sick again. Even my addled brain began to realize how diabolically heroin operated, changing the body's chemical balance: I felt great if I took it, horrible if I didn't. I snorted more and the "cold" went away.

A heroin habit in 1958 wasn't expensive. One capsule cost three dollars, and five people could get off on it. Insidious as it is, I consider heroin less dangerous to society than cocaine. A degenerate heroin addict tends to nod off into a stupor, too sick or too benumbed to rouse himself to commit a crime, while a cocaine junkie becomes exceedingly aggressive and violent.

As we spent more time together, I grew very possessive of Gerri and jealous of her girlfriends and the johns she serviced. "Let's get out of the Village," I said.

"Okay," she said, "but we need an understanding. I won't just throw everything over. I'll still turn tricks until I'm sure we belong together. I need to maintain some independence, make my own money, and not depend on a man."

"I can support you."

"I don't know, Donald. We'll find out."

We took a basement apartment on West 96th Street. She continued as a call girl and I accompanied Danny and Louie on more hotel burglaries. Our heroin consumption increased. Neither of us really attended to business. We began to quarrel.

"I want you to start dressing like a woman," I said. "You're beautiful, but you look like a man in the clothes you wear."

Even when the heroin made her weak and sick, Gerri maintained an independence I both admired and resented. Mostly I resented it. One particularly terrible evening, coming off a heroin high, feeling both ugly and nostalgic, I called my ideal woman.

"Mother, it's Donald." My voice sounded disconnected, weird.

"Where are you?"

"New York City. We just got back from the Mediterranean."

I would learn she knew this wasn't true. The shore patrol had come looking for me.

"You sound strange," Mother said. "Are you all right, Donald?"

I looked at Gerri, curled into a fetal ball on our bed. I tried to light a cigarette, but couldn't hold the match steady. "I'm doing great, Mother," I said. Despite *ordering* the words to come out right, I sounded crazy.

"Oh, Donald." She started to cry.

"What's the matter? I'm fine."

"Donald . . . " But she couldn't say any more through the tears.

"I'll come to Pittsburgh and see you soon." Her sobs pounded in my head. "I'm doing real good," I said. "You'll see. Wait for me, and I'll show you how wonderful things are."

I banged and trembled the telephone receiver onto its cradle and looked at Gerri. I got a pencil and piece of paper and tried to write her a note, but no matter how hard I willed it, my hand wouldn't stop shaking.

I walked out into a cold October 1958 night and caught a cab to Times Square. Staggering into an office used by the shore patrol, I said, "My name is Donald Frankos. I'm AWOL and want to turn myself in."

The man behind the desk, a graying navy lifer, looked almost fatherly. "How old are you, son?" he asked.

I had to think it over, then, "I'm nineteen, sir, nineteen years old."

Chapter 4

MY FIRST MURDERS

THE MARINES WHO RAN THE BROOKLYN NAVY YARD BRIG, just across the Brooklyn Bridge from Manhattan, barked us to attention at 4:30 A.M. for inspection and punched any inmate who didn't keep his gaze fixed straight ahead. It happened to me. Because I suffered from heroin withdrawal and couldn't stand stiff as a board, a marine sergeant judged me a wiseass, smacked me in the face, and dragged me to solitary confinement, a chicken-wire cage so small it had to be entered on hands and knees.

I stayed in isolation five days on a strict bread-and-water diet. My strength and youth pulled me through, but mainly, I later realized, I made it because the navy wasn't trying to break me completely. Prisoners slept in dormitories, not cells, and the food didn't come to us rotten and maggoty. The government wanted us functional when we got released. The hard-time penitentiaries that awaited me *did* want to crush their inmates and had no concern what kind of monsters they ultimately turned back onto the streets.

I cold-turkeyed the heroin addiction within two weeks of release back into the general population of the brig. Many years later, using a takeoff on the joke about kicking the cigarette habit, I said that giving up heroin "was easy, I've done it a dozen times." And always the same way, cold turkey, in the same place, a prison. I lied shamelessly, though, when I said it was easy.

My court-martial had resulted in a ninety-day sentence, and I quickly learned to exercise caution when dealing with some of the inmates. A black guy sauntered over and punched me in the stomach. A terrific shot that knocked the wind out of me.

"You don't like what I did?" he asked.

"No," I said.

"That's too bad. I'm going to do it again, and keep doing it until you like it."

He drew back to hit me a second time, but I opened up on him—hard, fast punches, and he sank to his knees. Once more I had demonstrated to myself that I possessed unusual physical capabilities, and for the first time I almost enjoyed the feeling. Still, admonitions culled from my childhood made me uneasy.

Mother learned of my confinement and came to visit me. She didn't say anything about my being in the brig, and neither did I. She was just happy my voice didn't sound crazy, as it had the night I'd turned myself in. Needless to say, during this visit I didn't mention my criminal activities.

After serving the ninety days, I received orders to report to Providence, Rhode Island, where I would ship out to Denmark aboard an aircraft carrier. The navy gave me a bus ticket, $50, and forty-eight hours to reach the ship. Just enough time, I figured, to say goodbye to Gerri and Danny McCrossin. But when I got to Greenwich Village, I found out we had said our final farewells *before* I went into the brig: they were both dead. Danny had been shot during a burglary, and Gerri had arrived DOA at Bellevue from a heroin overdose. Louie One-Arm gave me the news about Danny, and I heard about Gerri from the bartender at Club Paris.

I rode the bus to Rhode Island in a daze, blaming myself for the death of my friends. If I hadn't turned myself in to the navy, maybe things would have worked out differently for Gerri; and maybe my being with Danny on that fatal job could have kept him alive. I checked in at the base, wandered around the facility, decided I'd be driven mad with grief on that carrier, and went back to the bus station where I bought a return ticket to Manhattan.

The next three nights I spent drinking in midtown dives, eating ten-cent hot dogs, selling blood to buy space in an Eighth Avenue flophouse, and getting in a couple of fights. On the fourth day I was shooting pool in a grimy 44th Street bar when my old friend Jimmy walked in looking like a million bucks. Jimmy had kicked the shit out of me when I was a kid, and I remembered his ambition of becoming a gangster. Judging from the expensive duds and big diamond ring he sported, I guessed he had arrived.

Jimmy bought me a drink and I briefly caught him up on my life. He was slightly impressed, said he had heard about the doorman and the cop at the Club Paris. Danny McCrossin he had known personally.

"You don't look or smell so good," he said.

"I've been drinking. Usually I bathe two, three times a day." This was true. I'd always been strong on cleanliness.

"Get yourself straightened up," Jimmy said. "I might have some work for you."

He said he dealt heroin, and told me I could sell for him. I said okay.

The longer we talked, the more he liked the idea of my working for him. "Fuck it!" he said, peeling off $500 from a wad he carried. "Buy some clothes and find a decent place to stay. You could be a good-looking guy, and I might have just the spot for you. Meet me at three tomorrow in front of Hanson's Drug Store on 51st Street and Seventh Avenue."

Dealing dope, I rubbed elbows with more legitimate famous people in the next few months than during any other time of my life. I mean stars. Comedians. Singers. Actors. A *Who's Who* of black and white entertainers I won't name here because they are alive, many of them still doing quite well. They came to the busy front of Hanson's Drug Store in their big cars, or I delivered to their homes and apartments. On a couple of occasions Jimmy sent me out of town, where a headliner was doing a gig and needed the stuff badly. Soon Jimmy let me give out my own phone number, and these show-business personalities called me direct.

Of course, I couldn't just stand on 51st Street in front of Hanson's with pocketsful of junk. I stashed it in various places, like phone booths at the Port Authority terminal, and when a customer paid, I told him where to pick up the stuff. I had drugs stored all over Manhattan and kept careful records of where, what, and how much.

I gave drugs to many people who, instead of paying later, started dodging me and buying from another dealer. On some occasions heavy users I carried would come back with stories of being all strung out and dying for a fix, and I'd break down and shell out. I paid for what I gave away, but Jimmy still didn't like it. "Listen," he said, "you can't be generous. You gotta be strictly business. I don't care if a dame's the most famous and beautiful thing on two legs, she's gonna mooch off you again and again until finally she *can't* pay. That goes for men too. You can't let fame influence a transaction. Business comes first when dealing with junkies. You have to be cold in this type of life. If you're easy, they'll crap all over you."

But giving away drugs counted as a minor problem. A cop started shaking me down for $500 a week. Jimmy said, "Pay him. It's the cost of doing business. If another cop horns in, or this guy gets too greedy, we'll do something about it. Right now five hundred buys us peace."

Not exactly. In May 1959 I was walking on Eighth Avenue when two patrolmen and a plainclothes detective stopped me. One of the patrolmen put his hand in my jacket pocket, pulled out twenty-five policy slips, and said, "Look what we've got here! Get in the car, motherfucker. We're taking a ride to the precinct."

I ended up in court, although I had no idea where the policy slips had come from, and the judge—not knowing I was AWOL—informed me that possession of more than *twenty-four* policy slips constituted a felony. As I pondered this ominous information, the prosecutor took me aside and offered a deal: cop out to a misdemeanor and receive "only sixty days" at Rikers Island. On Jimmy's advice, I took the offense.

They first brought me to the Tombs at 125 White Street near City Hall in Lower Manhattan. This was a *real* prison. A dank twelve-story fortress of despair, also called the Black Hole, it served as my nightmare introduction into what "doing time" really meant. Infested with rats, roaches, and lice, the real danger came from the inmates themselves, some of them violent sociopaths but most driven mad by a place even *Time* magazine called a "dungeon."

Never in my life had I experienced anything like the Tombs. Wall-to-wall bodies; constant fighting; ignorant, brutal, corrupt guards; horrendous food. Breakfast consisted of reconstituted powdered milk, two slices of stale, crumble-in-your-fingers bread, rancid margarine, and sour, watery coffee. Lunch: a stomach-turning pigtail, mashed lima beans, and two more slices of stale bread. Dinner: a scoop of greasy, bone-filled hash and more bread from the same loaf.

Most of the cells were six by seven feet, less space than allotted a hyena in the Bronx Zoo, and occupied by three people. The floors of these cubicles became mass graveyards for cockroaches crunched underfoot.

They put me in a cell with *five* other inmates. One guy slept sitting up on the toilet bowl; another slumped on a metal chair; a third folded himself onto a little table; the fourth inmate slept on the bottom bunk; the fifth slept on the top; and I curled up on the only space left, the floor.

The men in this cramped cage were sick from drugs, gagging and vomiting all over themselves and me. When I lay on the floor one of them peed on my feet.

Many of the men in the Tombs weren't dangerous at all. They had been picked up for a traffic violation or petty theft and couldn't pay a $25 bond. Their sentences, had they been able to get to court for sentencing, would have been probation or a few days at most. Instead they languished for months, side by side with vicious criminals who *were* dangerous. Suicide, a frequent occurrence, presented itself to some inmates as preferable to their hellish existence.

One thing the Tombs had in abundance: weapons. Inmates fashioned knives from bedsprings. Not a day went by that someone wasn't shanked, or that I didn't cover my ears to shut out the screams of a prisoner being raped.

Finally, after I had spent two terror-filled weeks in the Tombs, correction officers herded a group of us into a van for an airless ride to the ferry to Rikers Island.

Rikers Island held a massive penal facility with separate cellblocks for youth and women, and a cluster of five-story, smokestack-topped buildings for male offenders. Located near LaGuardia Airport, the gray, forbidding prison structures seemed to warn, "Abandon hope all ye who enter here."

The inmate clerk assigning cells told me, "I'm gonna put you with a white guy, because our whites stay with whites, blacks go with blacks, Spanish with Spanish. This is the policy over here, and it's a good one. Otherwise, everybody would kill each other." He shook his head. "Tell me, where you from?"

"The West Side," I said.

"A few West Siders will come to see you. They'll check out what type of person you are. If you measure up, if you're good people, they'll let you hang around with them."

They put me in an eight-by-eight-foot steel-and-concrete cell and tossed me a couple of wool blankets. An hour later a trusty told me to undress. "Time for your shower," he said. "Take your clothes off."

"I gotta undress here?"

"You need to be sprayed."

He sprayed me all over with stinging disinfectant, under my balls, up my ass, even on my face and eyelids. "Stuff kills lice," he said. Then he added, after leading me to the common shower room, a place thick with the smell of semen, "Be careful in here." The shower ranked as a likely place to get waylaid by homosexuals.

Rikers Island assaulted all five senses: (1) *hearing*, constantly attacked by loud, mind-deadening music, usually played by blacks, and the screams of inmates being beaten, knifed, or killed; (2) *sight*, cell after cell of society's dregs packed up against one another in dirty dungeons; (3) *touch*, everything slimy, filthy, hard, never an object soft and clean, not even the bed; (4) *taste*, absolutely atrocious food, garbage not fit for the rats who ate much of it; and (5) *smell*, the worst of all, a devil's mix of shit, urine, and disinfectant—eyes could be shut, meals were only three times a day, but there was no escaping the stink.

Rikers Island could have been a gladiator school. Walking down the block from the shower to my cell, I saw *three fights occurring at once:* a white and a black guy going at each other with pipes; two blacks trying to rip each other apart with knives; and a pair of Spanish guys fencing with homemade screwdrivers. Cheering, wild-eyed prisoners stood in circles jumping up and down—like crazed bettors at a cockfight—watching the battle of their choice. The guards didn't seem to care.

Several times in those first few days at Rikers Island I felt hard, hateful eyes sizing me up. Penetrating stares from rough-looking strangers who wore proudly what police refer to as "distinguishing characteristics"—ornate tattoos, deep scars, missing fingers and teeth.

A week passed before a delegation of white guys came to visit. Their leader, an Irish hood named Joe O'Connor,* asked, "Where you from?"

"The West Side of New York," I answered.

"Who do you know?"

I mentioned my friend Jimmy.

"Jimmy's okay. Who else do you know?"

"His brother-in-law. Mikey."

"Yeah. Mikey."

"I knew Danny McCrossin. I worked with him."

"All right," O'Connor said. "You stay with us. We can school you on how to do time, and what to expect in this fuckin' prison."

The first thing I learned was that a "class system" existed at Rikers Island: "good guys" didn't rat and could take care of themselves in a fight; "bad guys" weren't violent and didn't know anybody. The good guys had free rein to beat up and extort the bad guys.

O'Connor warned me about the "prison combat zone," a

*This name has been changed.

grouping of picnic tables right outside our cellblock area. "Don't walk out there alone," he said. "You'll need four or five guys with you. Otherwise, count on getting jumped, hit over the head, or knifed. You know how to use your hands?"

"Not much." I didn't want anybody trying me.

"Well, learn what you can. There's a lot of racial tension here. It's best to keep your mouth shut in this institution. If you see black guys serving chow on the main line, don't pick up nothing from them. I don't care if it's meat. You don't touch nothing they serve. And don't talk to no black guys. Don't associate with them, because when a black guy comes in, they tell him the same things about us. See, the racism is both ways. It's not only us, it's them too. The key word is *beware*."

I asked about exercise and O'Connor said there was a gym, but the prison authorities had closed it. Too much violence. Then he continued telling me about how I should behave to survive in Rikers: "If a black *or* a white guy looks at you wrong, you *have* to fight him. If he talks bad to you or disrespects you in any way, you *must* go after him. And if it comes down to killing him, do it. Remember this: if you don't kill him, he'll kill you."

I would hear the same orientation speech from gangsters in other joints. The time came when *I* instructed newcomers.

O'Connor gave me more lessons: "Take an oath to never inform on nobody in here or outside, no matter if you're in the right. You can't squeal on no correction officers, even if they beat you to the ground or you see them pounding on your best friend."

Following O'Connor's advice, I had some fights. Once I responded to a black guy staring at me; another time an inmate called me "cocksucker" and I went after him. I knocked both these men cold with my bare fists, and began believing O'Connor had it right. If I fought, the day would come when I no longer had to.

"If you aren't in top shape," O'Connor had said, "you can't handle the adversity." Taking his words as gospel, I joined the white guys in the back section of the cellblock and did a lot of chins, push-ups, and deep knee bends. Each ethnic group worked out in a separate section, and vigorously defended territorial rights.

Our diet certainly wasn't conducive to bodybuilding. We had ten minutes to eat the garbage on our plates that told us what day it was. Saturdays they served tongue. On Friday we got a bowl of fish, boiled white potatoes with sprouting eyes, and wax beans. An unstomachable kidney stew was the Wednesday staple. The big meal of the week was Sunday's "murderburger," a gristly patty made from a mixture of the lowest grade beef and ground-up pork bones.

What an inmate did on the outside counted for or against him in prison. An ace bank robber or jewel thief was held in considerable esteem. The highest respect went to hit men and mob enforcers. On the opposite end of the spectrum, the lowest of the low, were the rapists and child molesters. A man sentenced for sexually abusing a woman or youngster may as well have walked into the joint with a neon sign blinking "TREAT ME LIKE SHIT. MAKE MY LIFE MISERABLE."

Still, there were plenty of sadists who enjoyed making life miserable for *anyone* who seemed to them "different." These differences included showing basic civility to others, a desire for privacy, too much intelligence, too little intelligence, and especially the wrong skin color. You couldn't win with the latter. Whites were prey to blacks, and vice versa.

I would like to say my month and a half of hell at Rikers Island wised me up and that I was smart enough to mend my ways. But it didn't happen. When I got out, I hooked up again with Louie One-Arm.

On our second job, at the Hotel Bristol, we hit a jackpot. In the top dresser underneath the clothing of a permanent resident, I found a "valuable book." Instead of gems of wisdom, the hollowed-out pages secreted pearls of another kind: brooches and necklaces set with precious stones, gold charms, and gold bracelets. Plus, I found $6,000 in cash.

Louie was overjoyed. He fenced the jewelry and my share came to another $7,500. We agreed the score called for celebration: he went to the racetrack; I caught a cab to LaGuardia Airport and a plane to Pittsburgh.

I took my mother out to dinner at a swanky restaurant, with candlelight and even a strolling violinist, and saw tears in her eyes before our food arrived. "What's the matter?" I asked, thinking something might be wrong with her marriage.

"It's you, Donald."

"I'm doing fine, Mother."

"You . . . you look like a gangster. You're dressing like the hoodlums I see in movies."

"That's the style in New York these days." I began to squirm under my mother's all-seeing eye and changed the subject. "Here's something for you," I said, balling a thousand dollars into her hand. "My card-game winnings on the ship."

She wouldn't take it and admonished me for gambling, though she suspected worse. Toward the end of the very uncomfortable dinner, I finally persuaded her to take the money—she must have needed it badly—but she kept worrying about my clothes and the way I talked.

When it came time to leave, I said, "I'll be back soon. The next time I'll give you even more money."

"I wish you wouldn't," she said.

"What? Bring you money? Can't you use it?"

"I wish you wouldn't visit me." Tears rolled down her cheeks.

"Mother . . . "

"Donald, don't come here again."

And that's the last time I saw the woman I called my mother. It broke her heart seeing what I was becoming, and I guess also she wanted to cut all ties with the Frangos family. I pretty much honored her wish, although a few times I tried to contact her. She wouldn't have it—she refused to see or talk to me. Nevertheless, she has remained through all the years the single warmest memory I have.

I think Mother's dead now. In 1989, from prison, I hired a private investigator who reported that Social Security had no current record of her.

Back in Manhattan, feeling my last link with the civilized world had been severed, I closeted myself in the apartment during the day and walked the streets alone at night, trying to figure out what to do with my life. After seventy-two hours of soul-searching, I made a conscious decision to be a crook, a damn good one. I decided there was no other way for me to make so much money and at the same time not be beholden to anybody. No Uncle Gus, no navy, no anybody telling me what to do. I said to myself, *Forget needing to hear Mother say, "You're a good boy, Donald." From now on, as Tony the Greek, you will earn the praise and respect of fellow criminals.* Thus I began plotting my course through the world of crime, vowing there would be no turning back, and no regrets.

I was twenty years old, about the age college students decide the profession they intend to pursue.

I went to see my friend Jimmy and asked if the $8,000 I had remaining from the Hotel Bristol robbery would buy me a partnership in a portion of his drug trade.

"Why not?" he said. "I'm beginning to sell in Harlem, and you can have some of the action there."

Jimmy showed me how to cut heroin with milk sugar and quinine. I spent long hours each day in a hot, unventilated room loading hundreds of capsules for street pushers to sell for $1.50 and $3 each. Money quickly began pouring in from black buyers in Harlem. Unfortunately, while I was cutting the heroin, I got hooked on the fumes, and soon I was snorting more than ever.

About this time I met a young East Side madam named Mary who once had posed for *Playboy*. I sold her drugs she wanted for her girls, took her out a few times, and ended up moving into her bordello in the East Seventies, a large, modern, specially designed apartment with six bedrooms feeding off a reception area/living room with a bar. The girls felt safer with the protection I provided, and I had access to the best sex money could buy.

I found myself enjoying every bite of the slice I'd carved out of the Big Apple. I made $2,000 a week in the partnership with

Jimmy, and I met a steady stream of colorful underworld characters: hustlers, pimps, stickup artists, crossroaders—hoods from all over the country who came to us for drugs.

In fact, I considered myself a real man of the world until two shore patrolmen spotted me and pulled me in; officially, the navy still had dibs on me. Incredibly, the spit-polish shine on my black leather shoes—a serviceman's chore I had learned too well—caught their attention as I strolled through the Port Authority bus terminal. I tried to bullshit my way around the shore patrolmen, but soon they had my name and case history and took me to the Brooklyn Navy Yard brig.

In September 1959, I was sentenced to three years at the naval and marine prison in Portsmouth, New Hampshire. Prior to transfer there, however, I acted repentant and managed to secure a job as a trusty. Then I caught the eye of a sergeant major who sent me on his personal errands, and from one of these trips I simply didn't return. I headed back to the life of petty hustler and drug dealer. Back to Jimmy, to Mary, to the same apartment/bordello.

My life-style had been leading inexorably toward a certain type of crime, but I was surprised when the moment arrived. Mary told me that a black pimp had become a problem for several of her girls. He had ripped their wigs off, stolen the money they hid underneath, and threatened to keep it up if they didn't agree to work for him.

"You have to kill this pimp," Mary told me.

I didn't even argue with her. I hunted him down, caught him from behind on Broadway in the early morning hours, and drove a knife into his heart. He crumpled at my feet, like a punctured flour sack, and no one chased me as I jogged off into the night.

The police made only the most perfunctory effort to solve the homicide. They didn't care, and I never became a suspect—I doubt they knew I existed. Most detectives, though they won't admit it, think in the same manner as criminals: good riddance to that scumbag pimp, our congratulations to the guy who stuck him.

Society says I should have remorse for the murders I committed, but I'm not sure I do. Even if I ignored the dubious qualities of those I hit, there is the fact that I viewed myself as a soldier and my victim as the enemy, and in that warrior context there can be no regret; rather, I felt a sense of mission accomplished.

I can't say either that my first killing, committed at age twenty, was harder than the others or that it sticks in my memory. I went out and did it and that was that. I enjoyed the praise and recognition it brought. Clearly I had become that most envied criminal, a cold-blooded hit man, and daily I saw my newfound status reflected in the deferent, fearful eyes of others. *Respect.*

Mary operated under the loose auspices of a Genovese crime family captain, and she told me he had been impressed with my performance. She said there were two white pimps he wanted me to take care of and, eager to please, I whacked them on consecutive nights, again using a knife. The chances now were that Vito Genovese himself knew my name. Crime bosses are always on the lookout for killers.

In November 1959, I decided to move out of Mary's apartment. I was worn down from the drugs, partying, tricks, girls coming and going, and johns ringing the bell at four or five in the morning. It was too much, packaging and delivering drugs all day, playing the entire night. The heroin use had slowed my pace, and increasingly it was a struggle even to get out of bed.

"You need help," a hooker friend told me. "Check into Manhattan General and go through detox."

I gave my real name at the hospital, not realizing it ran criminal checks on drug addicts. The receptionist told me to sit tight, and I did, stupidly, from 1:00 P.M. to 5:00 P.M. when a pair of plainclothes cops showed up to arrest me.

I was just seasoned enough to know how ludicrous my arrests had so far been, hardly the way Machine Gun Jack McGurn got taken: I had been busted on a beach; I'd turned myself in; I'd been framed; I'd been ratted out by my own spit-shined shoes; and now I had sat like a fool waiting for the cops to find time to pick me up.

The navy slapped on two more years to run consecutively with the three I already owed. On the train to Portsmouth, New Hampshire, a marine guard told me, "Now you're going to a man's prison. Wait till you get a load of this place."

The marine was blowing smoke. Once I cold-turkeyed the heroin habit, I joined the boxing team and quickly fought my way to the prison middleweight division championship. I won the title with a second-round knockout of a Mexican considered the toughest guy in the joint.

Prison authorities, who always seemed impressed by a good boxer, gave me an easy job as bartender in the officers' club. Then I caught a much bigger break when the staff psychiatrist interviewed me and discovered my history of drug abuse. His report stated I was "physically and mentally incapable" of ever serving in the navy and recommended I receive a commutation of my sentence and an undesirable discharge.

After six months of red-tape unravelings, the navy sent me on my way. An officer advised me to stop by Stillman's Gym in New York and continue boxing, but I ignored his rehabilitation suggestion and headed straight back for Jimmy.

Why did I always go back? Because the life was glamorous and exciting, big money could be made, and I didn't imagine I'd get caught again. No matter how many times a gangster is busted, he always thinks he'll be more clever the next time. I *guarantee* he doesn't think, "Goddamn, I'm falling into the same old routine, and for sure I'll be back in the joint soon."

"What do you think I should do?" I asked Jimmy.

"I know what you *shouldn't* do," he said. "Don't go back to that pimp scene. It's no good for you. Try a real man's job: big-time stickups. I'm working on hijacking a truck filled with musical instruments. Should be a piece of cake."

The first part of the heist went just like he said it would—I drove the truck away while the driver ate lunch. But when I arrived at the Apollo Theater in Harlem, the supposed buyer turned out to be a cop, which *wasn't* the way Jimmy had said it would be.

Now I figured I faced some real hard time.

Chapter 5

CHIN GIGANTE HELPS OUT

"WHAT'S YOUR PROBLEM, ASSHOLE? WHY THE FUCK DO YOU keep looking at me?"

The occasion was my first night in the New York City Workhouse (NYCW) on Hart Island in the Bronx; the speaker was the gangster in the bunk next to mine, a husky hood named Rocky Moro.* *He* had been maliciously eyeing *me*. Not in the mood to play staredown or any other jailhouse game, I jumped to my feet and said, "All right, cocksucker, let's go to the back right now and throw down."

"Hold on!" said a gray-haired gangster, inserting himself between us. "Don't fight each other. Use your brains. We gotta stay strong against *them*."

My antagonist itched to start swinging, and so did I, but the older inmate's wisdom made sense. Grumbling, we sank down on our bunks, conserving energy to battle "them," the numerous blacks who shared our dormitory floor.

*This name has been changed.

Thanks to my friend Jimmy's connections, stealing the musical instruments resulted in a minor ninety-day sentence in the New York City Workhouse, a dirty, dreary place with bad food, terrible accommodations, brutal guards, and constant threats from other inmates. In other words, par for the course.

Prisoners at Hart Island's NYCW were kept in seven three-story dormitories, 120 inmates to a floor. Those on the second and third tiers climbed to their quarters on outside fire escapes. Two other buildings—a hospital and a solitary-confinement section—completed the complex. Packed in large open rooms with no bars and no racial segregation, inmates roamed freely, engaging in fist and knife fights around the clock. I soon learned to sleep with one eye open and to awaken at the slightest sound of anyone approaching my bed.

After getting off to a bad start with him, the guy I spent the most time with at Hart Island was Rocky Moro. A good-looking blond-haired half-Italian with a pockmarked face, Moro was serving sixty days for numbers. Little could I have guessed that this run-of-the-mill street thug would, like a latter-day John Gotti, murder his way up the ladder of organized crime. Nor was I yet privy to Moro's closely guarded secret: half-Irish roots that, if known, would have precluded his membership in the Mafia. At that time I only saw his huge fists, arms like Popeye's, thick fire-hydrant legs, and fierce, mean eyes. Moro was a 200-pound mass of bad temper and solid muscle.

On my second night in NYCW, Moro, incensed by the blasting music from a radio, shouted, "Turn that damn noise off!"

"Fuck you, white boy!" an anonymous voice replied angrily.

"Yom," Moro said to me, shaking his head. (Yom, a shortened Italian word for eggplant, is used derogatorily by Mafiosi toward blacks.) He marched over to the nearby cluster of five blacks, lifted the offending radio above his head, and smashed it to pieces on the floor. Right away the blacks jumped all over Moro, smacking him with lead pipes produced as if by magic. I grabbed my own pipe and waded into the melee, swinging hard and wildly at the men who were clubbing Moro. They had split his forehead wide open, and blood stained his blond hair red.

The NYCW "goon squad"—an appropriate name the inmates gave a special organized group of the toughest guards—broke up the battle, but not before Moro and I were winning. Since the episode was hardly uncommon, the hacks didn't reprimand any of us.

The guys playing that ear-numbing music were wrong; and Moro, I, or any one of the 113 other inmates sharing our floor had every right to object. But voicing a complaint behind bars is a waste of time: guards invariably turn a deaf ear and, besides, the prison animals causing the trouble understand only one form of communication, violence directed at them.

It hadn't taken long to absorb the lesson first taught me by Joe O'Connor on Rikers Island, that violence constituted the only means of survival in these joints; nor had it required superior intellect to judge that winning beat losing. When I went after those blacks in defense of Rocky Moro, I had already learned how to block out fear and enter a conflict without concern for my own safety. I pumped myself up silently. *You may get killed, but die like a man.* Not caring gave me a big advantage, and I steeled myself to do anything to win—slash a throat with a razor, pluck out an eyeball, squeeze a guy's balls to mush. Drawing first blood helped. Usually, unless opponents were just plain crazy or totally disoriented from drugs, they backed off after seeing themselves bleed.

If Moro and I hadn't made an early stand against the music, violations of our rights would have increased. For instance, the blacks might have ordered us to surrender our cigarettes and, if we complied, their demands would have escalated until we were reduced to groveling foot servants and convenient bent-over butt-fucks whenever they got horny. I'd already seen it happen to weak inmates unable to resist intimidation, and over the years witnessed it ad infinitum. For many prisoners who wouldn't, or couldn't, stand their ground, suicide became the only alternative.

Put an average guy in one of these prisons and within six months he will wind up a good street fighter, a doormat, or dead. Joe Schmoe from the suburbs will find himself extorted every week and sexually abused every day. There's no being a decent individual whom the animals will leave alone. They'll suck Schmoe absolutely dry, take away his dignity and pride and every cent he has. It starts when someone tells him, "You're going to put one hundred dollars in our commissary every Friday. And your wife will send five thousand dollars to an address we'll give you."

Demands for payment never stop. They'll beat the shit out of Schmoe and make him suck their dicks, whether he pays the money or not. State prisons used to be the worst, but federal joints are catching up because of new types of wild men such as Latin American drug dealers, the Mexican Mafia, Cuban boat people, Vietnamese extortionists, and the Aryan Brothers.

I've seen it happen a hundred times. Joe Schmoe—maybe he swindled an insurance company, a white-collar scam—hears a young tough say, "Give up the radio, cocksucker, or I'll cut your throat." Schmoe loses no matter what he does; he dies if he refuses, or suffers a lingering death if he gives in. Behind prison walls there is no mercy for the weak and powerless, no respite from the demands of the hood who has nothing but disgust for his victim's weaknesses. Guys in the joint will sodomize a ninety-year-old man.

Forget about asking the guards for help. They don't want to hear about problems and try to avoid beefs with young toughs. If Schmoe complains, guards spread the word that he's a rat. Or a hack will say, "Hey, motherfucker, you telling me this stuff happens while I'm on duty? You trying to get me in trouble?"

I recommend violence to anyone unfortunate enough to end up in prison. Usually if an inmate fights back the first time—say he cuts his attacker with a razor—he has a good chance of being left alone. Prison predators reason that there are too many easy marks, so why harass someone nutty enough to fight back?

It took a few years for me to work myself into a genuine terror whom inmates wanted to be around for protection from other prisoners. Getting incarcerated in penitentiaries made me a tough guy and taught me real violence: how to smash a man's kneecaps with my foot, shatter his larynx with my fingers, bite off an ear or part of a face. The more confidence-building success I had, the more respect I earned from everyone—the whites, the blacks, and the Latins.

One thing I didn't need a lesson for was understanding on whose side I stood: always *with* the inmates, *against* the hacks. I never became confused about which group deserved my loyalty.

Showing appreciation for my coming to his assistance, Rocky Moro arranged for me to work with his Hart Island crew burying bodies in potter's field, the final resting place for indigents with no known relatives, or prisoners with families who would not claim them. The corpses were given a number—no gravestone, not even a name. Known names were recorded elsewhere, next to the number, in case relatives appeared or had a change of heart. We planted the thin wood coffins, stacked 7 deep, in rows of 50: 350 to a trench.

Each weekday morning we grave diggers trudged in ragged lines away from the dormitory a mile up a lonely dirt road to the burial ground, from which we could see the neighboring island where Typhoid Mary (Mary Mallon) had been confined. Thirty years earlier her isolation from society had been a cause célèbre. Various rights groups had rallied to protest her exile as a pariah.

Regulations required that we open each box and examine the body before burying it. The sight of the corpses, many of them carved-up remnants of crude autopsies performed by medical students and instructors, would have turned a strong stomach inside out, but the guys in our crew possessed the clinical detachment of coroners.

The opening of one pine box sent Rocky Moro into convulsions of laughter. After several minutes of bringing himself under control, he explained that here lay the remains of Chris Tabo, a hood he had killed in a dispute over money. Rocky flipped out his cock and peed on the box. "Chris," he giggled triumphantly, "I told you I'd piss on your grave."

Potter's field had a Catholic hole, a Protestant hole, a Jewish hole, a hole for babies, and a hole for body parts. Some times we just had arms or legs, which went into the body-parts hole.

Even made guys wanted to be on the burial detail. The stench was sickening, but they considered it a score job because of the extra privileges—especially being away from the hacks who wouldn't, so to speak, be found dead in this place.

The job, like all others, paid zero, which meant the city employed slave labor. A few politicians fought to secure wages for prisoners who did work that otherwise civilians would have performed (getting off jobless rolls); ultimately the government did agree to pay: usually five cents for an eight-hour day.

We didn't just bury bodies, we also dug them up. The worst was a fat man we'd planted just a few hours before his family claimed him. Of course, his heavy body was at the bottom of the grave, so we had to move six coffins off his. Then we slid chains underneath, brought it up, and stepped gingerly with the casket all the way to the waiting hearse.

Each evening after a trek back down to the dormitory, which in the 1940s had housed Nazi prisoners of war, we took showers to rid ourselves of the stench. Then we heated bologna-and-cheese sandwiches, provided by the mortician, on steam radiators next to the wall. Nights were spent shooting craps for cigarettes, playing cards, reading, or getting to know one another. Moro never tired of relating the activity that most turned him on: obtaining a trio of sixteen-year-old Puerto Rican girls and caking their vaginas with cocaine for him to lick.

Moro got released from NYCW before I did, insisting on his last day that I go to work for him when I came out. Prospective wiseguys like him—the same held true all the way up to godfather—could never have enough tough people in their employ.

I knew Rocky Moro as mean and very ambitious. His goal, which he vastly exceeded, involved becoming a made member of the Bonanno family. Despite his negative personality traits, he promised I would earn $2,000 a week with him, and that sounded good to me.

As soon as I got released from NYCW, I went to work for Moro. I knew that if I was to achieve my goal of moving up the criminal totem pole, I needed to be accepted by guys like him, so I acted accordingly, mainly as a loyal, elemental force carrying out orders unquestioningly. I could still be shocked and disgusted, however; an example occurred on my first day out of jail.

I met Moro in downtown Manhattan, and he was drunk. I'll never forget this scene. On a gray afternoon with light mist falling, we walked along Delancey in the Bowery. I listened as he outlined my duties as a loan-shark collector. Nobody was on the street except for a dirty, very pathetic skid-row wino stumbling toward us. Rocky said to me, "Watch this." In a pleasant voice he asked the bum how he was doing, but before the guy could reply Moro punched him in the face and knocked him down. Then he took out a pistol, leaned over, and shot the guy in the head, for absolutely no reason.

I killed five people with and/or for Rocky Moro, either competing unconnected loan sharks or stickup guys ripping off Moro's collectors. These heavy-handed but effective messages to stay off Moro's turf enhanced both our reputations as tough guys.

I also did some head cracking when borrowers fell too far behind with payments. Often they were stone gamblers, deli or restaurant owners, sweatshop operators, or small trucking industry entrepreneurs. It amazed me how quickly debtors could produce cash when previously they claimed the well was dry. Of course, loaning money to businesses constituted good business, because when the payments really did become impossible to meet, Moro found himself owning legitimate enterprises.

In 1961 I broke away from Moro, deciding that this violent alcoholic simply represented too much trouble. I had grown tired of his drunken behavior and constant babblings about how he planned to get made. I couldn't be made—I wasn't 100 percent Italian, though neither was he—and actually counted myself lucky being an independent, without all the demands of a crime family. For one thing, a Mafia soldier had to share his earnings with a variety of bosses. Plus, he signed on forever; once in, only dying got him out.

Like nearly every gangster I met, I fantasized about the "big score" providing me with some undefined utopian retirement. Not until years later did I understand that I, too, had joined for life, as surely as any wiseguy, simply because I enjoyed the thrills, liked most of the people I hung out with, and would have been thoroughly bored without the daily rush of living on the edge, outside the law. I believe a major reason people drink or use drugs is because they enjoy it; booze and narcotics give pleasure, or at least escape, and so too does the criminal life with its lack of stifling strictures and excellent income. If nothing else, my life was exciting: I knew it and I loved it.

After leaving Moro I hooked up with a gang of armed robbers, five in all, including Mario Massulo, an associate of rising Genovese soldier Vincent "Chin" Gigante. Interestingly, all five of these men died violent deaths; looking back, I'm surprised I didn't.

Our crew burglarized homes and apartments of high-dollar drug dealers and usually took plenty of junk, cash, and jewels. We tried to avoid mob-connected dealers because of our loose association with Gigante, who tipped us on some of the places to strike; but mistakes occurred—once we had to return the merchandise. Generally, however, we were a bold and cocky gang that didn't give a damn about the Mafia or anything else. The police didn't care if we fleeced drug pushers, and the victims certainly weren't going to report the loss.

One time we stuck up a fourth-floor apartment in the West Eighties near Broadway where several Jamaican drug dealers and their families lived. Two of our crew, dressed as cops, pounded on the door. A woman peered out through a peephole, then called for Jesse, her husband. "What do you want?" Jesse asked through the closed door.

"Two ounces of pure."

"I don't know who you are."

"Police, you dumbass! Do we have to break down the door, motherfucker?"

Seeing the uniforms, Jesse opened up, and six of us poured in, guns drawn. We found four men, four women, and six kids inside. After smacking a couple of the men to attention, we shoved them against the wall and tied up all the adults, except for one woman we locked in the bathroom with the young children.

The key to pulling off a successful robbery, whether in a bank, jewelry store, or residence, is keeping people calm. After a minimum of rough handling to demonstrate who was in charge, I assured the Jamaicans they wouldn't be harmed *if* they cooperated. This was true enough. We had come to rob, not kill. Creating panic would only jeopardize our objective.

We started ransacking the residence, which was actually three adjacent units remodeled into one. From the outside I'd expected to find a dump, but the place was filled with costly furniture, hand-tied Oriental rugs, statuary, and even a bubbling indoor fountain. A corporate executive and his family could have lived here, if they didn't mind the shabby facade.

We found a kilo of heroin inside a big wedge of cheese, varying amounts hidden in flowerpots and lamp bases, and telltale signs that some of it had been hastily flushed down a toilet or thrown out the windows when the occupants had thought cops were at the door.

I was slitting the brocade upholstery of an expensive sofa when I heard one of the frightened youngsters crying in the bathroom. This wouldn't do at all. I untied a female prisoner and placed her with the child in a bedroom. Taking the woman aside, my voice soothing and my gestures nonthreatening, I said, "Keep the little kid quiet. We're not going to hurt anyone."

When I returned to the main living area, a pile of merchandise had accumulated on the floor: perhaps forty tailored suits, sixty pairs of alligator shoes, fifteen Zenith TVs, a container of fourteen-carat gold Bulova watches, and a half-dozen diamond rings. Also $10,000—literally, *cold* cash—from the freezer.

Suspecting there was more dope and more money, we forced three of the men to strip, rebound their wrists securely with venetian-blind cords, and herded them into an empty bathroom. I moved the two remaining women to a third bathroom. That left us

Jesse, the main Jamaican, who now didn't need to feel obligated to display courage in front of his associates and kin.

This head honcho sat, hands tied behind his back, on a once-elegant sofa that now spilled knife-riddled stuffing onto an Oriental rug. I stood over him and said, "Jesse, where's the rest of the bread? The rest of the junk?"

He didn't say a word. Sweat glistened on his forehead, and he looked into my eyes, calculating, trying to read me.

"Jesse, where are all the goods?" I touched my pistol to the bridge of his nose.

"No more," he said. His terrified eyes swept over the pile of merchandise on the floor. "You got everything."

I hopped onto his lap, straddled his legs, and clenched his torso with my knees—it's called "riding"—as I grabbed a handful of hair and yanked his head backward. I shoved the barrel of my gun against his eye and snarled, "Jesse, you've got exactly ten seconds to tell us where the goods are before I blow your eye right out of your fucking head."

"Okay!" he half shrieked, the pain of blue steel terrific against his naked eyeball.

I cracked the pistol on the side of his head to make sure he moved with appropriate speed, and he led us to a walk-in closet, then pointed to the back wall. A phony wall. We ripped into it and found almost $100,000, plus Canadian and German money, and three kilos of heroin. All told, this wasn't our biggest score, but neither did it tally as the smallest—about average from the house of a major drug dealer.

We carried everything, even the TVs, downstairs to the street where our truck was parked. Four guys jumped in the trailer with the goods, I rode up front with the driver, and we headed toward a warehouse run by wiseguys to unload all but the junk and cash. Not in a million years could any of us have imagined the craziness about to overtake us.

Unknown to the crew, one of the Jamaicans had worked free, gotten in his Cadillac, and was following our truck. While tailing us downtown at about 2:00 A.M., he managed to convey to a pair of cops in a patrol car that we had robbed him and were making a getaway. The officers radioed for backup and pulled us over. Before they reached the cab of our truck, *six* other police cars careened to a skidding halt, radios crackling, lights flashing, sirens blaring. We were surrounded.

"All right, motherfuckers," said one of the cops, "come out with your hands up." Soon all six of us were flat on the pavement, being kicked, poked with nightsticks, the usual routine. When they finally let us stand, the Jamaican fingered the entire crew.

A black cop arrived, took charge, and asked what we had stolen.

"Money," the Jamaican said.

"Anything else?"

"Only money."

I snickered to myself. The detective had already gotten an eyeful of the sizable stash of shoes, clothes, and TVs in the trailer—not to mention a few guns and the heroin—and surely knew we had stolen a load of hot merchandise.

This Jamaican, I thought confidently, won't be testifying against anybody. Greed had prompted the ill-conceived attempt to recover the money—he couldn't possibly claim the rest of the loot without buying some heavy trouble for himself—and I figured he would cool off once he considered his own precarious position. I was dead wrong.

"Sir," the black cop said to the Jamaican (*me* he had addressed the same way the first cop did, as "motherfucker"), "we've found other items in the truck."

"I know nothing about that. Money was all they took from us. Maybe the rest of the stuff came from another stickup."

I waited in vain for the cop to come down with both feet on this bum. Instead he nodded knowingly, as if indeed we might be stupidly cruising Manhattan with loot collected from several jobs. He took us to the precinct, and soon a bunch of the Jamaicans, even two of the children, showed up and identified us as the stickup men.

After our accusers left, a cop surrounded by other cops said, "All right, you cocksuckers, peel off your clothes, then come out one at a time, when we call you. You!" he pointed to me. "You're first."

"Fuck you," I said, not wanting them to think I'd take just any shit they dealt.

"Get those clothes off, you son of a bitch!"

"Fuck you, you faggot!"

"Cocksucker, we'll come in and take them off."

They didn't make a move, but I knew they would if I pushed any further. I gave them a few stares and then undressed.

When I came through the cell door, a big cop smacked me with his open hand, and I let go a shot that knocked him back four feet. I again hit him in the face, hard enough that he required medical attention, and then the other officers were all over me. I landed a few more good head and body punches before they wrestled me into handcuffs and started clubbing the soles of my feet, my back, and my ribs. Two of them held my arms while a third hit me in the gut.

Witnessing it all, my five crime partners later told people I never once begged, whimpered, or asked the cops to stop. Word reached gangsters and members of organized crime, who were impressed. Other events that occurred while I did time also enhanced my reputation. I got involved in so many fights while serving various stretches that a cellmate once said, "Greek, you're a legend in the New York prison system."

Two days after our arrest, a detective paid us a visit and Massulo gave him Chin Gigante's phone number. This convinced him that we were people he should help. Small-timers wouldn't know Chin, much less how to reach out to him.

An ex-professional boxer who weighed close to 300 pounds, Gigante in the early 1960s was a rising wiseguy destined to score big: ultimately he became godfather of the Genovese family. On May 2, 1957, however, attempting to execute a contract put out by Vito Genovese, Chin shot Frank Costello as he entered the lobby at 115 Central Park West on the corner of 72nd Street. Costello (real name Francesco Castiglia) had risen about as high as a Mafioso could—he had known Al Capone and had attended organized crime's *first national convention* in 1929. Costello represented the only competition Genovese faced to becoming primus inter pares among all American Mafia bosses.

But just as Gigante fired his .38, Costello moved, causing the bullet to graze the right side of his head. Because Costello went down as if axed, Chin thought him dead and sped away in a black Cadillac. Costello, honoring the code of *omerta*, refused to identify Gigante, yet the doorman at 115 Central Park West did—a very foolish act. But when Chin was tried for the shooting, his defense team effectively challenged the credibility of the doorman, and Gigante went free.

Gigante could pull off those kind of miracles, though his favorite ploy was the "bug act," pretending to be punch-drunk from his fighting days. Even when not under indictment, he prepared for those inevitable times (knowing the police watched him) by picking cigarette butts off the street and smoking them, gesturing wildly in the air, having long, loud arguments with himself, or dropping his pants to pee in the street. Chin wasn't crazy. He was a shrewd businessman and a cold, cunning, merciless killer.

Responding to the detective's call, Chin sent one of his men to see us. The man told us Chin said "not to worry," but we did plenty after reading the charges: possession of narcotics, menacing, unlawful imprisonment, robbery in the first degree, felonious assault in the first degree, and a lot more. Worse, the district attorney was calling it a "big case," which meant he aimed to further his career by giving us serious time.

Almost a month went by before the crime lab analyzed the heroin, time needed by Chin Gigante. Meanwhile, we were transferred to the Tombs.

The detective who had called Chin did his part to help us by raising a stink that the Jamaicans should also be indicted. The D.A. knew that that would blow most of the case against us, since the Jamaicans wouldn't be so eager to testify, but he realized the detective was right, even though he didn't know he was right for the wrong reasons.

Three months dragged by in that wretched hole called the

Tombs, during which several pretrial hearings got us nowhere. Finally we learned from Chin's man that the D.A. might want to make a deal.

"What kind of deal?" I asked.

"He didn't elaborate. But Chin says no, don't take it, just keep going through the motions."

Three months later the messenger from Chin told us the D.A. would recommend we get two years, with credit for time served. This sounded good to us—only two years for a "big case"—but we were once again told, "Chin advises you to wait."

A day or two before the scheduled opening of our trial, the D.A. offered not to prosecute, *to let us go,* if we pleaded guilty to lesser charges. Chin's man told us, "Chin says it's up to you."

"Why *wouldn't* we take this deal?" I asked.

"Maybe you want to be vindicated in court," he said dryly. "But the D.A. can obtain continuances, keep you here for awhile, though he knows he can't win. You think he's offering this sweet arrangement out of the kindness of his heart? He hates you guys."

"Why *is* he offering it?"

"He doesn't have any witnesses. They've all vanished."

"You mean . . . "

"They're okay. I think. Chin says they wanted to go back to Jamaica."

I heard that's what happened. A few visits from tough guys convinced them life would be shorter if they testified, so they backed off.

I thought this represented a remarkable coup, a stunning victory against insurmountable odds, since we had been caught red-handed with the stolen property. For awhile I stood in awe of the power of Chin Gigante. Actually, I learned, his feat on our behalf was all in a day's work for him.

Already my life had developed a pattern: each time I came out of jail running. I was a gangster who thrived on the underworld's atmosphere and excitement, not to mention the money. Aside from lucking into a big inheritance, few guys my age had bundles of cash like I did, or such pleasurable ways to spend them: fine cars, food, booze, drugs, and women.

The one thing I didn't love 100 percent was the killing, though I can't honestly say I hated it either. I killed because people I hung around respected hitters, and the reputation I acquired opened many doors for me. But I wasn't the type who got his thrills from murdering. I met plenty of these disgusting perverts, and sent a couple of them on to the next life.

By establishing some guidelines—never murder anyone who didn't deserve it, and never, *never* hurt women or children—I kept the conscience my mother had stirred from revolting against the crimes I committed. And I really did stick to my self-imposed rules. Several times I didn't kill a woman, even though the danger existed that she would testify against me.

After beating the Jamaican stickup case, I ran some numbers and worked as a collector for wiseguy loan sharks. I made a couple of thousand a week, but being a "cowboy," and treasuring my independence, I decided to solo on a score.

I was living at the Milton Hotel* in Manhattan. I learned that a Jewish mobster, operating his bookmaking business out of the newsstand/candy store, kept his take in the hotel safe. Once a week he made a withdrawal and delivered the money to his boss, a Genovese captain.

This bookie was highly regarded by the Mafia. Although Mafiosi snubbed black and Hispanic hoodlums, they viewed a good white money-maker with as much respect as a made guy.

I didn't care what the Mafia thought, nor was I deterred by gratitude that a Genovese family member had kept me out of prison. I figured the bookmaker would be picking up at least $75,000 from that safe, and grabbing it would be easy. *Fuck the Genoveses*, I said to myself. Since I'd wear a disguise, no one could identify me, and I didn't have to worry about the cops because the mob wouldn't report the heist.

The moment I snatched the money, everything went bad. A

*This name has been changed.

detective on stakeout in the hotel lobby heard the old bookie say, "Please don't shoot." That's when I noticed the cop for the first time. "Hold it right there!" he boomed, rising from his chair and fumbling for his gun. I darted out the door, cash in hand.

The detective was twenty yards behind and losing ground as he chased me westbound down the street, yelling "Halt! Police!" He never would have caught me, and didn't dare shoot on a crowded street, but suddenly a beer-truck driver who heard the cop shouting and saw me running blindsided me with a tackle that would have made New York Giants linebacker Sam Huff feel proud. By the time I recovered my feet, the detective had his revolver against my head.

My old friend Jimmy and Rocky Moro visited me in jail. Each said I'd made a serious mistake, taking that Genovese money, but they thought I had a way out.

"Plead guilty," Moro said. "It's the only chance you have."

"I don't think so," I said cockily, proving I had a great deal to learn. "I figure I'll drag the case out as long as I can. I'll go scot-free. Those mobsters won't testify."

"Jesus Christ, Greek," Jimmy said, "the least of your worries is their testimony. Listen to me, you dumb bastard. They'll *kill* you if you don't plead guilty right away. First and foremost, the Genoveses want their money back. As long as you tie up the case, the prosecutor will hold the cash as evidence. I'm telling you, plead guilty now. You're young. Maybe I can put in a word for you."

That's what he did. After Jimmy explained what a good guy I was, albeit green and impulsive, the Genovese captain agreed to forgive and forget.

I pled guilty to robbery and grand larceny and got sentenced to 2½ years in prison.

Chapter 6

THE DEATH HOUSE

GANGSTER FILMS OF THE THIRTIES AND FORTIES TOOK MILLIONS of moviegoers up the river with James Cagney, Edward G. Robinson, George Raft, and Humphrey Bogart for an inside look at the Big House at Sing Sing. Hollywood always dramatized some poor sap being dragged kicking and screaming to the electric chair, his pleas for mercy drowned out by the melancholy wail of a harmonica or an old black man humming a tear-jerking tune in the background.

That was all bullshit.

The only person I ever heard of who cried was Julius Rosenberg, the convicted atomic-bomb spy. He cried for his wife, Ethel, who followed him to the chair and, actually, her execution was worse than he could have imagined, because it took a long time to kill her. They didn't hit her with enough juice the first try and had to do it a total of five times.

After being transported thirty miles up the Hudson River to Sing Sing to serve my sentence for the Milton Hotel stickup, I learned a lot about the death house and executions. Authorities assigned me a job in the prison library, and my duties included delivering books, newspapers, and magazines to individuals waiting to be executed. Therefore, I frequently entered this ultrasecure building, and I grew fascinated with the inmates, their personalities, and the crimes that had landed them in this dread spot.

My own housing consisted of a six-by-eight-foot cell in A Block, which comprised six tiers, forty cells to a tier. Wake-up bells rang at 6:45, 7:00, and 7:15 A.M. Anyone able to sleep through them was rousted out by a guard's club banging against the steel bars of his cell.

After breakfast—powdered eggs, stale bread, a mug of undrinkable coffee—we headed through a tunnel attached to the mess hall down hundreds of stairs to reach our jobs. It was a dangerous walk. Knifings and pipings were commonplace; the only hack supervising the trek positioned himself safely at our journey's end.

Each morning I reported to the three-story education building, far down the hill upon which were perched the various cellblocks, with a commanding view of the Hudson. On the first floor of the building where I worked was a print shop; the second floor consisted of classrooms; and the third was the library. Three times a week a death-house hack delivered written requests for reading material, which I gathered up and personally carried to the condemned prisoners in a separate building only thirty feet from the library.

The death house was an island unto itself on the Sing Sing property, an ugly two-story blockhouse squatting on barren soil about fifty yards from the river. I had to pass through *four sets* of double-locked gates to reach the inmates, who waited for their walk to the electric chair in eight-by-twelve-foot cages. Since solid steel walls prevented eye contact, the prisoners communicated with each other by shouting or passing notes out the barred front of their cells. Some 612 Sing Sing inmates had already gone to their deaths when I arrived, and the grim count increased by two before stopping.

One of these was Freddie Wood, a career criminal I got to know very well. On June 30, 1960, he had bludgeoned a pair of Queens robbery victims to death in their apartment. Since Wood was out on parole at the time, the parole board subsequently tightened up on releases, specifically disregarding "earned good time." Consequently, until his execution, Wood's peers probably ranked him as the most unpopular prisoner in the New York State penal system.

But no one is totally evil, and the fifty-two-year-old Wood—I tried on my visits to spend a few minutes with each inmate—made some astute observations about the life he had come to know best: "All the brutalization and dehumanization you see in these prisons is for a reason. It's part of the system to take these young guys and break them down, and then to send them back into society so crazy and violent to where they're gonna commit even worse crimes than they did before. That's why there's nothin' prison officials like better than a crime wave. 'Cause that's the only way they're gonna get more guns and more money."

Freddie Wood was no exception to the rule that a condemned inmate doesn't sleep the night before his execution. He knows there will soon be plenty of time to rest, and each second becomes precious.

Wood ordered pot roast for his last meal and, though he didn't smoke, five packs of cigarettes (the maximum allowed), which he gave to other prisoners. Hoping to dull the pain of death, he requested liquor and pills. No chance, the warden told him. The alcohol ban traced to the previous century when Commodore Elbridge T. Gerry, a member of the New York Yacht Club, chaired a committee to recommend the "most humane" method of execution. "In the moral aspect," the committee noted, "the gross impropriety of sending a man into the presence of his Maker intoxicated is too obvious to require comment."

Freddie Wood, whom I considered a friend, earned himself a niche in prison lore with a statement made just before they led him to the chair. "Gentlemen," he said, "tonight you will have the opportunity to witness an experiment designed to measure the effect of electricity on Wood."

Jerry "The Jew" Rosenberg, who became one of the closest friends I ever had, was in the death house at this time. He later was the subject of a biography by Stephen Bello, titled *Doing Life*, which contained Rosenberg's unforgettable description of the night Wood died:

> They came for him at nine fifty-five on the nose, and I watched every step he took. You could hear the generators revving up and the exhaust fans in the ceiling roaring to carry away the smoke. But Freddie never looked back. There was a tremendous sense of dignity about him all the way, and I'll always carry with me the sight of him disappearing through that door—with the chair just waiting for him and the leather straps coiled neatly on the arms.
>
> A few minutes later the lights dimmed for twenty seconds. There was a brief pause, and then they dimmed again—this time for the full two minutes.
>
> It was a terrible night. And that's when I finally realized the state wasn't playing games.

Jerry Rosenberg mentioned me in *Doing Life*. "Thank God I had my good friends in there with me. Especially the Greek. He stood watch over me. Donald 'the Greek' Frankos is his real name. Looks something like an Anthony Quinn type of character, only younger—dry sense of humor, the best in the world.

"Years later I defended him in a murder case where we made new law in the Second Circuit. As usual, the guy who got whacked was a stool pigeon, a low-life bastard who'd been at it for years. They needed blood for the guy. They announced it on the prison speaker. And not one guy gave blood. That's the kind of solidarity we had over there at the time."

My favorite stop on my death-house rounds was Jerry Rosenberg's cell. Invariably he asked for a tall stack of reading material (I carried the books, magazines, and newspapers in a mail sack), and he seemed always happy to be able to talk with someone.

Jerry and his partner Anthony Portelli (also awaiting execution), had been convicted of the May 18, 1962, murders of NYPD detectives Luke Fallon and John Finnegan during the robbery of

Boro Park Tobacco, a distributor of candy and wholesale cigarettes. Portelli, the prosecution said, was the shooter, but the law deemed Jerry Rosenberg equally guilty. Press coverage of the case galvanized much of New York City against the defendants, since Fallon, especially, had been a popular officer with thirty years on the force.

Jerry was always talking about his case; more specifically, how he could get the decision overturned. He told me the police beat two witnesses to obtain their testimony. One of them, Richard Melville, claimed he had been punched and clubbed, burned with cigarettes, and forced to stand naked in a station-house basement with a weight tied around his balls. "This beating," said Kings County Judge Samuel Leibowitz, "would do credit—if I can call it credit—to a Gestapo wretch in Hitler's concentration camp."

It was clear each time I stopped to chat with Jerry that he didn't intend to go quietly to the chair. After his arrival at the death house—amid a mob of jeering, cursing guards who wanted to tear the "cop-killer" apart—he spent a couple of months in his steel cage screaming obscenities, ranting, and throwing whatever he could lay his hands on. This behavior earned him a few predictable beatings and nothing more.

A little guy, 5'7" and 140 pounds, the twenty-eight-year-old Rosenberg gradually began listening to wiser heads in adjoining cells. "Cocksuckering and motherfuckering the hacks won't get you anywhere," they told him. "Study the law. See if you can learn something that might help you. *Don't* count on your lawyers, who aren't, *can't be*, as concerned for your welfare as you are."

Did Jerry take this advice?

Did he! This fourth-grade dropout, who at age thirteen ran numbers and dealt stolen cameras, ultimately obtained *two* law degrees from correspondence courses he took in the joint and became the most famous jailhouse lawyer in the world. The 1986 made-for-TV movie about his life, starring Tony Danza, correctly credited him with representing hundreds of criminal defendants.

In the death house, Jerry buried himself in books and urged the habit on me whenever I visited, as did another of my prison heroes, a murderer named Francis Bloeth (more on him later). It said something about these two that they fretted over *me*.

Jerry the Jew became a *great* lawyer. If he had been practicing on the outside he would have ranked with the stars of his profession.

Prison officials hated him, and not just because he was an irreverent cutup refusing to be impressed by their authority. They hated him because he constantly upset their cozy status quo, filing and winning a blizzard of lawsuits. Many of the privileges a prisoner has today—such as the right to consult regularly with his attorney (which previously depended on a warden's whim), to see a psychiatrist, and to send and receive mail—were enforced from actions filed by Jerry Rosenberg.

In March 1979, he won a parole for Bonanno crime family boss Carmine Galante, a miracle legal feat that had proved beyond the capability of Galante's own high-powered, expensive lawyers. Usually, though, Jerry didn't care about the problems of big shots like Galante. He preferred working for indigent Puerto Ricans, who couldn't receive mail because prison authorities often didn't employ censors able to read Spanish.

Perhaps Jerry's most outrageous stroke as a lawyer was one documented in the July 11, 1988, *People* magazine. His death sentence had long before been commuted to life, and he argued in New York State Supreme Court that since his heart had stopped during open-heart surgery, he had already died and, therefore, had served his life sentence.

"Death is an irreversible condition," Assistant Attorney General Kenneth Goldman stated sensibly.

"If it was irreversible," Jerry shot back, "I wouldn't be here arguing this case."

Being naturally sociable and curious (probably the reasons I met so many unusual characters—in a different milieu I might have been called a busybody), I enjoyed talking with most of the death row inmates—fourteen men (eleven white) and one woman—as I made my rounds. Only two of these were genuinely unpleasant, repulsive individuals. One was what we call a "cell gangster," a guy who kept threatening to beat the shit out of anyone who came near him. Of course, no one *could* get near him, so the loudmouth felt pretty secure.

The other unpopular inmate was Winston Moseley, a real creep. He had been sentenced to death for killing Catherine "Kitty" Genovese in Kew Gardens, Queens, in the early hours of March 13, 1964. People all over the world still talk about this murder as a prime example of the apathy, callousness, and even cruelty that animals of the same species display toward one another. *Thirty-eight* residents of respectable Kew Gardens who were aware of the attack on Ms. Genovese not only refused to go to the aid of the screaming, begging woman, but didn't even bother to call the police. The victim would likely be alive today if just one neighbor had acted. Moseley originally had stabbed her repeatedly, but she still lived when he left her on the darkened sidewalk. Worse than a vampire returning for the kill, he came back ten minutes later, found her cringing and bleeding in a narrow stairwell, and carved her apart. He drank blood from the dying woman's vagina and attempted to rape the corpse. When the cops arrived they found an abattoir.

Moseley admitted to police that he had killed another woman, Annie Mae Johnson, shooting her eight times, committing acts of oral necrophilia, and setting her on fire. What the police probably didn't know was that he boasted to his fellow death-house inmates that he had slaughtered six more women in similarly hideous ways.

A short, thin, unimposing man, the almost supernaturally powerful Moseley crouched on all fours in his cell and with an expressionless face and monotone voice recounted exploits no one wanted to hear. I attempted several times to find something human in this man. I would relay a piece of news from the outside world—Moseley could read only the simplest of words, never asked for books or magazines—and he'd stare at me with dead, evil eyes. "What a beautiful flow of crimson," he'd breathe, "when I worked the knife up her pussy."

Judge J. Irwin Shapiro omitted the traditional closing words—"May God have mercy on your soul"—when he sentenced Moseley to die. Instead he said, "I don't believe in capital punishment, but I feel this may be improper when I see this monster. I wouldn't hesitate to pull the switch on him myself."

Kitty Genovese's killer again made the news briefly in 1968 when he escaped by overpowering two guards at a hospital where he was being treated for self-inflicted stab wounds. Hundreds of lawmen surrounded the suburban home where he hid out and raped a hostage before his capture.

Despite Moseley, I preferred the atmosphere in the death house to that pervading the prison's general-population blocks, where racism powered a mighty engine of hate. *Groups* wanted to fight each other at Sing Sing; only enlightened prison policies prevented a bloodbath. In the death house, violence was never even contemplated by the condemned prisoners, a fact the hacks attributed to extraordinary supervision. But I think the phenomenon occurred because, facing a terrible shared fate, the inmates cared for one another. In any case, my rounds brought me in contact with some remarkable people.

Carmine Di Biasi

AKA Sonny Pinto, Di Biasi would beat the electric chair and live to pump the fatal bullets into Joe "Crazy Joey" Gallo. Pinto, an awesome killer, stood a handsome 5'8" with dark eyes and curly hair. A highly intelligent man, his taste in literature centered on the classics: Flaubert, Tolstoy, Dostoevsky, Franz Kafka.

As a veteran hitter for mob boss Joe Colombo, Pinto was by nature a closemouthed gangster, but even he always had encouraging words that boosted morale in the death house. I enjoyed talking to him about guys we knew on the outside. This very neat, compulsively clean killer knew everybody.

"I understand you ran with Rocky Moro," he said.

"Yeah." I wondered how he knew that.

"A drunken bully. You don't belong with him," Pinto said.

Sonny, in his thirties, awaited execution for having murdered Michael Errichiello in 1951 in the Mayfair Boys Civic and Social Club on Mulberry Street in Manhattan. He'd shot Errichiello three times: in the head, the stomach, and the heart. Realizing he had a witness to the homicide, Pinto had also shot Rocco Tisi. However, Tisi survived and testified against him seven years later, after the elusive Sonny tired of hiding out (he nonetheless took contracts while dodging the cops) and turned himself in. Giving up was a mistake, he judged from his death-house cell, though ultimately it worked out for him: his conviction got reversed on a technicality and he was acquitted in the retrial.

Francis Bloeth

Francis Bloeth was the most admired criminal in the death house, maybe in all of Sing Sing, not for his murders but for how he completely turned his life around in prison. Bloeth's killing spree on Long Island and subsequent chilling confession to his wife and law-enforcement officials earned him nationwide media exposure, typified by the following story in the August 24, 1959, *Newsweek*:

> "All right, they saw me. They had to die. That was it."
>
> These words ended a two-week reign of terror on suburban Long Island, which began shortly after 10:00 P.M. on July 31, when Hans Hachman, 54, was shot dead in his delicatessen in Islip. In all, there were three remorseless killings, netting a total of $357, but robbery was not the motive.
>
> "I wanted to kill," Bloeth said.
>
> **His Last Bullet:** As Bloeth began his spine-chilling confession, the kneeling woman was helped to her feet and led away to spare her the ordeal of listening. She was the killer's wife, Jane, 25, mother of his 8-month-old daughter.
>
> Besides the Hachman killing, Bloeth quickly admitted shooting to death Lawrence Kircher, 53, counterman in the

> Diane diner in Smithtown on Aug. 5, and Mrs. Irene Currier, 50, in her restaurant in Westhampton on Aug. 8.
>
> "I would have killed more but I was out of ammunition and I was afraid to buy more," he said.
>
> In disbelief, police heard Bloeth explain that he originally had planned to strangle Mrs. Currier to save his last bullet for someone else.

A grim portrait indeed of a man who had changed dramatically by the time I met him and would even more as years went by. Entering prison a functional illiterate, Bloeth scored the highest I.Q. in the New York State penal system (the thickest books I brought into the death house always went to him), and he eclipsed even Jerry Rosenberg's academic accomplishments behind bars—I think he earned three university degrees. In fact, it was Frank Bloeth who urged Jerry the Jew to go into law. After Rosenberg's cell-busting rampage, Bloeth said, "That violent shit will get you nowhere. They know how to meet you with violence. They got soldiers and you don't got shit. They could easily kill you in here; you're in their backyard. You want to get at them? The only way you'll do it is with *this*." Bloeth passed down a law book to Rosenberg, who could scarcely read at the time.

Frank Bloeth was a very close friend of mine. We were together in the riot at Auburn Prison and he also participated in the Attica uprising. He and the bomb maker Sam Melville helped draw up the list of grievances at Attica: Why can't we have tutors? Why can't we have high school equivalency tests? Why can't we have college programs?

This man, who used to strangle cats and first got busted at age thirteen for stealing money from a church poor box, somehow had achieved genuine rehabilitation. Transforming into a thoroughly admirable individual, he earnestly tried to help other inmates. Most amazing of all, he was that rarest of persons who experienced heartfelt sorrow for his crimes. He told me, "I never would have known remorse or grief if I hadn't educated myself. Without expanding my mind, I would have kept on thinking who gives a fuck that I killed those people. But now I see that you don't *take* a man's life, you *give* him life."

Bloeth loved the shit out of me and a lot of others. "I wish I could get you into education," he said.

But he never did, though not for lack of trying. At that time I was skimping to make it on the money I'd accumulated and fighting blacks and greaseballs all fucking day long. Like a know-it-all teen turning a deaf ear to parental warnings about pitfalls of a road already traveled, I chose to deal with all my day-to-day problems. I was living in the jungle struggle of the general population; Bloeth was more removed from it. When he finally got released from the death house, he would sit down and talk to the tough guys because we respected him. I knew that even though Francis Bloeth was one of us, a convict, he was rehabilitating himself, while we merely marked time. He said to me, more convincingly than anyone ever did, "Greek, this is no life for you. You're going to die if you keep being a tough guy. I know you feel you need to maintain that image, but you don't. Look at me: I murdered three people, and I don't want to ever kill again. I'm sorry and wonder why I did it. I took those lives and now their kids and their grandkids and their friends and loved ones are suffering. And I think of how much my own family suffers because of my crimes."

Bloeth had two lawyers who liked him, and professors came from all over the country to see what made this brilliant man tick. With so many people ultimately pushing for his parole, he got all his bids running consecutively, and after twenty years made it back onto the street.

He became a model citizen, working with the underprivileged, especially prisoners. His message to inmates: "Crime does not pay; don't glorify it. The only thing you got going for you is the time. So let it work *for* you. Get into books, my friends. That's the only way to escape the bullshit these people put you in, these revolving doors. It's called recidivism. Look the word up. Take it seriously."

Today he is still active helping ex-cons, more effectively than any program the state ever set up.

I didn't follow Bloeth's advice, but everything he said made sense. When I first went into prison I desperately needed job training and counseling, but neither were available. Not the right kind, anyway. The training I received sucked me deeper into a life of crime. I learned how to make a living, albeit an illegal one, employing a new set of rules. I also found a family, one that didn't reject me because I got into trouble. I discovered a brotherhood that was loyal, helpful, understanding. We had common interests and I enjoyed their company. I was a criminal and other criminals taught me to be a better one.

Hank Dusablon

Another high-IQ inmate, the chalk-faced, burly Dusablon had been condemned to die for the murders of Martin Himmelstein, owner of Roma Liquor Store in Manhattan, and his employee, Cesar Largo, during a holdup. These weren't Dusablon's only murders. He and his partner Emanuel Samperi had also killed shopkeepers in Woburn, Massachusetts; the Bronx; Queens; and another in Manhattan.

Dusablon, a yoga buff (he'd put himself into a trance in front of my eyes) and astrology fanatic, told me he could leave his body whenever he wanted. I didn't argue with him. Though he said he killed because "dead men tell no tales," he was always a gentleman in the death house, extremely clean and neat. When I dropped a cigarette ash in front of his cell, he reached outside and swept it up.

Dusablon was the most optimistic of the condemned inmates. His study of the stars convinced him, correctly as it turned out, that the death penalty would soon be outlawed, and his never-wavering optimism made him a popular man even with the cold-eyed Sonny Pinto. When Dusablon did get released into the general population, he became involved in several serious knife fights with inmates who objected to his "bullshit."

Emanuel Samperi

"Are you being a good boy today?" I'd greet the twenty-eight-year-old Samperi as I made my rounds.

"Oh yes," he'd say in a shy, giggling voice. "Yes I am, Mr. Greek."

Samperi, Dusablon's odd-fellow partner, was a short, dark-complected, dumpy man who hated taking a shower. Seriously retarded, he should never have been sentenced to death, even though he was capable of the most mindless, vicious murders.

Charles Glinton

A wealthy man, Glinton, forty, received the death sentence for tossing his twenty-one-year-old roommate, José Rivera, out of a fifth-story Manhattan window. The police said the motive was a life-insurance policy naming Glinton as beneficiary; but the defendant, a devil worshiper, claimed to the court, to his fellow death-house inmates, and to me that Jesus Christ had ordered him to do it. Not unexpectedly, the court didn't buy this defense. A college graduate, immersed in the occult, he often spouted ritualistic mumbo jumbo. Whether or not this was a "bug act" to beat the chair, I can't say.

Anthony Portelli

Jerry the Jew's partner, the alleged shooter of those two cops, Portelli more resembled a Catskills stand-up comic than a killer. Roly-poly, built like a pear, he usually greeted me with, "I'm going to get in shape, Greek. Watch." He'd do two squats and quit.

If the main purpose of capital punishment, as some contend, is to prevent condemned men from killing again, the state missed the boat trying to execute Rosenberg and Portelli. They weren't violent people at all. I know they could be released, live a million years, and never kill. The scared kid who panicked and shot two cops when they caught him in the middle of a robbery had died a long time ago. Someone different was locked up now.

Anyway, Portelli joked and laughed *all* the time, surely to hide his fear, and like Jerry he couldn't fight a lick; yet there was strength in this little man. He was also similar to Rosenberg, whom he adored, in that he identified 100 percent with the inmates against the hacks—and was always there when a friend needed a hand.

Salvador Agron

The Cape Man. For many New Yorkers he became the very symbol of evil.

On September 2, 1959, Agron and eight other Puerto Rican youths were arrested for their involvement in the knife murders of two boys on a West 45th Street playground between Ninth and Tenth Avenues. The motive: revenge for alleged mistreatment of Puerto Ricans by Hell's Kitchen Italian and Irish youngsters.

An angry mob surrounded Agron when he arrived at the police station. His murders had stirred enormous public outrage, and the sixteen-year-old took a terrific beating in the press.

It was revealed that Agron, a homosexual whose preference ran to very young children, had been seen wearing a nurse's black cape lined in red satin (thus the name Cape Man; others called him Dracula). This was bizarre enough, but what shocked everyone was the weapon he carried: a twelve-inch silver-mounted Mexican dagger.

The Cape Man was still a kid when I knew him, and not tough at all. He was very afraid of dying, and several times he cried when I tried to lift his spirits. The other condemned men also felt compassion for him. Most of them had been in gang fights—that's what the playground incident really had been—and knew this tall, shy, skinny kid was no Dracula.

Governor Nelson Rockefeller, pressured by groups and individuals that included Eleanor Roosevelt, commuted Agron's sentence to life imprisonment. During the Cape Man's new and misnamed punishment, he succeeded in an escape attempt and, ultimately, in winning parole in 1979.

Nathan Jackson

A small-time black stickup man, Jackson killed Patrolman William J. Ramos, Jr., during a gunfight outside a Brooklyn hotel on June 14, 1960. The robbery, Jackson's third of the night (the first two netted $173), featured the taking of six hostages and $63. One of the victims broke a window and alerted police before Jackson could even leave the hotel.

I liked Nathan Jackson. He got undone by a moment of madness, a "pistol duel" the *New York Times* called it, and received the ultimate sentence for a crime he wouldn't have committed had he not been caught up in a high-pressure situation of his own making. He himself had been shot three times. Although still in considerable pain from his wounds, Jackson always had a friendly greeting when I delivered his magazines, and his "up" outlook contributed to the death house's strangely positive atmosphere. Part of this, I'm sure, was "whistling through the graveyard" behavior, but regrettably such brotherhood and solidarity occurred in the general population only during strikes and riots.

Nora Elliott

Authorities kept this attractive black woman, Nathan Jackson's common-law wife and accomplice in the Ramos killing, on the second floor of the death house in what amounted to absolute solitary confinement. I delivered her mystery novels to a matron who in turn carried them up to her.

All I knew about Nora was a smiling face and a waving hand.

She watched for me at the window of her cell when I came from the library to the death house, and as I arrived she would wave through the bars.

I studied with morbid fascination the immediate reality of the death house from a front-row seat, and its history from books and documents found in the library. William Kemmler was the first to die in the electric chair, August 6, 1890, at Auburn (all executions were soon moved to the newly constructed facility at Sing Sing, where one of the men put to death had helped build the place).

Before Kemmler took his final walk he witnessed an unseemly battle between entrepreneurs Thomas A. Edison and George P. Westinghouse over whose type of electrical current should be employed to fry the condemned. Edison's Edison Electric Light Company furnished *direct* current, and he claimed that alternating current was so dangerous its only real value lay in killing people quickly. Edison argued that Westinghouse should get the contract *and* the bad publicity sure to ensue. Westinghouse, for his part, opposed the concept of the electric chair entirely and argued that hanging was the best means of execution.

The *real* struggle was over which man's company would be chosen to install electric systems for the nation's municipalities. Edison hoped to win these immensely lucrative contracts by showing that alternating current was unsafe. Westinghouse, who knew a.c. was stronger than d.c. but feared a public relations disaster, eventually won the contract for supplying power to New York City *and* the electric chair at Auburn. Despite Edison's claims, a.c. was both more efficient and less expensive.

Mistress killer William Kemmler—"I'm guilty and must be punished"—took a seventeen-second jolt of Westinghouse juice and fell still. "That will do," said Dr. E.C. Spitzka, an attending physician. "Turn off the current. He is dead."

"There," said another attending medical man, Alfred Southwick (a dentist), pointing at Kemmler. "There is the culmination of ten years' work and study. We live in a higher civilization from this day."

Kemmler started to groan and thrash about.

"Turn on the current instantly!" Dr. Spitzka shouted. "This man is not dead!"

Back on went the voltage. The Erie County District Attorney ran out of the room in horror. A United Press reporter fainted. Although Dr. Southwick predicted, "No sir, I do not consider that this will be the last execution by electricity, there will be lots of them," newspapers of the day were not so impressed. The New York *Sun* wrote, "Civilization will find other lines on which to manifest progress." The London *Times* said, "It would be impossible to imagine a more revolting exhibition." The London *Standard* suggested that Kemmler's death would "send a thrill of indignation throughout the civilized world."

Not enough to stop it, though. More than 600 condemned individuals followed Kemmler to the chair, and it didn't get any prettier.

Poignant stories abound about people who died in the electric chair. Several prisoners underwent life-saving treatment and operations in order for the state to keep them alive so *it* could kill them. The main job of the death-house guards is suicide prevention.

The humor in the death house can be remarkable. One individual scheduled for the electric chair said, "Life is a joke, Warden," and then quoted Shakespeare's Julius Caesar:

> He that cuts off twenty years of life
> Cuts off so many years of fearing death.

A one-legged condemned man willed his wooden leg to a reporter he disliked, saying he hoped the journalist would some day need it.

Another man was married just minutes before going to the chair. Still another inmate's last request, which the warden granted, was "for a guard who could smile instead of look gloomy" to accompany him to the death chamber.

And then there was inmate 70292 who obtained his wish to commit "legal suicide" by confessing to a murder he didn't commit.

What I remember most about the death house were the warmth and camaraderie of the prisoners, plus the dignity they maintained while readying themselves for the end. They were interesting people and I considered most of them friends, but there were many more (horrifyingly) fascinating individuals in Sing Sing's general population.

Chapter 7

SING SING

ON A STARK, WINDY, UNFORGIVING AFTERNOON IN LATE autumn 1963, I stood on the sidelines of the football field that doubled as a baseball diamond near the gray waters of the frigid Hudson River, cheering for my team, the all-white Spartans, against the all-black Senegalese.

It was a bad idea, this football game contested on a dirt field pocked with pebbles and rocks and officiated by old-timer inmates who knew better than to aggravate anyone by calling penalties. The players wore no uniforms and had one piece of equipment, the pigskin. Except for a game against the hacks, neither of these teams could have found more hated competition.

There were good athletes on the field. Our tight end was a former star NBA basketball player jailed for rigging point spreads. Still, athletic skills didn't count as much as toughness and meanness in these Sing Sing gridiron duels.

I paced behind the Spartans bench. Normally I was the team's starting halfback, but I was sidelined with a cracked hand from a mess hall fistfight. The fight had been with a Puerto Rican inmate who had jumped ahead of me in the chow line, a blatant insult I couldn't overlook unless I wanted to eat more serious shit later. Episodes like this didn't occur because a guy was hungry; they were tests, and how the offended prisoner graded determined his treatment in the future.

The football game, tied 0–0 in the second quarter, more resembled a gang fight than a sports competition. The hitting was simply ferocious. The two teams' hatred for each other was matched by that of their rooting sections, which hurled insults across the playing field. A big loudmouth black inmate named Barracuda kept screaming at the Senegalese, "Kill those white motherfuckers!"

"Kill those nigger motherfuckers!" I shouted back. Soon it became a chorus: "Kill those nigger motherfuckers!"

Barracuda pointed across the field at me. "I'll bust your fucking white head wide open!" he yelled.

Fuck this shit, I thought. I marched around the perimeter to where the blacks stood. Ten whites, including Willie "The Ape" and Sally D'Ambrosio (loan-shark "muscle" and hit man, respectively), trailed me.

"Hey, my man," I growled at Barracuda, "let's you and me go behind the bleachers."

He brought about fifteen guys with him.

Seeing the rumble developing from across the field, a second loan-shark enforcer named Sally rounded up five of his crew and hurried over.

The game continued along predictable lines as a black player got kicked in the head, and a white spit teeth from his bleeding mouth. The zebras—referees—claimed not to have seen any fouls. These officials hadn't survived years in the stir by being stupid.

Barracuda didn't know I had a pipe stashed behind the bleachers, near the red brick wall over which a touring Babe Ruth had hit Sing Sing's longest home run, by the gym Warner Brothers had donated after filming a prison flick starring John Garfield.

Using my good hand, I hit Barracuda first, a hard left hook, and his head struck the back of the wooden bleachers. I gave him four more hooks that put him on the ground. When I leaned over to pop him again, he grabbed my balls, *lifted me up by the balls,* and body-slammed me onto a slab of concrete that encircled a sewer drain. He cut my face with three or four solid punches before Willie the Ape pulled him off, whereupon a black inmate jumped on Willie's back. Ronnie "Guinea" Cusano brandished a knife and suddenly everyone had blades. I saw blood dripping from my face and lost control. I grabbed my stashed pipe and cracked Barracuda on the head, driving him to his knees. I kept hitting him, and this genuinely tough guy began to whimper.

The other inmates faced one another in a tense standoff, interrupted by the occasional thrust of a blade, and the only sounds were the cracks of my pipe against Barracuda's arms, legs, and back. Before I could kill Barracuda, Willie the Ape—his features more simian than human—pulled me off, and the two groups backed leerily away.

Barracuda, needing treatment for a broken jaw, broken nose, cracked ribs, and concussion, convalesced many weeks in an outside hospital, but he honored the inmate code by not ratting me out.

Actually, he figured he didn't need to give the officials my name to exact his revenge. During the aftermath of the rumble, most black inmates learned what had happened and wanted to kill me. One of them likely would have succeeded if Tony D, a wiseguy in the Profaci organization, hadn't called for a sitdown with a black leader named Shingles. Tony argued that Barracuda had started the fight with his first "motherfucker," an argument Shingles countered with, "Frankos called him nigger." Finally, the arbitrators agreed to squash the budding race war to prevent the inevitable retaliatory bloodshed in which, as Shingles put it, "the hacks will be the only winners."

Twenty-one days after the battle behind the bleachers, I got in a fight that carried more serious consequences. It occurred in the Powerhouse Rec, a big five-story building that had been the prison's first death house. Monday through Friday the Sing Sing band occupied the top floor and serenaded prisoners as they marched from the workshops up the hill to dinner.

On weekends inmates packed into the smoky first floor, approximately the size of a basketball court, and played checkers, chess, and cards, while Mafiosi in aprons cooked huge pots of spaghetti. Musicians practiced off to the side, and sundry groups huddled in corners, plotting scores they intended to pull or bullshitting about exploits on the outside. At this time, the recent John Kennedy assassination was the hottest topic of conversation.

The Powerhouse Rec, a loud democratic meeting spot, saw a Mafia don digging into a piping-hot plate of lasagna at one table and someone being stabbed at another.

This day my partner at bridge, a would-be Mafioso named Scotty, objected to my raising his four-spades bid to six.

"You made a mistake," he growled.

"To hell with you," I said.

"Where the fuck did you learn to play?"

I threw my cards in his face, and he dove over the table headfirst against my nose. The force of his body drove me into a locker that fell on my leg, cracking the shin bone. Flat on my back, I hooked him twice to the face, held him by the hair and head-butted him, and with my free leg kneed him in the groin. "Goddamn!" Scotty screamed, reaching for his throbbing nuts. I jerked his head close to mine and butted him unconscious.

When I eased my numb right leg out from under the locker and saw blood spreading through my pants, I went wild again. This happened to me numerous times during fights; it was almost as though I blacked out. I grabbed a can of tomatoes and pounded the would-be Mafioso's face. A guard put his club to my throat and pulled me back, and in the heat of the moment I thought he was a friend of Scotty's. I threw him over my shoulder before realizing I'd made a potentially fatal mistake.

Hurting a hack can be tantamount to an inmate signing his own death warrant. Other hacks might seek him out and kill him. I apologized to this guard, and lucked out when he didn't report my attack on him. The upshot: Scotty spent forty-four days in the hospital, and I got sixty days licking my wounds in the "box," a solitary confinement that prohibited all human contact except with the trusty who three times a day delivered meals. This dungeon where I spent two months had no electric light, an iron bunk, a filthy, smelly toilet, and a single coarse wool blanket under which I expected to freeze.

Insane as my frequent fights might seem to someone on the outside, they were good career moves for two reasons: (1) they kept me alive so I could *have* a career, and (2) they caught the attention of various underworld people who were always looking to beef up their crews. Guys with schemes and a few brains were dime-a-dozen commodities, but genuine tough guys—and what does history boil down to other than the success of tough guys?—were truly to be treasured.

I'm not referring to bullies, dim-witted, slow-footed behemoths able to scare the shit out of some elderly loan-shark victim, but guys who won't back down from anybody. Who won't run during a shootout. Panic driving a getaway car. Who can kill and get away with it.

In particular, my march straight up to Barracuda and those blacks on the football field caught the eyes of several Mafioso. Earlier, in the death house, Sonny Pinto had given me some names to look up when I got out, but now there were several more offers. Johnny Dioguardi, a captain in the Genovese family (the man who ordered acid thrown in the face of labor columnist Victor Riesel), urged me to look up an associate of his in New York City. I was just twenty-six years old and tempted by this major mobster's interest in me. Suave and personable with no bullshit about him, he bore a startling resemblance to Rudolph Valentino.

Sally D'Ambrosio, a captain in the Colombo family (he was part of the crew that whacked Murder, Inc. head Albert Anastasia), pitched the pluses of association with his organization.

Most interesting of all, though, was Joe Gallo, nicknamed "Crazy Joey" by the cops. I had briefly met Joey at Rikers Island, but we became much closer at Sing Sing. "You *have* to join my crew," he urged each time I saw him. "We're headed for the fucking top."

Right.

Contrary to public perception, hit men do brag about their major scores—their egos wouldn't allow them to keep such secrets—to gangsters they trust. Later Joey gave me the lowdown on the Albert Anastasia hit, of which he was part.

Cocky, always swaggering, Joey could talk up a storm, and I always enjoyed listening to him in the Powerhouse Rec. A made member of the Profaci family (soon to be the Colombo family), Gallo had entered prison fresh from a bloody two-year battle against his boss, Joseph Profaci. Gallo had been badly outgunned—he had perhaps fifteen soldiers and five associates—but he'd fought like a tiger. Once he'd even kidnapped five of Profaci's most important men, but had released them after his boss had promised to negotiate Joey's grievances. Gallo, an outstanding money-maker, felt he deserved a bigger cut from Profaci enterprises and more independence—after all, his daring murder of Anastasia had helped put his boss on top.

Joey's eyes burned with hate and determination when he told how Profaci hadn't kept his word. Instead of negotiating, he'd sent killers to wipe out the troublesome little band. Gallo's crew had found itself under siege, holing up in a pair of tenements at 45-51 President Street near the South Brooklyn waterfront. The place bristled with arms and fortification, impenetrable against anything short of a military assault. Or, as it turned out, a criminal conviction.

Joey was serving a seven- to fourteen-year hitch for extortion. A colorful type of guy, 5'7", very thin, piercing blue eyes, he had a large mole on his left cheek and a receding hairline. Years earlier he had been called Joey the Blond because of his full head of blond hair.

Charismatic, a genuine tough guy, Joey recognized me right away at Sing Sing. Why not? One day on Rikers Island we had temporarily abandoned a card game for a handball workout at the back of the cellblock. When we'd returned, some inmates had taken our seats. We'd had words, which led to a free-for-all and our chasing them away with pipes.

Anyway, my prospects for employment when I got released from Sing Sing were excellent. I spent a lot of time thinking about what I'd do. Going straight never entered my mind: too much money to be made, fun to experience, high living far out of the reach of a wage earner.

The big score: it always came down to that. Grab enough cash and retire. I could still stay around these guys, I liked them, but maybe I'd have so much money that I wouldn't have to put myself at risk with the cops. Be close to the life but not *of* it.

Life at Sing Sing gradually assumed a bearable routine. I was "learning to serve time," though the prison deserved more credit than I did. Most joints, no matter how long you spend there, just aren't tolerable. Even inmates who have been straight all their lives can become violent homosexuals, and miserable conditions turn mildly antisocial criminals into packs of beasts.

Prisoners at Sing Sing were locked into their single cells approximately fifteen hours a day. We were let out at 7:15 A.M. for breakfast, and locked back in after a 4:00 P.M. dinner. The schedule suited me fine. One of the horrors of jail is prisoners wandering through corridors carrying knives and pipes. Unlocked cell doors invite rape and murder, a shank ripped throat to crotch through the body of an unsuspecting inmate.

As mentioned, the most dangerous moments came when we walked down the tunnel on our way to work. Jobs occupied us from 8:00 to 3:00, with a half hour for lunch, and then we had an hour for recreation before marching up to dinner. I always used the hour to jog in the main yard.

Staying in shape was a high priority for anyone serious about surviving. I was a physical-fitness fanatic in my cell: each night I ran in place for an hour, then did 1,000 push-ups, 1,000 sit-ups, and 1,000 deep knee bends. I became hard as the solid steel that surrounded me on three sides.

The only view from the cells were through the front (no one could see anyone else), through a wall consisting of mostly windows looking down and across the Hudson River. Occasionally I saw Nelson Rockefeller's yacht sail up the Hudson, and I had a clear view of the lovely estate of actress Helen Hayes.

Even the guards at Sing Sing evinced traces of civilized behavior. The reason was the prison's proximity to New York City, which guaranteed numerous liberal groups would protest any egregious treatment of inmates. A prisoner transferred to Dannemora near the Canadian border, a godawful hole, learned the difference. "You're not at Sing Sing any more, cocksucker," was the normal greeting. "No fucking commies to protect you here. Get out of line just a little bit and we'll kill you."

Sing Sing had many rules that made sense, like no loud music. Inmates had to wear earphones to hear that bam-bam-bam bullshit. The prevailing noise—heard all night long—was the flush of toilets.

The worst part of doing time is the constant tension fed by fear of being jumped. That was largely absent at Sing Sing, thanks to the long daily lockdowns. After my workout, I read a book a night—reading is absolutely the best way to make the hours fly—mostly mysteries and travel books.

Booze and drugs could be purchased from corrupt prison officials, but there wasn't much of this as we approached the mid-1960s. A few years later things changed: drugs were more readily available in the stir than on the streets, plus money could buy most of what we wanted. We could obtain meals from the finest restaurants, women (a girlfriend, prostitute, even a guard's wife), and weekend passes. I exaggerate not even a small bit.

Everything in A Block was painted institutional green, hardly something to complain about, but the food was very bad and there was not enough of it. I was always hungry. It was freezing cold in winter, boiling hot in summer, and a virtual Eden compared to most joints.

I met the closest friend I ever made during this first stretch at Sing Sing. His name was Joe Sullivan, and people called him Mad Dog, but never to his face. The son of a New York City police detective, he came from a family of cops, and early on his path diverged dramatically from theirs. Joe became the most prolific killer in American criminal history, not just in quantity (he may have murdered as many as 110 people), but also in quality. He pulled the trigger on many of the underworld's most famous hits.

Joe and I stayed together at Sing Sing for more than two years. He was about twenty-two years old when I met him and already had three (or five) notches on his gun, the tally in doubt because as a teenager he'd shot two rival gang members but had never learned if they'd died.

Joe grew up near John Gotti's neighborhood in Queens. He had a terrible childhood. His tough alcoholic Irish cop father frequently beat him, but the unceasing verbal abuse hurt worse. Detective Sullivan had Joe's life mapped out: his son would be a cop, no matter what the boy wanted. The more the father harangued, the harder the son resisted. Joe began pulling armed robberies at age twelve.

When I met Joe he was doing ten-to-thirty years for murder. He had already killed a cop in Texas and escaped from a prison in Trenton, New Jersey. After climbing over the wall, he'd gone to Queens and killed a guy in a bar.

Joe Sullivan's story, gleaned during many Powerhouse Rec talks, would be impossible to tell as fiction. He acquired the nickname Mad Dog because he foamed at the mouth even during normal conversations, and especially when committing murders. I did numerous hits with Joe, and he truly presented a terrifying sight to those victims who saw him coming. Mad Dog was a very aggressive killer—he went right after the target—but he behaved as deviously as a used-car salesman when the situation warranted. He possessed enough patience to impress Job. Whenever he entered prison, which was often, his first thoughts were about how to escape, a feat he accomplished several times. In 1971, a month before the famous riot, he became *the only person ever to escape from Attica*. He hid under crushing 100-pound sacks of flour and was chauffeured out the gates by an unsuspecting truck driver. By the time the police captured him, six weeks later in Greenwich Village, Joe had killed three more people.

As a young man Joe Sullivan had a drinking problem, but he never picked a fight nor did he back down from one. He was polite, soft-spoken, easygoing, very humble—a gentleman. If someone stepped on his foot, *he* would apologize.

In Sing Sing Joe often talked to me about his hatred for his father, and I related stories about Uncle Gus. Joe had resented being belittled more than he'd disliked the beatings. He said he often thought about his father when he shot people.

Joe stood 5'11" and weighed 180 pounds, with most of the weight in his legs. He had legs as powerful as pistons, and a thin, wiry, strong upper body. Veins popped up on his neck and arms; his stomach was flat as a sheet of steel. I never saw anything like him in my life. He did two thousand push-ups a day, worked with weights religiously, and pounded the stuffing out of heavy punching bags.

Joe was a terrific athlete: a sprinter, a high hurdler, and an outstanding football player. I played halfback on one of Joe's teams, the Assassins, and the old joke was a true one, all ours were home games. Visiting players, often small college teams, had to be searched before they were let into the prison. Sportswriters call the NFL Central the black-and-blue division, but they should have seen our games against a team of guards. We kicked their asses.

The prison basketball team, composed mostly of blacks was, according to professional referee Dom Vece, "good enough to hold its own in Madison Square Garden's college tournament at Christmas." And the boxing team always had a couple of standouts I thought might have become world champions had they been on the outside. Occasionally I even let myself wonder how I would have done.

Joe Sullivan's modus operandi involved shooting his victim, then cutting his throat from ear to ear with a razor-sharp knife to make sure he was dead. I got used to the white foam bubbling out of Joe's mouth as he leaned over his victim, but other hitters who accompanied him never did.

Like myself, Joe went free lance all the way. In fact, we made a pact in Sing Sing never to hook up with any specific gang. We didn't want that shit, where if the boss said, "I want to fuck your wife," we had to allow it.

Joe Sullivan had an on/off switch. Like Joey Gallo, he was a voracious reader, much of it poetry, and he could be holding an intelligent conversation with someone and change personalities in the blink of an eye. His face would harden, his eyes would blaze, and the perspicacious knew it was graceful-exit time.

"Sometimes I think about those killings I did," I once said to Mad Dog in the Powerhouse Rec. "I can't think of a good reason why."

"Brother Greek," he said, "somebody has to clean up the environment."

I don't think Joe kept a single thing from me. We were as close as two people can get. It was Ben Franklin, I believe, who uttered Joe's favorite quote: "Three can keep a secret if two of them are dead." But the fact is, even the most closemouthed murderer needs to share his innermost thoughts with someone, and I'm the person Joe chose.

Joe was a fearsome fistfighter, even in these early days, and inmates learned to leave him alone. An opponent, unless he killed us, couldn't really win against either of us because we'd come back the next time willing to commit murder.

At least nominally Sullivan professed the Catholic faith, and I joked that he could stop the heart of any priest he decided to be honest with in the confessional.

"You'd be surprised what I tell them," he said.

Maybe he did confess his murders. It couldn't have been zanier than the time I saw him as an altar boy serving at a prison mass.

I think two people occupied Joe's body, and he couldn't control the rage that kept boiling out of one of them. No, that isn't completely true. He could *call on* that rage when he had a contract to perform. Then the victim, if just for a moment, might see the sparkling eyes, foaming mouth, and terrible visage of this nonpareil murder machine.

Just before I was released from Sing Sing, Joe and I agreed to get together on the outside. He had a hundred ways he figured could gain his freedom, including escape. Neither of us imagined, when we did indeed hook up, the incredible, blood-soaked adventures we would share.

Chapter 8

THE LOUIE MOIA MURDER

"WHEN YOU GO OUT," SONNY PINTO TOLD ME, REFERRING TO my release, "look up my friend Johnny E. He'll have a couple hundred dollars to help you get on your feet."

I figured I would do that, give it a look, if only because Johnny E's location was convenient to the area of Manhattan where I wanted to live. But first I had chores to perform.

I left Sing Sing in June 1964, with a thick wad of messages that needed delivering. I called this guy's wife, that guy's friend, another guy's partner. Inmates were always getting out, and they considered it a solemn obligation to carry greetings, news, or instructions to people on the outside. These ranged from suggestions to a lawyer on an upcoming court action to orders for a murder. Prison officials, no matter how many phones they tapped or letters they opened, couldn't shut down this means of communication.

A week passed before I went to see Johnny E. He was a suave gangster with salt-and-pepper hair, very well dressed in a sharkskin suit, silk shirt and tie, and the pointy-toed shoes gangsters favored. He was that rare type of criminal who could speak without using obscenities, and he actually could meet a customer in his store—a pet shop—without giving his game away. Even many of the dons I met couldn't do this. Just a few words from the mouths of Chin Gigante, Tony Salerno, Junior Persico and, later, John Gotti, and the listener knew to whom he talked.

All I had when I visited Johnny was an unflattering state suit, so he took me downtown and bought me some stylish clothes. Instead of the $200 Sonny Pinto recommended, he laid $1,000 on me, most of which I used to rent an apartment on 98th Street near West End Avenue.

Johnny was a medium-level drug dealer. He paid me $300 a week mainly just to watch his back, because I had gotten a name as a tough guy. Johnny cackled when he recalled stories he'd heard of my fights with Barracuda and Scotty, the would-be Genovese wiseguy.

I snuffed out three rival drug dealers for Johnny. He paid $8,000 for the first, and the other two I did as favors. The killings didn't arouse any remorse. Maybe all the heroin I had again begun to snort deadened my conscience, or perhaps I'd just grown accustomed to murder. But I don't think so. I found a rationalization, something I referred to before, which I call the Soldier's Syndrome. A soldier usually isn't haunted when he kills in the service of his country—he has murdered an enemy, and that's how I viewed my victims. Additionally, the soldier gets honored for what he did, is lavished with respect, praise, and medals, which are not dissimilar to rewards I received. Soldiers are told the enemy is evil, often a questionable assertion, but I know the guys I killed fit the description.

Nor was I nervous on hits, except when I sensed danger to myself. A top boxer doesn't fear climbing into the ring with a second-rater, and my stomach only fluttered when I went after tough guys.

The first hit for Johnny E occurred at 3:30 A.M. on 110th Street and Broadway. This Puerto Rican drug dealer was waiting on the corner when I pulled up in a car. "I've got the package," I said. "Get in." When he did I wasted no time. I shot him in the face and hauled him away.

The second hit took place in midafternoon on 123rd Street near

Pleasant Avenue: an Italian drug dealer I shot on the narrow stairway leading to his apartment. Just after he fell dead, a young woman pushing a baby carriage appeared at the top of the steps. "Get the fuck back inside," I growled. She had gotten a good look at me, but I didn't kill her. I hefted the drug dealer's body onto my shoulders and carried it down to the car.

The third individual I killed for Johnny E was a half-crazy drug dealer nicknamed Charlie Off the Wall Ding Dong, who worked at a candy store on 119th Street. I persuaded him to get into a car to sell me two ounces of heroin, and as soon as his ass hit the seat, I put a slug in his left temple from about six inches away.

All three of these victims I buried in predug graves on the West Side between 46th and 47th Streets near the railroad tracks.

Johnny wanted only genuine tough guys on his payroll, stand-up people he could count on when things got rough—which they inevitably did. One of these, Johnny thought, was Louie Moia, a powerful bull-necked bruiser weighing about 250 pounds. The trouble was, during Moia's job interview, Johnny didn't dig deep enough into his past.

When Moia had been in prison, he'd spent a lot of time beating up inmates. Every time prison authorities had hauled him on the carpet he'd played the bug role, pretending to be crazy. The charges against him would be dropped when he got transferred to a state insane asylum.

Moia told psychiatrists he was a covert agent for the CIA, which intended to blow up all the penal institutions in the United States. These ravings, coupled with the violence he directed at prisoners, prompted the doctors to mark him down as a nut.

But when installed in hospitals for the criminally insane, Moia worked with certain violent correction officers. These officers would strap the prisoners they couldn't control—very tough, psychotic individuals—into straitjackets and beat them, sometimes practically to death. Or suffocate them. Louie Moia worked hand in hand with these officers.

Moia also played nice guy in the mental institutions when it suited him. He bilked inmates who didn't know what planet they lived on out of their commissary, and conned them into endorsing over their income-tax-return checks.

Patients were afraid of Moia and kept complaints to themselves. He physically and verbally abused them, hoping to goad someone into a fight. "Listen," he would say, "any time you want to mix it up, let's do it. You want to go with a knife? A pipe? Your hands? Fine. Any way you want will fucking suit me. But remember one thing, you pieces of shit. If I win, I'm going to kill you."

He wasn't bluffing. He beat a couple of inmates down, and while they were unconscious he kicked them to death.

Moia was released from a state hospital for the criminally insane about the time I joined Johnny E. Johnny asked if I knew him. I said yeah, I'd been introduced to him in the Tombs. So Johnny said, "We want this guy with us." Our mistake, as mentioned, was not knowing Moia's pedigree, all the sick things he did.

Eventually there were four of us: Joe Pagano, Johnny E, Moia, and me. Pagano ended up a captain in the Genovese crime family.

Johnny told Moia that if he would go with me to deliver some packages, he would never tell him they contained heroin. That's how Johnny talked. So Moia and I began making the rounds to different boroughs, dropping off packages and picking up money. We did business in the Bronx, Queens, and Harlem. Louie carried the packages and I watched his back, escorting him in and out of tough tenement houses. A buyer would come out of his flat, meet us in the hallway, then go back inside and get the money. When the count was right we handed over the goods.

These weren't big quantity deliveries, usually only an ounce or two. But we made ten or twelve drops a day. At this time heroin was very inexpensive, about $500 an ounce, and Johnny sold pure stuff. The buyer could cut the heroin and out of one ounce make five. People purchasing from Johnny E made a hefty profit.

We hid the heroin in a secret compartment in the trunk. The cops would have needed to tear the car apart to find it. Once we got stopped by members of a hardass detective squad, known for shooting and asking questions later. Wiseguys considered them the most dangerous police officers the city had, and also the most honest. They gave our car a thorough search the day they stopped us, but didn't find a thing.

Here's how the heroin trail ran: Johnny obtained the drug from Mafiosi who had been associated with Joe Valachi, the famous rat, who purchased his junk from Vito Genovese (in prison in Atlanta). Turkey was the source of the heroin, which got shipped from Greece to Sicily and on to New York City. Tony Anastasio, the brother of Albert Anastasia of Murder, Inc., fame (Tony used a different spelling of the last name), controlled the docks, so smuggling the heroin into the United States posed no problem.

With Vito Genovese in jail in Atlanta, Joe Pagano ran the heroin trade for him in Harlem. Johnny answered to Pagano, and Moia and I answered to Johnny. We were, in effect, wholesalers selling to retailers.

Moia and I had the most dangerous jobs. Two white guys going into Harlem ranked as a most onerous assignment, but the dumps we delivered to in Queens and the Bronx could prove just as deadly. I often wished I had five eyes in the back of my head to watch for take-off artists, thugs, and rival mobsters. Some of the cops, the honest ones, could also be a problem.

I didn't care for riding with Louie Moia, either. Probably he really was insane, but in a perverted, brutal way that earned him no sympathy. He was cunning, cruel, and murderous, and not in any manner that required courage. His victims were always weak, like those patients in the mental institutions. I didn't want to hear about how he clubbed a straitjacketed prisoner to death with a lead pipe, or how inventive he had been stealing some poor wretch's commissary.

Moia never used his "let's do it" speech on me. He knew I'd kill him.

Johnny called me one day at my apartment. "I have something very important to tell you," he said. "Come to the club."

I met him at the Italian Social Club on First Avenue. "Let's walk around the block," he said. "There's information you need to know."

We stepped out on the street and Johnny, looking very grim, got right to the point: "I think your sidekick Moia is working with the FBI."

"Who told you this?"

"A guy we pay. A cop."

I didn't think Johnny would lie to me about such a serious matter, nor was I surprised that his information came from the police. The wiseguys I hung around with joked often about the judges, prosecutors, and politicians they had "a piece of," public officials who at least in part owed their positions to the Mafia, or who had succumbed to the lure of the payoff.

"How sure are you about Louie?" I asked.

"We'll find out tonight. We're gonna frisk him."

Johnny made the arrangements. Then he and I plus a hitter named Spike picked up Moia at 122nd Street and Pleasant Avenue. Johnny had told Moia we would be bringing some heroin for him and me to deliver.

Moia didn't act nervous, even though he knew Spike's business, and that the instructions deviated from the usual method of picking up heroin. Maybe he didn't suspect anything; more likely, as we later learned, his confidence derived from knowledge that the FBI monitored everything from a surveillance car two blocks away.

Moia's casual manner should have alerted us. Usually he was very afraid of Johnny, whose father ranked as an important organized-crime figure in the neighborhood.

The dark-skinned Moia wore a short-sleeved Hawaiian shirt this warm, humid evening and carried a sport jacket over his arm. He got into the front seat of Johnny's white Thunderbird, with me and Spike sitting in the back. Instead of driving toward downtown Manhattan, Johnny headed for the Bronx.

"You got the junk?" Moia asked me. He figured, we later learned, that his FBI protection was listening.

But somehow we had lost the surveillance car—Johnny's cop

source subsequently told him the Bureau considered this a monstrous screwup, which indeed it was—and no outsider heard me answer, "Yeah, Johnny's got the stuff."

Around 135th Street, Johnny pulled up next to the curb and told Moia to drive. I could see Louie didn't like this arrangement at all. He started talking a lot, hoping the feds listened, but Johnny just directed him all the way to Westchester County, while Spike and I sat silently in the back.

Johnny gestured Moia into a dark, vacant parking lot. Then he opened the glove compartment, pretending to go for the heroin, but instead he pulled out a .38 snubnose and jammed it into Louie's stomach. "Put your hands on the steering wheel," he ordered, "and keep them there. Don't move a fucking muscle."

"Jesus Christ, Johnny, what's this all about?" Moia's face was flushed, sweat popping out all over, and the skin under his eyes twitched as if being stabbed by a dozen sharp pins.

Johnny reached underneath the seat, pulled out handcuffs, and fastened Louie's right wrist to the steering wheel. Moia looked like a man having a heart attack.

"Greek," Johnny said, "search his jacket."

In his inside breast pocket I found a transmitter with a tiny microphone sticking out of it. I handed it to Johnny, motioning that it was on and sending. Johnny unplugged the microphone, held it in front of Moia's face, and hissed, "What is this?"

"I don't know," Louie said. He was crying.

"Tell me what the fuck it is, motherfucker!"

"I don't know," Louie whimpered, his face now hideously contorted. He knew he had better stutter out some explanation. "I hung my jacket up in a restaurant. That's the only time I left my jacket. I see now, Johnny, that's a bug. Somebody must have bugged me in that restaurant. I swear to God, I didn't know."

Johnny had his face shoved right up against Moia's. "I'm going to tell you something, cocksucker," he said. "We paid off a cop, and he told us all about you." Johnny smashed the butt of his pistol into Moia's face, splitting open his nose and sending a spray of blood onto the windshield. "Motherfucker," he muttered.

Spike and I held pistols on Louie while Johnny rehandcuffed him behind the back and shoved him onto the floor of the passenger seat. Johnny got behind the wheel and headed upstate.

Louie cried and begged all the way. "I swear, Johnny, somebody planted that bug on me. I don't have anything to do with the cops. You know I wouldn't double-cross you like that. Please, Johnny, listen to what I'm saying."

Johnny punched the steering wheel of the T-bird, a gesture of hatred and disgust. Moia tried a new approach, invoking the influence of his father, an old wiseguy. "Pull off the road at the next pay phone, Johnny. Call my old man; he'll straighten all this out. He's got plenty of dough, and I'm sure he'll make it worth your while to think this thing over. I'll kick in some money too, though God in heaven knows I've done nothing wrong, nothing to harm you. Please, Johnny, for chrissake don't hurt me."

Except for Moia pleading, there wasn't a sound in that car. Johnny drove on through the night, his face fixed as a statue's. I felt nothing but contempt for Moia. He knew what happened to rats.

Johnny drove to a farm owned by Joe Pagano and pulled into a big barn. We dragged Moia out of the car and told him to sit on the ground. He was sobbing and begging, *please, please, please!* As happened later when I grabbed Buster DellaValle, Johnny literally had scared the shit out of Louie Moia, and the smell was awful.

Inside the barn, we tied Louie's legs to a workbench, took out a chainsaw, and cut off his right foot at the ankle. When the saw bit into Moia's flesh his shriek was the loudest and longest I've ever heard. It filled the empty barn and still rang in our ears as he gasped *Please! Please! Please!* and *Oh God!* until his brain mercifully shut down his senses and he passed out.

Next we cut off his left foot. Jimmy Coonan, an Irish West Side gangster, often dismembered bodies using *only* a knife, but a person doesn't need to think about it long to realize that a power saw is preferable.

We cut off Moia's arms. With Johnny's knee pressing against Moia's back, pushing him down but pulling the head up by the hair, we sawed halfway through his neck and took a break before finishing up.

Moia flopped around for maybe ten minutes before he bled out. Then we concluded the job, chopping him up and depositing the body parts in big plastic bags, which we buried on the farm.

Some times I can still hear Louie Moia scream. I can tell you, *I* don't like me whenever I remember that night.

I had plenty of money at this time, spending it as fast as I made it. The heroin habit, huge as it had become, didn't cost much. I usually took what I wanted from Johnny. But I'd begun gambling heavily—horses, ball games, dice, numbers—and living like Rockefeller.

I also was probably the biggest tipper in New York City. Regularly I left a $20 bill to pay for my scrambled eggs at the neighborhood diner in the morning, and street panhandlers often did double takes when they saw I'd given them a Jackson.

I dressed expensively and well, ate at the finest restaurants, and always drove a new car. Driving, unfortunately, didn't rank as one of my strong points, and in 1964 I totaled two vehicles in as many months. I simply walked away from the crumpled wrecks and headed for a wiseguy car dealer I knew to obtain a bargain on another one. I mean, a real bargain, since this was stolen merchandise. *Anything* I wanted I could purchase from wiseguys for a fraction of its price on the regular market, an arrangement made possible because *their* cost was zero.

At night I made the rounds at bars and nightclubs where organized-crime figures hung out. At the Ali Baba East, a pimp I knew introduced me to a guy named Petey who stood 6'4" and weighed 200 pounds. He was smart, however, and was highly respected by the Lucchese crime family, into which he ultimately got made.

"Greek, I heard about you," Petey said.

This no longer surprised me, having people tell me they recognized my name. The police, at least in their public pronouncements, never seemed able to solve organized-crime hits, but people who hung around the Mafia knew who did them. Like old ladies in a sewing circle, wiseguys gossiped among themselves about who whacked a guy, and why. I occasionally talked about my own business, though not often, but word sure got around. And in a way this wasn't all bad. Bosses always looked to hire good hitters, and since the Moia killing had cemented my reputation as an up-and-coming tough guy, more work got tossed in my direction. That's why I was talking to Petey at a quiet corner table in Ali Baba East.

"I need a new partner," Petey said, "for some jewelry stickups."

"I'm working for Johnny E."

"Keep working for him. These aren't everyday heists. You can fit them in."

Petey explained that he received tips on out-of-state diamond salesmen coming into New York City from places like Atlanta, Miami, and Los Angeles with briefcases full of jewels. The tipster might be the salesman himself, the salesman's boss, or somebody, usually in the Lucchese family, with information about the merchandise.

"I had a close call not long ago," Petey said, "and my partner froze on me. I got to find somebody who don't rattle. How about helping me, Greek?"

"What do I get?" I asked. "How much are we talking about?"

"I can't give you half. But we'll split our end of it, go fifty-fifty on everything."

Petey, I learned, was a *great* jewel thief. He had a roundabout method of explaining things, but it came down to our having to share one-third of the take with the individual providing the information (if it was the salesman's boss, he also collected the insurance money); another slice went to the Lucchese crime family, whether or not it provided the tip. "The cost of doing business," Petey called it. "We have to do the right thing," he emphasized, leaving unsaid what we could expect if we didn't give the mob its cut.

"How much are we talking about?" I repeated.

He had trouble with the figures. Finally I asked him how much the *total* take usually was, and he said, "Oh, yeah. The total. Averages about $150,000, Greek, maybe a little more, maybe a little less."

I agreed to the deal and Petey took me shopping. "You wear nice clothes, Greek," he said. "But for these jobs, let's soften your appearance."

Translation: you look too hard, like a tough guy, even a hit man; tone it down. Petey helped me select a new wardrobe. I had my hair cut short and my fingernails manicured, and I bought horn-rimmed glasses.

When we pulled a job, I—appearing to be a tastefully attired hotel guest or businessman waiting to meet a colleague—positioned myself nonchalantly on whatever couch or chair afforded the best view of the lobby while Petey took the elevator to the diamond salesman's room. There he'd grab the ice and smack the salesman—especially necessary if the victim doubled as the tipster—to assure his cooperation or make it look better when the cops came around asking questions. I watched his back, so to speak. If a hotel employee, security guard, or even a cop appeared to make a move for the floor on which Petey worked, I had to ward him off. Pull a pistol and put him against a wall, if necessary. And if that happened, I also needed to secure the desk clerk, who could lock the elevators so Petey couldn't get down.

The most likely time for trouble arose when Petey exited the elevator in the lobby. He would head straight for the getaway vehicle, and I had to make sure no one stopped him. We would drive two or three blocks in the stolen car, then switch to a different one.

I pulled three stickups with Petey before becoming involved in an incident much more dangerous. It was early in 1966 at Ninth Avenue and 49th Street. I was on my way to see an Irish girlfriend named Diane when an acquaintance stopped me and introduced his friend Jimmy Coonan. "The Greek is the kind of guy you're looking for," he told Coonan.

Coonan was just a kid, barely nineteen, 5'8" but with a powerful build. Solid legs. Thick, strong arms. I agreed to have a cup of coffee with him at C & J Restaurant near 52nd Street, where it took no special insight to size him up as aggressive, ambitious, and immature. He was, however, very respectful to me, a quality young toughs don't often possess. What struck me right away was an absence of bombast and youthful arrogance. He seemed very sincere; he spoke quietly without wasting words. A special kind of boy, I thought, who would go far if he stayed alive—which I didn't think he would.

This tough upstart teenager, a fearsome fistfighter, had set himself a high goal: he intended to become sole boss of all the Hell's Kitchen rackets—including numbers, extortion, shylocking, and bookmaking—plus take control of the Stagehands Union and various waterfront shakedowns.

I later wondered from what well Coonan drew his murderous juices. His parents were solidly middle-class—his father John was a certified public accountant with his own business (Coonan's Tax Service at 369 West 50th Street). His mother put in long hours at the firm. What happened to Jimmy, I decided, had occurred in a lesser degree to me: he saw how easily neighborhood gangsters obtained the good things in life, and compared their success to that of his always-strapped parents. What excitement did a CPA have? The hoods had plenty, and respect, money, and big cars besides.

Coonan didn't intend to work his way up to the top. He planned a coup d'état, a blow to the head, and in this case the head belonged to Mickey Spillane (no relation to the writer). Along with his "unseen" partner, John Sullivan, the handsome, politically connected Spillane ruled the roost in Hell's Kitchen. He delivered votes the Democrats needed to win elections, and once in office they left him alone.

By anyone's standards, Mickey Spillane was a ruthless killer, but Coonan rationalized that he needed to be hit because he was "too soft."

"I'd like you with me when it's done," he said.

"How much are you paying?" I said.

"For you, five thousand dollars."

That represented a lot of money to Coonan at this time. Later it would be chicken feed. He had pulled some stickups to finance himself and his tiny gang, terrorized some businessmen into paying for protection, and had a profitable counterfeiting operation, but his expenses were high. When he said I could run the bookmaking action at several theaters where the stagehands worked, I told him to count me in. What the hell. I was curious to see how he'd do.

Coonan was young but not stupid. He told me that he had cleared the Spillane hit with John Sullivan (he of the Buster DellaValle murder and, later, Jimmy Hoffa). Of course, Coonan planned to eliminate Sullivan when the dust settled, exactly what Sullivan intended for him.

Coonan, a master of saying what he meant and no more, revealed that he had arranged a meet with Spillane on a West 46th Street rooftop, within pebble-tossing distance of the tenement I'd lived in as a boy. The brash Coonan intended to gun Spillane down right there. Spillane, for his part, was going to warn the kid, cause any more trouble and I'll squash you like a bug.

We arrived early and took up positions on the rooftop. There were six of us, including Jimmy Coonan's brother Jackie and a Boston Irish hood who years later, in another crime the cops never solved, murdered Albert DiSalvo, believed to be the Boston Strangler, in a beef over drugs.

Five of us carried rifles in addition to our handguns. Coonan had a machine gun, which seemed overly dramatic to me.

It was a cold, dark blustery spring afternoon, and 46th Street stood virtually deserted. I wore a ski mask—if something went wrong, I didn't want to risk being recognized by Spillane or by some witness materialized from nowhere—and pep-talked myself into making every shot count.

Coonan crouched some ten feet away. No mask for him. His blond hair made him look like a Viking. In the week since I had first met him I'd learned to appreciate how formidable he was. An ice-cold killer. Even on the rooftop he aped every mannerism of Jimmy Cagney, his hero. Maybe his fearlessness derived from the belief that he lived in a movie.

Spillane's crew came in three cars. The Irish boss brought eight hitters with him, just in case, most of them imported from Boston. I caught a brief glance of him—tall, thin, built like a male model, wearing dark sunglasses—as he stepped out of his black Cadillac. Instantly Coonan was on his feet, spraying the street with bullets.

He didn't hit anybody, and to our amazement the Spillane crew dashed inside the tenement. They were coming up after us!

This suited Jimmy Coonan just fine. He had opened up too soon with that machine gun—not waiting for the signal that would have brought the more accurate rifle fire to bear—but didn't bother dwelling on a lost opportunity. We aimed at the trapdoor through which Spillane's killers would have to come before fanning out for the shoot-out. I suspected they believed Coonan had acted on his own.

We let two of them through the rooftop door before we blasted away. I hit one guy in the shoulder. I heard Jackie Coonan scream and saw him grab his leg. Our Boston hood hit another guy, but not well enough to put him down. Jimmy Coonan was firing like crazy, but inaccurately, and posed more of a danger to birds than Spillane's hoods.

It didn't matter. That second or so of gunfire sent them scrambling back into the building and down the stairs to their cars. We didn't wait around for a third chance. The 16th Precinct stood just a block away, and we could hear police sirens. We raced down a fire escape, dragging wounded Jackie Coonan with us, and made it safely to a nearby apartment owned by Jimmy's dad.

Jimmy and I got Jackie liquored up, sort of a makeshift preop anesthetic, and during the process got pretty loaded ourselves. Then, using a knife and heated spoon, I ignored Jackie's screams and cut the bullet out of his leg.

Jimmy Coonan asked me to hook up with him. "We'll ice that motherfucking Spillane," he said, "and then we'll be sitting pretty."

I thought it likely Spillane would be the one doing the icing. Soft-spoken and sinister, he possessed everything Jimmy Coonan didn't: influence—including partnerships with the Italians, manpower, and money. I'd once spotted him drinking white wine in a fashionable East Side saloon with the rising Genovese crime family wiseguy Fat Tony Salerno.

I think what saved Coonan and allowed him to grow up and fight another day was a mistaken-identity murder he committed shortly after the Spillane shootout. He and his gang mistook a pair of innocent barhoppers—Jerry Morales and Charles Canelstein—for associates of Spillane, kidnapped them, drove to Queens and, laughing hysterically, pumped more than a dozen bullets into them. Incredibly, Canelstein lived to testify against Jimmy, who plea-bargained a five- to ten-year sentence for felonious assault. Spillane mistakenly figured he would hear no more from pain-in-the-ass Jimmy Coonan.

I was about to head for prison myself, and maybe this too was just as well. My heroin habit had become so ferocious that I had begun carrying a stash in my rectum, in case I got arrested. I also shoved pills up my ass so I wouldn't go crazy in confinement.

It was still the good life—booze, broads, big cars, reserved tables at Aqueduct for the races, at Sardi's or Dempsey's for dinner—but subconsciously I feared the drugs would get me. I had nightmares of hit men chasing me down dark alleys, of running toward a distant cop standing underneath a light pole and screaming for him to arrest me. But whenever I reached the cop, I never told him about the murders. I blurted out silly crimes, like stealing a candy bar from Pop's Grocery. The hit men came closer and closer. The police officer seemed to know them. He was their friend.

I continued picking up and delivering packages for Johnny E, a much more dangerous job than heisting diamond salesmen, and potentially just as deadly as shooting it out with Spillane's killers. Also, with Louie Moia out of the picture, I was alone. I made deliveries during the day, brought the money to Johnny each evening, and collected the junk for the next day's work. Johnny paid me each night—usually $250—plus I received that $300 a week for being around him.

One day I got a call from my parole officer, McKean, who told me to come to his 42nd Street office to talk to him. A parolee hearing this knows he's either going to be locked up for a violation or ordered to rat on somebody.

"Listen," I said to Johnny. "McKean wants to see me. I don't know, but he might be locking me up."

"Tell you what I'll do," Johnny said. "If he does haul you in, I'll send down one of my girls." He had five girls working for him. "She'll put some money on the books for you, and you won't have to touch your own money. When you come out, you'll have that money. Count on it, I'll take care of you. I'll give you a hundred dollars a month for commissary," the maximum allowed.

I went to see McKean, a big burly guy who always treated parolees with respect. He told me to sit down and I did. He lifted up his huge body, lumbered over to where I sat, and handcuffed my hand to the chair. "I'm locking you up," he said.

"Why?" I asked.

"I had you followed a few weeks back, and we took a picture of you and Johnny E talking on 115th Street. Johnny is a known narcotics dealer, and we observed him giving you a package, which we assume contained heroin. It was either heroin or money, doesn't matter. Either way, you can't associate with that guy. We know he's not giving you a Dale Carnegie course in self-improvement, or training you to sell encyclopedias door-to-door. Johnny E means one thing: narcotics."

McKean told me to roll up my sleeves so he could check my arms. Then another parole officer came in and they ordered me to strip. But they didn't find a thing. Nothing.

"He must be snorting it," McKean said.

He arranged for my transfer to the Tombs. I didn't think I'd be there long, and knew it could have been for something far more serious than a parole violation. It could have been for murder.

Chapter 9

DANNEMORA

"JACKSON!"

"Here!"

"Ruskin!"

"Yo!"

"Franken!"

"Here!"

"Jones!"

No answer. The only sound was a cell door clanking. The meaty face of the guard who had been calling names turned a deeper red. "Jones!" he barked again, and when there was still no response a team of hacks spread through the ranks of newly arrived inmates assembled in the Tombs bullpen. When I heard the *thwack thwack thwack* of billy clubs, and a prisoner screaming, I knew they had located Jones. He had passed out—from booze, drugs, whatever—and they figured it was a good idea to wake him up so they could knock him out again. Actually, beating this wretch emphasized the balance of power to prisoners wondering who ran the show.

In 1966, inmates in New York City jails rarely sought help from groups like the American Civil Liberties Union (ACLU). Such groups wouldn't really fight for them, wouldn't go into court to seek injunctions. Quite simply, most lawyers feared the powerful Department of Correction, which they viewed as an arm of the police. A do-gooder attorney filing a petition for prisoners' rights might find his own life turned into a nightmare. His car might be vandalized, the windows of his home smashed, or his person assaulted by "individuals unknown." Anyone calling for an investigation of prisons likely would find *himself* investigated.

Judges didn't care. They were on the side of the guards and didn't want the boat rocked. Moreover, any prisoner with an ounce of sense knew that after the judge dismissed his case, he would be returned to the same hacks who originally had brutalized him.

After I answered with a bright, brisk "Here!" an admissions hack assigned me to murderers' row, the fourth floor, which housed the most violent of the violent, a number of them killers. Here I was reunited with Hank Dusablon and Salvador "Cape Man" Agron, who awaited Manhattan court appearances.

The Tombs was a house of negatives. No jobs. No recreation. No hope. Prisoners crouched in their two-man cells, freezing or sweltering, depending on the season. Lights burned twenty-four hours a day on murderers' row, illuminating fights that broke out almost hourly. Correction officers generally allowed the skirmishes to run their course. Guards didn't step in until most fights had ended, often with someone unconscious on the floor bleeding from knife wounds.

One very large effeminate guard considered the inmates his personal harem and coerced them into having sex with him. Two other hacks were outright sadists who got their kicks routinely hurting prisoners. Still, despite all the pain, misery, and suffering, I managed to leave the Tombs with one good memory: getting to know the famous bank robber Willie Sutton.

I sought Sutton out as soon as I learned he was at the Tombs. A little bright-eyed guy, just 5'7" and always talking, chain-smoking Willie rolled his cigarettes with Bull Durham tobacco, and dispensed mounds of legal advice to anyone intelligent enough to listen. Inmates rightly considered him a wise old head. He never had to worry about young toughs and homosexuals; people like me protected him.

Sutton had grown up in an Irish neighborhood near the docks in Brooklyn, and he sadly reminisced about the violent 1920s and 1930s. I didn't have the heart to tell him that things had gotten worse, much worse, but now I understand his misconceptions. I thought this year, 1966, was the most violent ever, and I couldn't have imagined the bloodbath waiting in the 1970s and 1980s when groups like the Westies, the Albanians, the Cubans, and the Colombians came to the fore. Willie had never engaged in violence, but he knew a lot of stories from the twenties and thirties and figured those days of Capone and Luciano were the country's bloodiest.

The bloodiest time is right now, the nineties, and the proof is everywhere to be seen: prisons bursting at the seams, packed with truly violent, don't-give-a-damn-about-anything young toughs; and politicians scrambling to raise money to build *more* prisons, although the percentage of citizens in jail in the United States is already higher than that of any other nation in the world.

Anyway, among many other stories, Willie told us about Dinny Meehan, "the only dock boss I can remember who died in bed. By which I mean that somebody slipped in through his bedroom window while he was asleep and put a bullet in his brain."

Old-time gangsters, especially bosses, loved Willie, though he wasn't at all like them. He was a gentleman, witty, nonviolent, a criminal who made Jesse James and John Dillinger appear to be amateurs in the bank-robbing business. Sutton's oft-quoted reply to why he robbed banks—"Because that's where the money is"—never failed to elicit side-splitting laughter from wiseguys.

Here's how highly the Mafia thought of Willie Sutton, who wasn't, couldn't be, and didn't want to be a made member: when an average citizen, a common Joe named Arnold Schuster, appeared on television to tell how he had done his "civic duty" by fingering Sutton to the cops, Albert Anastasia of Murder, Inc., had Schuster killed. The gentle Willie didn't approve of Anastasia's showboat move, and neither did I. Straight-arrow Schuster hadn't taken any vow of *omerta*; he'd just got in over his head. Probably he didn't think he was in any danger at all. I've always believed, though, that someone should have told him to keep his mug off TV.

"Greek," Sutton said to me one day when I visited his cell. "Do you happen to know the four stages of being a convict?"

I said I didn't.

"I'm talking about long-term convicts, and this applies to the great majority. I don't know why it holds true, but it does. First stage, they develop an interest in sports and keeping themselves in shape. They make their bodies strong and rock-hard because the weak, as you know, can't survive in here. Second stage, they learn to be jailhouse lawyers. They dive into law books, figuring brains instead of muscle will be their salvation. Of course, very few succeed. Third stage, they start carrying Bibles and preaching the word to others. Perhaps they really have found the Lord, but more likely they've heard that parole boards often have a soft spot for religious converts. They learn all the sanctimonious lingo and then find a chaplain or rabbi to put in a good word for them, which can't hurt. But usually this doesn't spring them either, so, fourth stage, they turn to each other for release through sex. After the plunge into homosexuality wears off and they see they're in the same horrible spot as before, they go stark raving mad and either get killed or commit suicide. Study a few of these guys, Greek, and in time you'll see I'm telling you the truth."

I did watch. Sure enough, I saw Willie's scenario unfold over and over again. But unlike the metamorphic stages of nature—where caterpillar changes to butterfly—life in our depraved cocoon underwent a reverse, degenerative process.

Early in 1967 I was happy to learn I'd be heading to Sing Sing to continue serving my indefinite sentence for parole violation. Also transferring there was Ronnie "Guinea" Cusano, who had fought Barracuda with me on the football field.

When I arrived at Sing Sing, various crews asked me to hook up with them. The Italians wanted me, and so did the Greeks and the Irish. The more tough guys a crew had, the less likely they'd be harassed by other groups, especially the blacks. I chose an Irish crew I thought the toughest.

After Cusano and I settled into the Big House, I was assigned a clerical job in the Catholic priest's office and Guinea went to work in the prison library. Guinea, who was proud of his Italian heritage and considered his nickname a compliment rather than a racial slur, minded his own business and tried to do his time—fifteen years for robbery—without incident. That was the case until he found himself an unwitting participant in a love triangle.

To make his boyfriend jealous, a black homosexual claimed Cusano had "made eyes" at him. When the enraged boyfriend, a tough dimwit called Pistol Pete, made too much noise about planning to stab Ronnie, the hacks slammed the idiot into the box. While in solitary confinement, Pistol Pete sent orders to his friend Boomer: "I want you to stab Ronnie Cusano for trying to get it on with my old lady."

This was the kind of petty nonsense that went on all the time in joints and made life virtually unbearable. Cusano hadn't done a thing wrong, but here was a fag threatening to kill him over an imagined beef.

It didn't take long for Guinea to get wind of Boomer's mission and realize he needed help. The next time I went to the library, he took me aside. "Greek," he whispered, "I'm in real trouble with this guy."

"Yeah, I heard. Keep your eyes peeled; I'll watch your back all I can."

I anticipated a bad scene, but two weeks rocked by: nothing from Boomer.

Cusano, tired of the anxiety of waiting, called Boomer out of the print shop. Boomer produced a knife, and I handed Cusano mine, which he drove deep into his enemy's stomach. Pistol Pete's enforcer dripped a blood trail to the nearest correction officer and fell across the top of his desk. Cusano leaped on Boomer's back and plunged the blade into him five more times.

Despite emergency medical efforts, Boomer bled to death. The guards led Cusano to solitary.

Killing an inmate usually resulted in a seven-year stretch, but at this time prosecutors who had too little to do in relatively crime-free Westchester County were eager to take offenders to trial. They offered Cusano ten years. He refused and ended up getting twelve.

Since I had provided Guinea the weapon and watched him use it, they considered me an accessory to murder. But when it came time to prosecute, none of the inmate witnesses would testify. The state decided that linking me to the crime would be iffy and too expensive to pursue, so no charges were filed.

As I think back on what insanity this whole episode was, I look around me today and realize that it's only gotten a hundred times worse.

At Sing Sing I renewed acquaintances with Joe Sullivan, Joe Gallo, and Jimmy Coonan, the very serious, soft-spoken Irish kid who later headed the Westies. I also became friends with Sally D'Ambrosio, whom I'd first met there in 1963. It was from Sally D that I first received the lowdown (later confirmed to me in every detail by Joe Gallo) about the 1957 hit on Albert Anastasia, the dreaded chieftain of Murder, Inc. Sally told me the police knew, but couldn't prove, that Joey Gallo did the murder. And they never did find out who else went on the hit, because, unlike today, few people informed. Yet wiseguys, and the guys around the wiseguys, knew who killed Anastasia, and I figure the whole world may as well know. Who can it hurt? The Anastasia murder, a killing the police never solved, even though the pressure was terrific because of international headlines, can be laid to rest once and for all.

The people on the killing were Joey Gallo and his brother Larry (probably the most capable of the Gallo brothers), Sally D himself, and Carmine "Junior" Persico. Quite a crew. A deadly quartet.

Junior Persico, nicknamed "the Snake" because his "bite" always proved deadly, became at age seventeen the youngest made member in Mafia history. Later Junior graduated to underboss and then boss of the Colombo crime family in a rise to power that didn't surprise anyone. What did amaze was how he conducted himself when he made it to the top. One advantage to being a boss: you use others to perform the dirty jobs, like killing. But Junior Persico, who thoroughly enjoyed the murders and the excitement of the kill, continued to go on hits even after he reached the summit. I later got to know Junior well when we shared a cell. He was the coldest of the cold-blooded killers.

Sally D'Ambrosio, another of Anastasia's executioners, was a Profaci soldier and nominally in charge of the assassination. But how could he really maintain control over such powerful personalities as Joey, Larry Gallo, and Junior Persico?

The hit on Anastasia, Sally told me, was ordered by Joe Profaci, with the approval of Vito Genovese and Carlo Gambino. Anastasia, who had some 100 killers at his beck and call, was king of the New York docks and a major extortionist and drug dealer with close ties to the exiled Lucky Luciano. Among many reasons for his death, Anastasia had been stealing soldiers from Profaci and, much more immediate, had a contract out on Profaci's life.

"Profaci took care of Anastasia," Sally said, "before Anastasia took care of him."

Anastasia's big mistake, one his pal Lucky Luciano had warned him against, was falling into a pattern. He always got his hair cut at the same place, thus enabling Joey Gallo and the others to plan the hit at the Park Sheraton.

They waited across the street for Anastasia to arrive. His chauffeur/bodyguard had been told, "Make yourself scarce, vanish, the moment your boss is seated in that barber chair." The guy knew he had to obey or get whacked too.

Teenage Junior Persico came in first, followed by Sally D and Joey Gallo (Larry Gallo, driving the getaway car, waited a few short blocks from the hotel). "Get the fuck down," Sally screamed at the shop's proprietor, "or I'll blow your fucking head off!"

Joey did most of the shooting—certainly he fired the fatal bullet into Anastasia's head—while Junior and Sally stood guard. Sally, who forced the barber to lie on the floor, was the last one out of the shop as they jumped into the car Larry Gallo drove and went to President Street.

In December 1969, two years after D'Ambrosio told me this story, he was tortured and murdered at a Colombo social club at 8648 18th Avenue, Brooklyn. A neighbor heard Sally's dying screams, and the FBI found his monogrammed, blood-stained shirt in what they called the "torture room." But the feds never recovered Sally's body. The story I heard was that Persico or his crew had done the job.

Mafia connections didn't weigh heavily in prison. Here it was everybody for himself, and some inmates were so wild they didn't give a fuck if a guy was godfather of godfathers. My considerable history of prison violence earned me a leadership position in my Irish crew, and I even conducted sitdowns with the heads of other inmate gangs.

The prison authorities took note of this, and I think that's why after I'd spent five months in Sing Sing they shackled me to Nunzio Provenzano and shipped us off to Dannemora, one of the toughest prisons in the world.

Nunzio, whose brother Tony later played a role in the Jimmy Hoffa murder, was a Teamsters official and a made member of the Genovese family. Although Nunzio and I had a minor fight while we were at Dannemora, he later suggested I look up his brother when I got out, that he'd have work for me in Union City, New Jersey, cracking heads for his Teamsters local.

Dannemora (official name: Clinton Correctional Facility), just a few miles from the Canadian border, ranked as a very dangerous prison, worse even than the Tombs. Inmates so tough no other prison wanted them got sent to Dannemora, where daily they played mini-Super Bowls of violence against the hacks, and against one another.

There was an institution for the criminally insane at Dannemora, which held guys who had been there for years and would never come out. Kept in straitjackets, they seldom saw a psychiatrist or nurse, and correction officers dispensed their medications. The most common method of subduing inmates was to choke them out.

Many of the guards at the asylum farmed their own spreads when they weren't brutalizing prisoners. Those in charge of the criminally insane kept their jobs for perhaps twenty years, never moving to the regular penitentiary next door, and exercised life-and-death control over their charges. The trusties, who at one time included Louie Moia, were noted for their savagery.

The toughest of the tough were imprisoned at Dannemora. I met a roly-poly eighty-year-old who once had been Al Capone's bodyguard, and Lucky Luciano's main killer, a little short guy who smiled a lot and had been in prison for decades (I once saw him pipe an inmate who pointed out what was only true, that Luciano had been a snitch).

All these old wiseguys gave the same advice: "The only thing you know is being a gangster. You got no other experience. When you get out, pull off a big score and then retire to Florida."

Among the black inmates at Dannemora were Thomas 15X Johnson, convicted of killing Malcolm X (he claimed he was innocent, and I believed him); plus Norman 3X Butler and Thomas Hagan, sentenced for the same crime.

I became a close friend of Thomas Johnson and he introduced me to Louis Farrakhan, who visited him in prison. Johnson said he had been taping Malcolm's speech that fatal day, that he didn't know the murder was about to come down. According to Johnson, there were *ten* shooters gathered in the ballroom, but only three or four of them fired.

I also became friends with Karate Bob, Malcolm X's bodyguard. Bob had to be locked up whenever Johnson came into the yard.

As at Sing Sing, one of the first choices I had to make at Dannemora was perhaps the most important: which group to join. Various Mafia soldiers wanted me with them, and so did Irish gangsters and the Greeks. All of them sought jailhouse tough guys for their group, and I fit the category in every respect. I once again chose the Irish, primarily because of two rough-and-ready brothers, Joe and John D, and my old pal Willie the Ape.

The Dannemora prison yard resembled a hobo jungle. There were many "courts," pieces of property on which unified groups had staked claims. On one plot would be Irish gangsters from Manhattan's West Side, on another were guys from Queens, and at others sat members of different Italian crime families. Each of these open-air campsites, with a garden, table, and boxes to sit on, were kept immaculately trim and clean—neat as a pin in the pen.

The courts reserved for whites were set against the forty-foot high prison walls, and in the middle of the yard were properties held by black inmates. They protected their turf as zealously as the whites guarded theirs. Anyone wanting to travel from one court to another had to obtain permission from crews in between, and woe to the new inmate who didn't understand this rule.

The courts were actually armed camps. Each member had weapons. Shunned inmates—rapists, child abusers, and individuals who had proved they wouldn't fight for their rights—straggled by themselves near the ball field. They didn't have the courage to set up and maintain their own court.

Not welcome on any of these courts were the muscle-bound, bodybuilder homosexuals with names like Shirley Temple, Mae West, Crying Shame, Hardhitting Hannah, and Scrap Iron. All of them were physically powerful people who spoke like women: "You better do what I tell you; otherwise we're going to fight."

I had two knife fights at Dannemora, bloody battles that once and for all solidified my reputation as a jailhouse tough guy. Both involved entering a shower stall from which only the victor could emerge, while other inmates stood outside to make certain one of the combatants didn't try to flee. My opponents didn't die, but after being released from the hospital, neither was ever quite the same. Of course, no one even thought of telling prison officials what happened.

A knife fighter's most immediately vulnerable body parts are his hands and arms. I always came to a fight wearing thickly padded gloves and with towels wrapped around my arms. I also strapped a telephone book under my shirt. Such hand-to-hand knife combat demanded tremendous courage, or colossal stupidity if viewed another way, and required arduous physical and mental preparation. *Physically* I needed to be loose; tensing up could be fatal. For me, this posed no problem, because I had confidence *and* experience. I was a veteran who had survived many tough situations before. *Mentally* I psyched myself into a murderous mood, my mind black as a pit; through my head would run: *this is no fucking joke, Greek, show no mercy.* Incredibly, one of the guys I fought seemed not to understand how serious this all was. An insipid smile on his face, his attitude indicated he'd wandered into a neighborhood gym for a few rounds of friendly sparring. The other guy wasn't so easy: a young, strapping Jamaican, full of machismo, he sneered at the wrapping I wore and attacked the instant the shower door closed. But I was always ready. I slashed each of these opponents to ribbons before they could inflict major damage.

During these knife fights and during all my prison "group fights"—when multiple bodies tangled like worms in a fish-bait can—I noticed the intense press of flesh emitted a familiar but elusive odor. Finally at Dannemora I identified the smell—no doubt caused by fear and tension—as the aroma wafting off a slow-simmering pot of chicken soup.

Winston Moseley, Kitty Genovese's killer, was locked at Dannemora, and he spent all his time by himself. It became routine for any inmate in his vicinity to spit on him or kick him if he could; most would gladly have killed him had the opportunity presented itself.

At Dannemora I met Philly Gambino, a Colombo soldier who had a fatal date with Joey Gallo waiting in his future, and Buster DellaValle, who had a date with me.

There were six football teams at the prison, three white and three black. I played halfback for the Irish and was voted MVP in one of our "Super Bowls." The other white teams were the Ramblers and the Hoosiers, and the black teams were (again) the Senegalese, the Watusi, and the Magnums. The games were like wars, extremely violent. Guys played with bones thrusting out their skin. Prison officials approved of these contests, reasoning that it was better for inmates to vent rage on one another than on the hacks.

Richard Nixon had been sworn in when I was finally released in 1969, given $40 and a state suit, and driven to the Greyhound bus station in Plattsburgh, New York. Numerous inmates never got further than downtown Plattsburgh.

What these poor saps did was truly stupid, but very sad as well. Many bought a bottle to celebrate and walked out of the liquor store into the arms of chuckling correction officers, who laid in wait to bust them for a parole violation. A few newly released inmates deserved what they got by attempting to supplement their $40 with a quick stickup.

As I boarded a bus to Manhattan, I knew I hadn't been rehabilitated at all. In fact, I was more dangerous—smarter, too, I hoped—than before, and I aimed to use all that "prison learning" to make the big score.

Chapter 10

THE FIVE MAFIA FAMILIES

AN EX-CON TRYING TO TURN HIS LIFE AROUND HAS A HARD row to hoe. Upon his release from prison—when the warden hands him little more than cab fare in folding money and an out-of-style state suit good for a poor impression at best—he might as well have FELON branded across his forehead, just in case someone doesn't immediately recognize him as an ex-con from his pallid face and weird haircut. Even if the ex-con had taken full advantage of "educational opportunities" and mastered a skill while inside, having to acknowledge a prison record to a prospective employer usually guarantees a quick turndown. For even the few who have help—a caring parole officer (a most rare phenomenon), understanding relatives, a strong support group, prearranged job placement—walking out the gates can be an overwhelming experience. A substantial stretch in a structured closed environment breaks a man's spirit, reduces him to the state of a Pavlovian dog, only able to respond to programmed stimuli. He has been told what time to wake up, eat, work, clean, relax, shower, sleep—practically when to fart. Then, suddenly, left to make all decisions alone, he can't hack it. He has trouble adjusting to the spaciousness of an average home or apartment, finds a forbidding vastness in the workplace. The good intentions and honest efforts of many ex-convicts are dashed by the lure of old haunts and the influence of former crime partners. One guy closeted himself in a cell-sized boardinghouse room, mindlessly spent his days scrubbing the walls clean, and refused even to venture out to a waiting job. For a myriad of real or imagined reasons, ex-cons, attempting to stay on the right side of the law, have a hard time from doing hard time.

Not me. I didn't want to go straight. No boring sessions with do-gooder social workers for this cookie. No bullshit therapy from a shrink who would say I hated my uncle. Forget denial and struggling to make ends meet on some begged-for, dead-end job. *You're a criminal, pure and simple*, I told myself, *so go for it whole hog.*

When I hit New York City, a wide range of high-paying opportunities spread before me like a sumptuous smorgasbord. Grateful to be an independent, I decided to sample as many of these options as I could. All my tough-guy stuff in prison, very little of it calculated, had reached the ears of the criminal element outside, making me a sought-after commodity in the underworld marketplace.

I thought I had it all figured out, though my plan was hardly original. It's one every street thug and wiseguy goes to sleep dreaming about: *Look for the Big Score. Grab a million or so and retire to the good life, safe from prison jungles.* The terrible downside to the life I considered fabulously exciting was being thrown into fucking jails.

I had no doubt that if I played my cards right, one way or another a retirement plan would present itself. Even if I didn't luck into a colossal jackpot, I felt confident that bearing down to three or four years of steady, lucrative activity and conserving earnings would do the trick. I could have plenty of money and still stay around these guys I admired, while never taking risks. I'd be respected as someone who'd scored and walked away untouched. Other mobsters would seek my advice. Maybe I'd put a little money on the street, a relatively safe activity, just to avoid boredom.

Similar to a pro athlete before multimillion-dollar guaranteed contracts, however, I knew the odds against my enjoying an ultra-profitable career were enormous. My end could come from a cop's service revolver, a Mafioso's bullet in the back of the head, or a switchblade cutting through the darkness of some back alley.

Working in my favor when I came out of Dannemora were offers from the five New York Italian crime families, and I managed to do business with all of them. Although each was cutthroat, fiercely competitive, and extremely protective of turf and enterprises, they often cooperated for mutual benefit or against a common enemy. Working closely *with*—but not part *of*—these organizations, I obtained an overview few have achieved.

A typical Mafioso sees only one solution for a problem, any problem, no matter how small: kill it. If a guy thinks he's been cheated on a drug deal, or on the split of goods from a heist, his thoughts automatically turn murderous. Motherfucker can't screw me and get away with it, he tells himself.

According to unwritten Mafia law, only godfathers are supposed to sanction hits, based on the assumption that the dons are more restrained than their hotheaded underlings. A Carlo Gambino, for example, Mario Puzo's thinly disguised Don Vito Corleone, knows that the killing can quickly get out of hand, thus forcing a response from politicians and police. If every soldier, every captain, went to his godfather for approval for a hit, 99 percent would be turned down. "Ah, fuck it, just forget it," Carlo Gambino would say, unless *he* was the one being shortchanged on the deal.

Also, the "wronged" subordinate could find *his* life endangered if he went squawking to the godfather. His beef likely stemmed from an activity the don wouldn't approve. Maybe he is dealing drugs on the sly. Muscling into someone else's loan-shark territory. Running an unauthorized book.

"You wanna whack this scumbag because he took sixty percent of that fucking jewel heist, right?"

"Right."

"You got forty percent?"

"Right."

"How much did *I* get, you thieving cocksucker? Not a fucking dime!"

That's why I was frequently summoned. Most of the murders I committed for the Mafia were contracted by *captains* who couldn't trust their own soldiers to kill and keep quiet about it.

Some of the hits, of course, were at the behest of top bananas, the godfathers themselves. When a don wanted to distance his family from a murder, he would choose from a select group of the most trusted outsiders, efficient, stand-up guys the bosses believed would never talk.

I made this underworld list of free-lance hitters. Word-of-mouth reports about no-nonsense actions in the slam and on the street got me on it, and the position was solidified and greatly enhanced by my overt, bone-deep hatred of rats. My having permanently silenced a few blabbermouths made a Mafioso in the market to farm out a hit feel safe picking me as his triggerman. The bosses knew they could count on my silence. They also felt that if they told me something I would never repeat it to anyone.

I knew and lived by the code of *omerta*: you don't tell on anyone, even if it's a cop or a fag. You don't rat on guards, no matter how brutal they are.

I carefully guarded my reputation as a zipped lip. Once I was called to a prison waiting room, where I learned two FBI agents wanted to talk to me. I started screaming for the correction officer to slip me out of there. Word might get out that I had been seen with the FBI, and at least that guard could attest that I wouldn't speak to them.

Being marked as a rat is worse than being a child molester. There have been inmates who weren't rats, but stood accused by a powerful enemy, who killed themselves because of the bad rap. It seemed preferable to them to choose their own way of dying rather than to leave it up to some mobster. (The individual pointing the finger had better possess good proof. If he's lying and found out, he will be quickly killed, so serious is the accusation.)

A Genovese wiseguy named Louie had me checked out through 16th Precinct cops on his payroll. He asked if I fed them information, and they said *What, are you kidding*? I had to beat the shit out of Louie after I found out what he'd done.

But most gangsters can tell who has the strengths and who has the weaknesses. They just have to observe for a while. It helped that people liked me, and that I'd built a reputation too solid to attack.

My 1969 reentry into criminal activities was financed by a lot more than the $40 the state handed me when I exited Dannemora.

I had met Lucchese godfather Carmine Tramunti in prison, and he arranged for heroin and $10,000 to be waiting for me when I came out. I sold most of the heroin, used the rest. The money went for clothes, an apartment, good furniture.

I considered Tramunti one of my mentors. He was always scheming how to make more money, talking openly about various innovative scams, like a professor in a crime school. A gentleman, known affectionately as Mr. Gribbs, Tramunti bore a remarkable facial resemblance to comedian Jonathan Winters—a likeness that was only skin-deep. Mr. Gribbs was no joker.

Made in the 1940s by Tommy Lucchese himself, Tramunti okayed million-dollar deals with the nod of his head. In fact, he preferred that method. That way a bug couldn't pick up his voice. His family thrived on airport, hotel, bank, loan-company, and armored-car robberies; dealt heroin; owned nightclubs, caterers, and limousine services; and operated bookmaking establishments. Tramunti lived in Queens but often, dressed in his trademark sharkskin suit, used the Stage Delicatessen to personally direct his favorite racket: the organization's loan-shark business in Manhattan. Lucchese loans carried the highest interest rates in the city, and the family's collectors (including myself) were the most ruthlessly efficient. If the shylock *liked* a customer, he might charge $20 a week on a $100 loan. If he didn't give a fuck about him, the interest was $40.

Whenever I saw Carmine Tramunti—usually at the Stage Deli—we'd bullshit about some sporting event that we viewed from different sides of the coin toss, so to speak. Whereas I always worked out to keep my body in shape, loved playing contact games, and followed careers of pro athletes, the sedentary Tramunti didn't give a damn about the various players, teams, statistics, and trades. His interest and sports expertise derived strictly from money to be made.

The Luccheses had their hooks into professional boxing. Frankie Carbo, a family hit man, along with Blinky Palermo and St. Louis mobster John Vitale, had owned heavyweight champion Sonny Liston, and I never met a hoodlum who wasn't convinced that Liston, following Carbo's orders, threw both his fights with Muhammad Ali. One scam man, Patsy Lepera, bet against Liston in the first fight. "This guy didn't just take a dive," Lepera said, "he did a one and a half off the high board. It was so bad I figured we blew everything. But no, everybody got paid off. We had to give up forty percent for the information. I come out with seventy-five thousand dollars."

The second Liston/Ali fight (the first ended with the apparently unhurt Liston refusing to budge off his stool) was an even bigger stinker. The mob fighter went down in the first round from a punch nobody saw.

It was Frankie Carbo who "persuaded" Jake LaMotta to dump his 1947 fight with Billy Fox, though LaMotta wisely didn't mention Carbo when admitting the infamous fix in *Raging Bull.*

Al Weill, Rocky Marciano's manager, got his marching orders directly from Carbo. After he retired undefeated, Marciano admitted that during his career he had turned over half of his income to the Mafia.

At the deli after Tramunti and I verbally reran the Celtics/Knicks game from the night before, or quibbled about the field of Heismann Trophy candidates, the godfather would get serious and discuss various defaulters on loans made by his man Victor Amuso.

Collecting for Tramunti always featured a certain sameness. I remember one Broadway lunch counter owner in particular, though he could have been a score of others.

"How ya doin', buddy?" I said to the portly man hunched over his cash register.

"Who are you?" he asked, trying to feign ignorance as his eyes sparkled with fear behind the glasses he wore. His hands trembled; sweat gathered on his forehead. I'd seen it all before: acute terror.

"Victor Amuso sent me and my buddy Red to see you." I gestured backward at Red Kelly, a 5'11", 300-pound creature with flaming red hair, cold blue eyes, tree-stump legs, battering ram arms, and no neck. Red Kelly truly was the toughest street enforcer who ever lived, a legend. He dispassionately killed people with his bare hands or a baseball bat. Years later I mentioned Kelly to an interviewing detective who said, "Just hearing that name gives me the shakes." I believe if Kelly and Mike Tyson had ever fought on the street, Kelly would have been the one left standing.

"We want to talk to you alone," I said to the restaurateur, no menace in my voice. None was necessary.

"Okay. How about my office?"

He led us on rubbery legs to a little room in the back. I sat across from him at the desk; the expressionless Kelly, looking six-feet wide, stood behind me.

"You gonna pay this money?" I asked.

"Yes. Of course." He wiped sweat off his upper lip. "I *want* to pay. It'll be just a few more days."

"You're two weeks late."

"I've got problems. I need a little more time." Like *everyone*, he was afraid to look directly at Red, but he could hear the brute shuffling his feet impatiently.

"Vic's got bills due," I said mildly. "He can't give you no more time."

"Tell Vic I've got something going Tuesday. I'm almost sure I'll have the money by then."

"It can't work that way. You have to pay now." I was uncomfortable in the soft-guy role, but it was the only one I could play when making calls with Red, who was every ounce the hard guy and couldn't fake anything else.

"Red," I said, "this cocksucker don't want to pay Vic."

Kelly lumbered around the desk and grabbed the fat man by the neck. "You got two choices," he said in a voice that could freeze hell. "Within thirty minutes you either give us your business or the money. If you don't, we'll kill you, but first we'll break every bone in your body. Then, count on it, motherfucker, we'll whack your wife and kids."

The guy had to believe Red. *I* believed him. I worried that the choking businessman would suffer a seizure. This borrower, who had used $40,000 (juice had quickly boosted the amount owed to $75,000) from the Lucchese coffers to modernize and expand his lunch counter, was convulsed and gasping for air, but Red, still squeezing his neck, cuffed him quiet. "We ain't playing a game, you piece of shit. We'll kill you and everybody in your fucking family. Get this straight. Vic don't give a damn about your money. He'd rather make an example of you to other assholes. You got exactly thirty minutes, motherfucker."

Red, looking disgusted, let loose of the guy's throat. I feared the owner wouldn't make it. But after a minute or so he pulled himself together enough to ask, "Could you leave me alone so I can make a few phone calls?"

That suited me fine. Obviously he'd have to do some begging to raise the money, and he didn't want anyone to witness his embarrassment. The important thing was the cash, no matter Red saying, "Vic don't give a damn" about it. Vic did give a damn.

It never ceased to amaze me how quickly a strapped, poor-mouthing late payer could raise money when Red tightened the screws. We had the cash, all of it, in *twenty-nine* minutes.

Reestablishing contacts after my 1969 release, I got dressed one morning and decided it was time to further bend the parole regulation prohibiting association with ex-cons and look up another man I had done time with at Dannemora: Bonanno godfather Philip "Rusty" Rastelli.

While we were locked in together, Rastelli had said, "After we get out, Greek, you must come and visit me." So I placed a few calls. Soon his familiar voice on the other end of the line was issuing a renewed invitation, and we agreed to meet that evening at a Brooklyn nightclub called the 18th Hole.

As I worked off the day hopping from place to place in Manhattan, mostly collecting for Tramunti, I thought a lot about this other godfather, a distinguished-looking little guy, 5'8" with silver gray hair; he was known as a street diplomat—someone able to restore peace between warring factions.

Rastelli had been made by Joe Bonanno, a man whose intelligence he far exceeded. Now the crime family he headed—200 made members (soldiers, captains, underbosses), plus perhaps 500 associates—ranked as the smallest of the five New York Italian organizations, but was still much larger than any criminal family outside the city. Carlos Marcello in New Orleans and Santo Trafficante in Florida, to name just two bosses, were considered very small operators compared to Rastelli. Generally, an organization's violence is measured by the number of soldiers it has; however, this too is relative. Any group counting the likes of Rocky Moro and Sonny Red Indelicato (he once drove an ice pick so far through a victim's chest and into the floor beneath him that tire irons had to be used to pry the body loose) among its membership cannot be minimized or ignored.

At Dannemora, Rusty had assumed the status of an ordinary garden-variety con, not a godfather. I never saw him push his weight around by ordering or paying an inmate to scrub his toilet or run errands. Instead, he treated everyone he met as an equal. He did the time and the chores, which should have—but didn't—set an example for lesser Mafioso.

An obese piece-of-shit made drug dealer, part of the famous Pleasant Avenue connection, named Fat Gigi Inglese told me one day in the yard to get water for coffee. "You don't tell nobody to bring water," I snarled. "In here, you fat motherfucking pig, everybody is the same." I buried my fist up to the wrist in his large, doughy midsection, and he stumbled away gasping for breath.

Later Fat Gigi complained to Rastelli, saying I had "disrespected" him, but Rusty, who had witnessed the incident, laughed and brushed it off.

The people Rusty trusted most were those who had, like him, done a lot of time. Often he invited some of us guys from other courts over to his strip of property to talk and sample his excellent

Italian cooking. "You are very lucky, my friend Greek," he said, sliding a plate of fettuccini in front of me, "because you don't have to answer to no one. You are your own boss. Our lives are very similar except I have to answer to people I don't even like." Then he looked squarely into my eyes and added, "Let me give you a piece of advice: never bow down to no Mafioso. Show him respect, but don't be afraid of him, because he will play on your fears and break you."

At 10:00 P.M. when I entered the 18th Hole, I had no trouble spotting Rusty. Dressed in a white-on-white shirt and wearing an expensive gold watch as his only jewelry, he sat at a table chain-smoking L&M cigarettes and leisurely sipping Chivas Regal. This quiet godfather who had spent long years in prison and committed many murders always spoke in whispers. As usual, he greeted me by telling a joke.

"Know what I'd like to be when I'm reincarnated?" he asked.

"What?"

"A horse."

"Why?"

"So I can have a big cock."

He belched, laughed, and belched again. Although a little rough around the edges, this godfather would have been judged by etiquette expert Emily Post as a cultural ambassador compared to his copower in the Bonanno organization, Carmine Galante, a man whose murder he later ordered. Sonny Red Indelicato's coked-up son, Bruno, known for using cyanide-tipped bullets, headed the team that killed Galante at Joe and Mary's Restaurant in Brooklyn.

Rastelli was a deadly little guy. He even had his wife hit when he learned she was wagging her tongue to the feds. "Hey," he said about his spouse's demise, "you play, you gotta pay."

During our reunion at the nightclub, Rastelli talked of jobs in which I might participate (his only conversational topic was crime). Had we been different people at another place in time, Philip Rastelli could have been viewed as an employment-agency interviewer matching applicant Donald Frankos's qualifications to current job-market openings. But here we were, a godfather and a gangster, drinking at a Brooklyn nightspot discussing which branch of his criminal empire—heroin trade (the family's bread and butter); unions representing waitresses and bartenders; bookmaking; concrete and construction companies—would best serve his needs and mine. We ultimately settled on hijackings, a Bonanno staple.

The hijackings I participated in were pieces of cake. First, a Bonanno soldier would give the driver of a valuable shipment one of those classic Mafia offers he couldn't refuse: "Take five percent of what we get for the load, or we'll grab what we fucking want and whack you just for the fun of it."

What could the driver do? He knew the Mafia didn't bluff or play around. The cops couldn't do anything to protect him or his family, which he'd have to move to distant points if he chose not to cooperate.

Usually the driver parked his load at a designated truck stop, went inside for a strong cup of coffee, and returned to find his rig missing. Before the authorities had finished writing a stolen-vehicle report, we would have the truck safely tucked in a Bonanno warehouse. Often the driver was so pleased with his share that he steered business our way.

The night Rastelli signed me on in the 18th Hole, I confided my ambition of making a big score and getting out. He conceded it *had* been done before, and even allowed that I might be able to save enough from a series of smaller jobs to set myself up for life. Certainly I had the energy and connections to work as often as I wanted.

"I hope you succeed, Greek," he said, but I could tell he didn't think I would.

Regardless, I was soon too busy working for him and other mobsters to worry about it. As always, the biggest part of my problem involved liking too much what I did, the excitement and glamour of living by my wits, on the edge. I should have been more selective, not jumped at every opportunity that came along.

In 1969 I broke a few skulls for the Colombo family, headed at the time by Joseph Colombo; delivered drugs for the Gambinos; and committed murder for the Genoveses, run by Fat Tony Salerno and Funzi Tieri—my friend John Sullivan was Fat Tony's main hitter, and John passed contracts on to me.

I opened two bank accounts, rented several safe-deposit boxes, and gave money to a few trusted friends to hold for me. If I hadn't been living so high—women, the racetracks, expensive clothes, the best restaurants—I would have been a more effective saver, but what the hell, these were the perks of my profession. I was also a soft touch for any hood with a hard-luck story.

Sleep obviously didn't rank high on my list of priorities, remarkable since I had again begun using heroin. Like an Energizer-powered toy, I kept going and going and going. I took assignments, mainly drug runs, from the Puerto Rican mob headed by Spanish Raymond Marquez, who controlled heroin distribution in Latin sections of Harlem. I picked the heroin up from a guy named Philly "Rags" and delivered it to Puerto Rican crews. The filthy rich Philly Rags, a millionaire many times over, had blue eyes, a receding hairline, and no regrets that he couldn't be made because his mother was Polish. Philly Rags had many sources for heroin, including police officers who stole the drugs off people they arrested and from evidence rooms.

It is believed (although it was never proven) that a member of New York City's elite Special Investigating Unit (SIU) of the department's narcotics division was the person who swiped almost every ounce of heroin confiscated in the famous French Connection case. Of the approximately seventy men in SIU, fifty-two (not including various rats in the unit who purchased immunity by snitching out their brother cops) ended up being indicted for felonies. According to findings of the crime-fighting Knapp Commission, almost every member of SIU was corrupt.

Besides dealing drugs, New York's finest also engaged in extortion. One detective explained why he felt safe shaking down the Mafia itself. "They talk a lot of shit," this cop said. "They're tough. We're tougher. We've got the biggest fucking gang in the world. There are thirty-two thousand of us."

Wiseguys I bullshitted with late at night in bars disputed that "biggest fucking gang in the world" assertion. To them, the biggest gang was the U.S. government, which they called "that crew in Washington." "How the fuck are they different from us?" I frequently heard hoodlums lament. "Damn crooks are extorting every tax-paying sucker in the country. Instead of breaking legs once in a while, they send assholes to prison so they can get raped or killed."

Despite all this, most wiseguys, and all bosses, were very patriotic. Not only did they feel America was the "Land of Opportunity"—look how well they were doing—but they believed the government was merely a larger version of themselves, if not quite so effective. Didn't mob areas have lower street-crime rates? Shit, it wasn't safe even a block from the White House. Put Carlo Gambino in charge and people would see some real crime prevention.

Anyway, I received $1,500 for every kilo of heroin I carried from Philly Rags to Spanish Raymond, and I figured that even with the lavish lifestyle I once again had adopted, a few years on the outside would fund that dreamed-of retirement. But being a "mule" was hazardous—there were always takeoff guys looking to ambush couriers and grab their junk—and I considered the job more dangerous than most hits, which I usually could control by choosing the time and place.

For example, on 114th Street between Fifth Avenue and Madison, I shot and killed a gangster who had been moving in on Spanish Raymond's numbers business. No sweat. And, as usual, no remorse. I knew the world wouldn't miss this scumbag.

Having acquired a reputation for knowing my way around Harlem, I was recruited to deliver Genovese family heroin to The General, a major supplier of blacks. Often I went with Blackie DellaValle, Buster's brother, who a few years later got whacked on orders from The General. Blackie and I received $1,000 each per delivery and felt free to steal whatever we needed for our own consumption. Several times I squirreled drug-delivery money into a safe-deposit box or one of my bank accounts. I needed to be careful, in case I was arrested, to have cash available for the prison commissary, so I increased the number of people who held money for me. No one is more pathetic than a convict without funds for commissary.

I killed a pimp for The General, another victim no one will mourn, a gay guy in a lavender suit whose presence in the neighborhood offended The General's sensitivities. It seemed to me most New York City pimps were gay. Many of those I knew had prostitute mothers who raised them in bordellos.

Like I said, most gangsters have just one solution for a problem. Kill it. I whacked still another pimp, also in 1969, as a favor for a big-time fence who sold pistols stolen from the docks to West Side Irish gangsters. The pimp's "crime" had been upsetting the fence's mother, who spotted him on a Tenth Avenue street corner as she walked to Sunday Mass.

Joe Sullivan would have called it a Neighborhood Beautification Project.

I had nearly $60,000 stashed away, despite my extravagant spending, when everything turned sour for me in early 1970. To satisfy my parole officer, I had a no-show job as an assistant foreman in a mid-Manhattan sweatshop controlled by the mob. Thus I always had a pay stub when I checked in weekly.

Little good it did me.

"Sit down," the parole officer said, when I ducked my head in his door.

He called in three more parole officers. I knew what was coming; despair, starting in the pit of my stomach, spread through my whole body.

"Stand up," I was commanded.

I did.

"Empty your pockets."

I did.

"We're arresting you for consorting with known criminals," my parole officer said. He held up $300 they had taken from my pocket. "Where did you get this?"

"I saved it from my paycheck."

"Yeah. And I inherited a million bucks from an old maid aunt last week. Get undressed, you lying cocksucker."

When their strip search failed to locate any track marks, one of them groped up my rectum and came out with a packet of heroin.

"You're working with Philly Rags selling that poison. Do you want to come with us, or do you want to go back to prison?"

"Lock me up," I said, outraged that they'd think I might turn rat. "I'd rather spend my whole life behind bars than work for you."

I didn't let them see the tremendous depression I felt at the thought of going back (a second time for a lousy parole violation) to one of their filthy jails.

Chapter 11

THE AUBURN RIOT

I GOT TIGHT WITH JOEY GALLO WHEN WE LOCKED BY EACH other in A Block at the Auburn Correctional Facility, thirty miles west of Syracuse in the Finger Lakes region, where a judge sent me for that second parole violation. I occupied cell 20, he cell 21.

We conversed frequently, always as equals. I had a larger crew of guys around me than Joey did, and mine weren't bought. He paid certain cons to watch his back, and others he promised work when they were released. My people stuck with me because they knew no one would fuck with them. I advocated an all-for-one philosophy—the *group* against anyone who hassled us—and never hesitated to lead an attack. Everyone knew, if it came down to it, that I would kill an enemy.

The tensions at Auburn were terrific, and prisoners, especially blacks and Latins, began considering a prison uprising. Often Gallo and I discussed the tinderbox situation, and what we'd do if a riot broke out and inmates started taking hostages. Joey had a goodly number of black prisoners around him and talked a tough game. He would be right alongside his "brothers," he said, and God help the correction officers. I kept quiet and wondered. The horrible conditions affected everyone, but the blacks and Latins most of all.

Prisoners' complaints started with the guards, the people they encountered day in and day out. Hacks anywhere are a particularly scummy lot, I believe, but some of the ones at Auburn established new low standards. They enjoyed beating inmates with clubs; yes, *enjoyed*, because why else did they do it *every time* they dragged a prisoner, no matter how docile, to isolation?

The typical guard had wanted to be a police officer, but had been rejected. I do not exaggerate when I say the average hack is crude and lazy. He mostly sits on his ass all day long, often reading girlie magazines. Occasionally he'll stir himself to intimidate an inmate or to search an inmate's personal property. Nothing pleases the guard more than to find a picture of a wife or girlfriend, preferably clad in underwear or nude. The hack coming upon such a treasure then could be seen passing it around to his comrades, and be heard loudly discussing the female's physical merits.

It does no good explaining Auburn or other institutions to say there were exceptions, a few decent and dedicated correction officers. There were. But it seemed the majority were animals. A favorite pastime of many was watching inmates take showers. One officer found excuses to throw prisoners into isolation if they refused to perform oral sex on him.

Everything about Auburn invited an uprising. The prison had been built in *1817*, and conditions ranged from suffocating jungle heat to freezing Arctic cold. If a guy threw a blanket over his head while trying to sleep, the guards tossed him in the hole.

The arbitrary issuance of punishment stood high on every inmate's list of complaints. An inmate could be placed in isolation for spitting on the grass, for keeping a diary, for anything that aggravated a hack. What displeased a guard most were jailhouse lawyers who drew up petitions and writs, anything that might help a fellow prisoner obtain his rights.

Higher-ups in the correction system, we believed, sanctioned and encouraged the beatings, the isolation, and the bread-and-water routines the guards put jailhouse lawyers through. Authorities didn't want the multitude of abuses made public.

The practice of divide-and-conquer ruled at Auburn. Guards encouraged strict segregation of the races in the mess hall and the athletic field, writing down the name of anyone who associated with a different group. Inmates got accorded disparate treatment in the hope that prisoners would resent one another instead of their keepers. Separate rules applied even to wiseguys: those from New York City were constantly harassed for petty rules violations, while made guys from Rochester or Buffalo got cut a bit more slack. The reason: anyone from New York City was regarded as a threat to the status quo and, therefore, had to be kept down. There were civil liberties organizations to which the authorities feared these more sophisticated big-city criminals would turn.

The food at Auburn was terrible, even for a state institution: lots of beets, week-old bread, colored water passing for coffee, and small (thankfully) gobs of greenish-brown meat.

But the clothing situation ranked worse. Inmates weren't asking for Savile Row suits, just something more substantial than threadbare rags to keep them warm during the bitter upstate winters.

Miserable as life was for whites, fairness compelled us to admit that others had it worse. The blacks and Puerto Ricans complained, rightly, that the New York State prison system employed no black or Spanish deputy wardens, wardens, or commissioners; and that while 70 percent of the inmates were black or Puerto Rican, there was a minuscule number of black and Spanish-speaking guards. The hacks, most of whom came from farm backgrounds, found it difficult to communicate with inner-city blacks and impossible to talk to Puerto Ricans, the most oppressed of all. Mail, for example, vitally important to every prisoner, often took months to get delivered because the prison censors couldn't read Spanish.

The miserable conditions and the racial hostility of the guards might not by themselves have guaranteed a prison explosion. But something new had been added to the mix: young, tough, relatively bright agitators with experience on the outside confronting authority. These were Young Lords, Black Panthers, and Black Muslims, and they weren't so easily cowed into silence.

Waiting for The Riot—I felt in my bones it would happen—I spent a lot of time visiting Joey Gallo in his cell, and he often came to mine. No matter how brutal hacks might be, we were always able to bribe them into bringing us forbidden loot—alcohol, dope, good food—and, more important, into staying out of our way. These lowlifes weren't even good businessmen: for $20, less than we'd tip a waiter at a restaurant, they'd "mule" to us virtually anything we wanted. I wasn't short of money, thanks to my "retirement fund," and Joey had a large constant flow of cash from outside enterprises he ran from prison.

Gallo had taken up painting, trying to become an artist and broaden his surprisingly considerable horizons. He also read a great deal: Jean-Paul Sartre, Albert Camus, Ayn Rand. Joey's philosophy: if you're a cab driver, be the best cab driver in the world; if you're a gangster, be the best. Don't settle for second rate.

Having already learned that reading was the quickest way to chew up prison time, I lost myself in tales by Agatha Christie and Ian Fleming. Joey scoffed at my choices of mysteries and spy thrillers and said, "Read *War and Peace*, read Alexander Dumas, read Victor Hugo. If you expand your mind with good books, you'll dislike being around the people you hang out with. In other words, you'll get out of the shitty ghetto life you're in. Learn about education and intellect. Extricate yourself from this trap that makes you suffer." He sounded like the death house's Frank Bloeth.

"I'm not suffering," I said.

"You're not suffering? Take another look, pal. You're a pathetic son of a bitch, locked up like some wild animal in a miserable fucking cage."

"So the fuck are you, Joey."

"Yeah, but I have peace of mind, and freedom. When I fantasize, my imagination takes me out of here. You're too involved with this place and its politics. In *my* mind I'm not even here. I'm free. You're never going to be free unless you quit reading those

Agatha Christie books and stop hanging out with the guys, talking all that shit."

"Get off my back," I said. "Okay. I'll read one of your fucking books."

He handed me *The Prince* by Machiavelli, a pocket dictionary, a pen, and a notepad. "If you find a word you don't understand, Greek, write it down and look it up. Even if it takes three weeks to get through this book, at least you'll understand what the hell you're reading."

Joey fascinated me. He could put twenty-dollar words together in a sentence and structure it to sound nice, comfortable to the ears. A good orator, he had a real knack for swaying and persuading listeners. He could stand in front of twenty or thirty people and spellbind them,

When I finished *The Prince*, Joey delivered one of his lectures. "Greek, did you know this is Nixon's bible? Yeah, he loves it. All political-science majors study Machiavelli. But his philosophy isn't limited to use in government or the military. You can practice it among ordinary people, anybody can. His thing was divide and conquer, even among the ranks. Always have them guessing your next move. *The Prince* teaches to stay with your own, and hire outside people, mercenaries, to do your work for you. Don't use the crew you're involved with. Hire others and let them take the weight."

Joey enjoyed tutoring me on the principles of his hero Machiavelli, and I taught Joey how to play bridge. But the other guys in the game didn't cotton to Gallo. They took me aside and filled my ears with tales of his kinky sex habits, stories I credited to jealousy or a jailhouse gossip mill gone haywire. Even seeing his constant entourage of young black fags didn't convince me. I was a little too blinded by Joey's successes in self-education *and* the Mafia.

I arranged a job for Joey with me in dresser-shop shipping as an elevator operator. Inmates made dressers and tabletops, including some for Governor Rockefeller's wife. All Joey and I did was carry the furniture down on an elevator to waiting trucks.

The rest of the day we cooked on a hot plate, listened to the radio, and played cards. I used to beat the shit out of Joey at Greek poker. We never bet money because once you start gambling it's good-bye friendship. Settling up can result in time-wasting, dangerous hassles: "If you don't pay the money you owe me by tonight, I'm coming after you." That type of shit. I'd be looking for a guy, and he'd be trying to duck me.

Joey said he owned this and that, operated these restaurants and controlled those businesses. "Greek, I got a couple games you can run if you come with me when you get out."

He also said, "I should be able to make you a captain. You know, things are changing in the families about pure Italian pedigrees." He meant it, and that's one of the big reasons the Mafia rubbed him out. His favorite topic of conversation involved how he would shoot himself to the top of the Colombo crime family, using blacks and tough guys like me.

"I don't know, Joey," I kept hedging. "I like my independence."

I'll never forget the day I inadvertently confirmed the rumors circulating about Joey's sexuality. I was on my way to see a guy in the tobacco shop, near where they made the New York State license plates. As I walked through the shipping department, I heard groans coming from one of the big cardboard dresser boxes. I eased over to the box, looked inside, and caught Joey butt-fucking a black guy, about twenty-six years old, who did chins and punched the bag all day long. There my friend was, right in front of my eyes, with his ass up in the air pumping away.

Joey got off the black guy real quick. I was embarrassed for him. "Hey, Greek," he said, blushing, "what can I tell you? This is my thing. I like it."

"You're no good, Joey," I said. "You got me giving you my coffee, you're using my coffee cups, and you're kissing these fucking guys. You're disrespecting me. Everybody told me you're a scumbag, you're no fucking good, you're evil. I keep you as a friend, and you're fucking these guys behind my back and using my coffee cups. Maybe these guys got some disease."

I had more to say when we returned to the block. "I'm not a

gossip, so I won't hurt you by telling the whole fucking joint I busted you on the kid. It sickens me to even think about fucking a kid in the ass that way. Joey, you're a very sick guy. I don't want to be around a person like you."

But I *was* around him, at work and in our adjoining cells, so gradually things smoothed over. After that incident, however, we went through a cooling-off period and didn't talk a lot. Without his incessant silver-tongued hype about my making fast money in the Mafia and rising above my gutter mentality, I began seeing more clearly the complex kaleidoscope of contrasts contained in Joey Gallo. He was a person who could describe gouging a man's guts out with the same eloquent ease that he discussed classical literature. This master of manipulation used words beautifully to get what he wanted, and Joey wanted it all, especially in the area of physical pleasure.

Joey was bisexual, I realized. He liked women, enjoyed having a flashy dame on his arm in public, but he was possessive and verbally abusive: "Hey, cunt, get down on your knees and suck my prick!" As for male sex partners in the slam, he adored young Puerto Ricans who weren't homosexual—they were a real challenge to him. His favorites were dark black men, athletic types with shaved heads, whom he was always looking to sodomize.

One day Gallo told a young friend of mine, Richie, to give him a haircut. After Richie finished, Gallo ordered this guy Willie the Russian, "Give the kid two cartons of cigarettes."

To Joey, everybody had a price tag and could be bought with booze or cigarettes (he had an unending supply of both). But guys like Richie weren't for sale. I went to Joey and said, "Why did you offer Richie the smokes? Didn't I tell you not to bribe my friends? They do favors out of the kindness of their hearts."

"Well, it's okay," Joey said.

"It ain't okay. Don't you offer none of my friends nothing."

Another time Joey smacked this old man, Carmine, in the face. Carmine, a long-time wiseguy, had been in the joint twenty-five years, and Joey wanted to show he could push around what he considered a Mafia has-been. Carmine dragged his aging frame

Frankos, in 1979, during his career as a boxing trainer at Eastern State Prison in Naponoch, NY. His assistant is on the left, two boxers on the right and above. *Photo courtesy of Donald Frankos*

November, 1988. Frankos participating in his favorite exercise: jogging. Because he was in the Witness Protection Program, he was only allowed in a small yard—which he had all to himself. *Photo courtesy of Donald Frankos*

Authors William Hoffman (left) and Lake Headley with Frankos's cousin, Alice Pohl, the family historian. *Photo by John Hoffman*

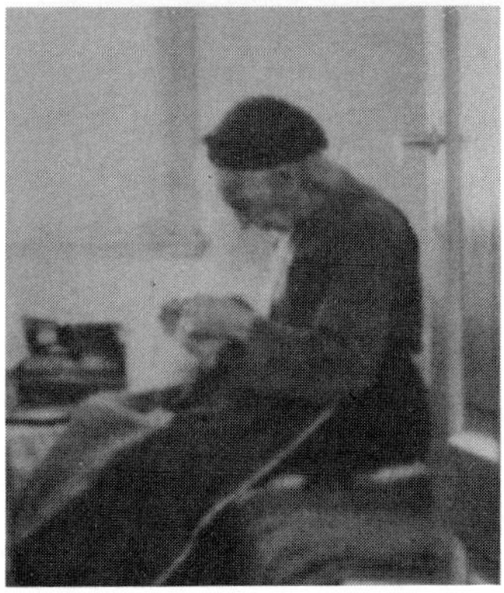

Elena Frangos, Donald Frankos's aunt, in Chios, Greece. She was over 100 years old at the time of this photo. *Photo courtesy of Donald Frankos*

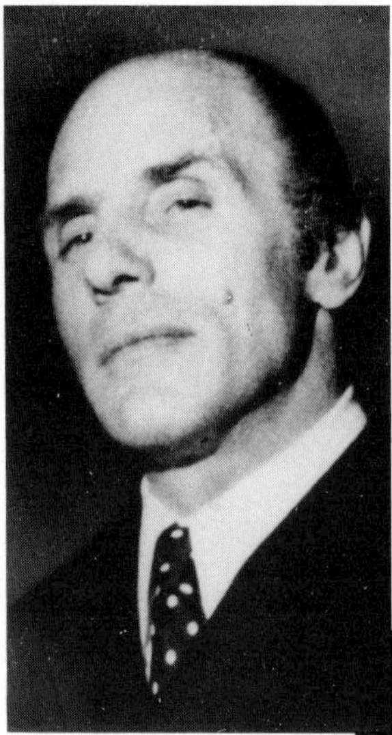

Frankos's sometime friend, Joey Gallo, gunned down in 1972 by Sonny Pinto at Umberto's Clam House. Until now, this case has gone unsolved. *AP/Wide World Photos*

Drug kingpin Leroy "Nicky" Barnes posing with Frank James (left) and Ishmael Mohammed (center), two men he later ratted on. *AP/Wide World Photos*

Frankos with Jimmy Coonan. Coonan, head of the notorious Westies, participated in many murders after this June 1973 photo, including that of Jimmy Hoffa. *Photo courtesy of Donald Frankos*

Joe "Mad Dog" Sullivan, in chains, being led into Onondaga County courthouse to face murder charges in 1982. *AP/Wide World Photos*

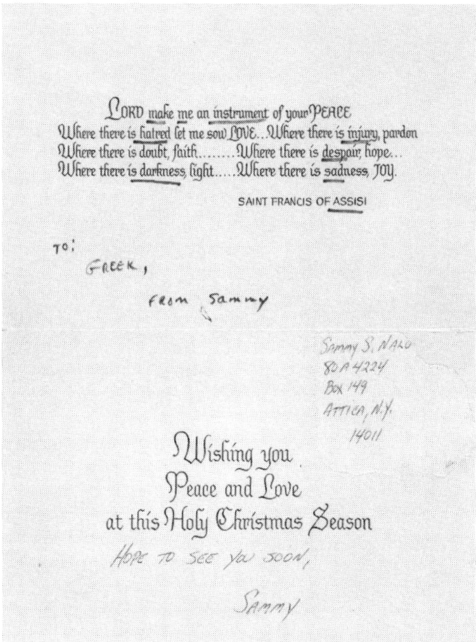

LORD make me an instrument of your PEACE
Where there is hatred let me sow LOVE...Where there is injury, pardon
Where there is doubt, faith........Where there is despair, hope...
Where there is darkness, light.....Where there is sadness, JOY.
SAINT FRANCIS OF ASSISI
TO:
GREEK,
FROM Sammy
Sammy S. NALO
80A4224
Box 149
ATTICA, N.Y.
14011
Wishing you
Peace and Love
at this Holy Christmas Season
HOPE TO SEE YOU SOON,
SAMMY

Coded 1983 Christmas card from Sammy Nalo telling Frankos to kill, or arrange for the killing of, Bobby Comfort (the contract was never executed). Comfort was a participant, with Frankos and Nalo, in the Hotel Pierre robbery. *Photo courtesy of Donald Frankos*

Thomas Bilotti, an aide to Gambino godfather Paul Castellano, lies dead outside Sparks Restaurant in Manhattan. The gunning down of Bilotti and Castellano, ordered by John Gotti, paved the way for Gotti to take control of the Gambino crime family. *AP/Wide World Photos*

John Gotti on trial for racketeering in 1987. He was ultimately convicted in 1992 for racketeering and murder and is serving a life sentence without parole. *AP/Wide World Photos*

Salvatore "Sammy Bull" Gravano, Gambino underboss who turned government witness and was critical to the 1992 conviction of Gotti. *AP/Wide World Photos*

"Fat Tony" Salerno, the late Genovese godfather who ordered Hoffa's murder, being led from federal court in Manhattan in 1985. Salerno, at that time, had become the richest mobster in U.S. history. *AP/Wide World Photos*

Jimmy Hoffa on trial for jury tampering in the late 1960s. He was convicted and jailed but released by presidential order of Richard Nixon in 1972. His disappearance in July 1975 has until now been a mystery. *AP/Wide World Photos*

Anthony "Tony Jack" Giacalone in 1975. Tony Jack, Hoffa's rabbi, set the Teamster up for murder. *AP/Wide World Photos*

Chuckie O'Brien, Hoffa's "foster son." *AP/Wide World Photos*

Frankos in prison. *Courtesy Donald Frankos*

around doing errands for Joey and was punched because he forgot to deliver that day's copy of the *New York Times*.

This really set me off. I got right in Joey's face and said, "Smack him again, and I'm smacking *you*. You should be ashamed of yourself for hitting Carmine and making him feel like a piece of shit in front of black guys and outsiders. That's disrespectful. Who do you think you are, taking advantage of that old man?"

"It won't happen again, Greek. I promise."

"You better believe it won't, 'cause I'll come after you."

Joey knew I'd keep my word, and I knew not to take his promises seriously. He was a treacherous, conniving little son of a bitch who'd shaft anybody he thought was a serious threat to him. For instance, he had a friend mail a package to an inmate bearing the return address of one of the inmate's relatives. Of course, all incoming parcels were searched by the guards before prisoners got them. So when Joey's target signed for his "care package" of homemade cookies from Aunt Susie, the hacks produced the ounce of heroin they had found inside and threw him in the hole.

Or Joey would have a shiv planted in a cell, then send one of his gofers to squeal about it. A hack would shake down the cell, find the secreted weapon, and toss the "owner" in solitary.

The bag of tricks Joey used in his process of elimination was deep. He politely invited guys into his cell and poisoned them. I saw him do it.

"Hey, buddy," he called to an inmate named Whitey, "come here. I got something for you."

"How you been doin', Joey?" Whitey asked as he sat down to catch up on the news.

"Fine. Help yourself to some food," said the gracious host, extending an attractively arranged platter of smoked meat, fresh vegetables, and cheese.

Whitey ate the strychnine-laced antipasto and nearly died.

A friend of mine brought Joey poisoned lasagna, and Joey offered him anchovies marinated in strychnine. I almost split my sides to keep from laughing as I listened to their standoff, each giving reasons for not being hungry and encouraging the other to dig in.

Other times it wasn't so funny, at least not to Joey's unsuspecting guests or the two blacks he forced to test his food. *Three* different times Hulk and Kareem had their stomachs pumped at the hospital.

I had to stay sharp with Joey every minute. He was forever bending my ear about all the wiseguys he intended to "square up with" when he got out, how he was going to take what belonged to him, and that he needed "good people" like me to help him. Maybe so, but I didn't think he would forget the times I'd backed him down; and besides wanting to remain independent, I didn't relish keeping one eye over my shoulder, looking for a Joey Gallo hitter. I turned him down and he was pissed.

On November 4, 1970, the riot broke out. Black inmates, refusing to take any more shit, started it, and soon everybody joined. There were 1,675 men locked in Auburn, and that's how many rebelled.

The uprising didn't begin spontaneously, though once it was under way a number of prisoners did pretty much what they wanted. The trouble began at 8:00 A.M. in the prison yard when, as prearranged, about 400 black inmates refused to report to work. They figured others would join them, especially the Puerto Ricans, but were surprised by the overwhelming response from whites.

Soon every building except the administration building was under the somewhat tenuous control of inmates. They grabbed hostages and construction workers, taking them to the middle of the yard. Prisoners soaked them with gasoline, ignited torches, and shouted a warning to the hacks positioned on roofs: "If you don't fucking get down from there, we're going to kill your friends!" Those guards with machine guns retreated from sight.

I want to say right now, all the stuff written about Joey Gallo being a hero in the Auburn riot was bullshit. I first saw him in the back of A Block where two guards had been laid out cold on the floor. Joey said to me, "Greek, why don't we let bygones be bygones? Since we're going to die anyway, let's shake hands so we can be friends in the next life."

I said, "Who the fuck wants to be your friend in the next life, you punk motherfucker?"

Rather than getting mad, Joey just laughed.

"Listen," I said, "I've got to take care of my people," referring to the 100 white guys who in this situation would look to me to provide leadership. "I'm going into the yard to help draw up our demands. I want you to round up all the whites you can find—even the piece-of-shit white guys—and bring them together against the wall by the cellblock."

The four cellblocks at Auburn formed a square with a yard in the middle. Gesturing and shouting over the din, I positioned the young kids in front of the old men and middle-aged guys in front of the kids. I surrounded everybody with forty or fifty of the really tough guys, including Jimmy Coonan. The idea was to shield the "elders," some prematurely aged from years of the prison injustices we protested—yet let them make a stand.

The air crackled with hostility and tension. I felt sure the authorities would attack with clubs, tear gas, and guns. They weren't going to wait around, and our only protection was the hostages. Already state troopers had arrived to buttress the hacks, and I knew the combined forces were whipping themselves into a frenzy.

Across the yard from us were the Spanish guys, a lot of them Young Lords. To our right and left were three factions of blacks: the Muslims, the Five Percenters, and the Black Panthers. The blacks numbered about 1,100; the Puerto Ricans about 300. Also, there was a mixed bag of some 50 renegades who didn't belong to any segment.

Thomas Johnson, the black convicted of killing Malcolm X (I had met Johnson earlier at Dannemora), represented the Muslims. A guy named Raul served as mouthpiece for the Young Lords, and the Panthers had a fellow named Fleer. The other respective groups chose their own leaders, and we set up a table and microphone and started writing down demands.

It had to drive the hacks crazy, watching us conduct business at that table and knowing that the liberal media would probably treat us seriously. We deserved truncheons and a boot in the nuts, the hole—their solution to everything—not bleeding-heart publicity.

Besides addressing the problems I enumerated earlier, we demanded more books and lower commissary prices. Psychiatric care: a key demand, and foolish for the state not to provide. Like it or not, most of the inmates would one day be released, only to reenter society more dangerous than before.

What did we hope to gain? I've often been asked. The answer is, just what we said: livable conditions, a little respect, and an end to the constant beatings. The inmates didn't rise up frivolously; they risked their lives (hearing the massed forces against us shouting, cursing, and threatening, who could doubt it?) because existence was intolerable.

In drawing up the demands, we agreed that complaints from each group—the blacks, whites, and Spanish—should be presented as a whole. A black guy named Kelly and a white guy named Bobby, who was good with the law, incorporated the separate grievance lists into a single document. It had to amaze the administration that inmate solidarity extended to job assignments, a favorite divide-and-conquer tactic our keepers believed would forever keep inmates separated. As a matter of practice, blacks and Latins had been given the hardest, filthiest jobs, but here we were united even in putting an end to that.

Thomas Johnson called the warden, Harry Fritz, and read the demands. Fritz said, "I think we'll be all right." He added that providing a plane to Algeria—a demand I thought lessened the impact of the document and gave the other side a propaganda weapon—was out of the question. A few inmates, who feared retaliation and considered themselves political prisoners, would just have to live without that plane. The only other demand Fritz didn't agree to negotiate, because he had no say in the matter, was for Governor Rockefeller to visit the joint (ultimately Rockefeller refused to come, just as he later refused to meet with prisoners at Attica).

Warden Fritz feared the situation would explode before an accommodation could be reached. The inmates had resorted to fighting among themselves, settling old scores, and the hacks and state troopers itched to come after us. They yelled every imaginable obscenity, shouted "We'll kill your asses! We'll cut your fucking hearts out!" Given the ugly, supercharged atmosphere, anything was possible. They considered us subhuman, murderous vermin; and our collective opinion of them wasn't any higher.

Thomas Johnson and I went to B Block to check on two injured correction officers being held by black inmates. "We need to carry these hacks up to the infirmary," Johnson said.

"The hell you say!" growled one of the prisoners, shielding a battered officer like a half-starved predator unwilling to share downed prey. "Fuck the first aid!" said another. "We're gonna kill these honkie motherfuckers!"

"Forget that bullshit." I said. "You'll get nothing done that way, and you'll set everybody back. If you *hurt* an officer, that's tough for him. But if you *kill* one, we're not gonna get cock. Nothing. So I tell you, no, no killing!"

Whether my words temporarily addled or convinced the vengeance-seeking captors, I don't know. But they offered no resistance when Johnson and I and a few others began escorting the guards plus a couple of construction workers to whatever makeshift emergency medical treatment was available.

At the infirmary we found what resembled an army M.A.S.H. unit pillaged by the enemy: soiled sheets falling off beds, bloody bandages and opened medical supplies littering the floor, cut and bludgeoned inmates doctoring one another, cries for mercy. One guy, who had been thrown off a second-story tier and crash-landed on his head, was in bad shape. I didn't think he'd make it.

In the dispensary we saw the pharmaceutical cabinet atilt, its smashed doors wide open and shelves picked clean. Looters, attempting to kill mounting fear or birth courage, had washed down handsful of pills.

Meanwhile the joint rumbled in chaos. As I hurried up and down tiers, from cellblock to cellblock, and through the yard, the prevailing tone of overheard comments confirmed my gloomy suspicion: we were into some serious trouble. Drugs, releasing long-suppressed resentment of the hacks, had some inmates talking massacre. A guard had already been attacked sexually, and cooler prisoner heads couldn't stop all of the beatings.

Even more ominous than the rantings and ravings *inside* was the heat we felt intensifying and pressing harder from *outside* the wall. The state troopers, tough guys in the mold of a SWAT team, were being joined by local Auburn police, all of them comrades-in-arms. Having frequently associated with the guards and their families in condemning what many residents considered a blight on their fair community, these cops had become acquaintances, drinking buddies, *friends* of the men we held hostage. For years they had swapped stories about the "animals in the cage" and nurtured a mutual hatred for the prison population. Now, the longer this congregation of law and order enforcers marked time, the closer their loathing for us moved toward lynch-mob mentality.

"We're coming in in twenty minutes to kill everybody in this motherfucker!" boomed a voice over the loudspeaker. Then tear gas exploded in the yard.

Throats and eyes burning in the noxious cloud, we braced for the attack, which I figured would come sooner than they said.

Twenty minutes later, nothing.

"Goddamn," said one of my crew members nervously, "I sure would like one more smoke before I die. Hey, George, you got any butts?" "Fuck no," replied George, "I split my last one with Lefty an hour ago."

In the role of outgunned army Sergeant Frankos eager to ease pain by granting a last request from troops, I wove a path through the mob of milling, angry inmates to A Block, stripped a pillowcase from a bunk, and quickly stuffed it with cartons of cigarettes.

As I came out of the block, I saw a correction officer, one of the few nice guards in the joint, lying on the floor. His right eye was out of its socket, dangling against his cheekbone, and he moaned as blood trickled from his mouth, nose, and ears—hemorrhages caused from inmates flogging him almost to death with his own keys. "Can you hear me?" I said, leaning over. He tried to look up with the good eye and groaned loudly in pain, serious pain.

Despite being in peak condition at this time, I was a 160-pound jogger, not a weight lifter. I wrestled the correction officer, who weighed well over 200 pounds, onto my shoulders, tried to stand up, and thought my nutsack would come out my ass. Deciding there was no way to carry him by myself, I called to a passing black inmate, "Help me with this wounded guy. We'll have hell to pay if we leave him here to die."

The prisoner hoisted the hack onto my shoulders and absorbed part of the load. As we carried him out in the yard, an announcement came over the public address: "Emergency! Emergency! Frankos, report to C Block immediately! The warden's on the phone!"

I looked around, wondering what to do with the hack, and saw coming toward me none other than Joey Gallo, accompanied by two cons. I'll never forget this scene. It was pouring rain, a dreary, miserable fucking morning, tear gas smoke all over the yard, a dark, dark sky—they named it Black Wednesday. I had the correction officer's blood all over me, and that goo crap coming out of his eye streaked my back. I put him down in front of a fence and said to Joey, "Pick this guy up and take him to safety."

Gallo, scheming with that Machiavellian mind, said, "This cocksucker is going to get me out of here." He and his bodyguards carried the officer up to a locked door that separated the rioters from the authorities.

"Open up!" Joey demanded. "This guard is bleeding and needs help."

"Move away from the door!" someone yelled back.

"No! I need to bring him in!"

"You're not coming in. Leave him on the floor and back off. We'll take care of him."

"I've got him right here," said Joey, who wanted to be on the side of those holding the guns when the shooting started. "Just let me in!"

"Get lost, buddy, or we'll blow you to kingdom come!"

No one who knew this master conniver ever called him stupid. "Okay, hold your fire. Just remember," he said, "my name is Joe Gallo. I saved this officer's life."

"Pal, we don't give a shit if you're President Nixon."

"Gallo! Joe Gallo! I want it on the record. Don't forget that name."

The hack didn't forget, and later his testimony about Joey's "heroism" helped spring Gallo from the joint.

The next time I saw Joey, he stood in the yard wearing a New York Yankees baseball cap and dark glasses. *What's the deal with the getup*? I asked myself. *That little fucker's up to something*. Knowing Joey as well as I did, I quickly figured out why he had conspicuously accessorized his standard prison-issue clothes: to make sure the soon-to-attack storm troopers wouldn't mistake him for us.

I had talked to Warden Fritz, and he repeated his promise to "consider" all our demands except that plane to Algeria. Inmates controlled virtually the entire prison, though with no illusions about maintaining the stronghold against a determined assault, and I didn't know if the warden's *promise* would be enough to coax the rioters back into their cells.

Various inmates, standing in the cold and rain, gave speeches—airing their most bothersome gripes. Thomas Johnson asked me to talk. Surrounded by hundreds of prisoners, who in turn were encircled by guards and police on the wall, I swallowed hard, stepped up to the microphone, and delivered the longest speech of my life: "We did the right thing with this riot. They give us no education, no decent clothes, the food sucks, they beat the shit out of us whenever they want. But I warn you, we can't afford to fight among ourselves and kill each other. That's what the administration wants, to divide us and conquer us. Listen to me carefully: nobody rapes no inmate; nobody brutalizes no guard. We want to make this clean so the press will say, 'They're human beings who want what's coming to them.' Nothing big like go-go girls or pink Cadillacs; we just want to survive in here. We can't let the press or the administrators in Albany say, 'Don't you see what they done? We told you. They're raping each other, killing each other, murdering the hacks. They are animals. Why should we give them anything?' So we done this thing, and it was the right thing. Now let's stay together, and face what we've got to face together, and come away with a victory."

The men talked animatedly among themselves. That's the way it worked. A guy presented his ideas, then everybody in the ranks agreed or disagreed.

"All right," Thomas Johnson said, "we have brother Joe Gallo over here." I looked at Joey, who had been knocked off balance by this announcement and appeared to be trying to shrink out of sight, make himself invisible. "Brother Gallo," Thomas Johnson said, "say a few words to your friends."

Most inmates booed as he started toward the microphone. They knew him as a divisive little bastard who used people. A few cheered, guys like Hulk and Lucky—blacks he had associated with his crew.

Here's what Joey said: "Gentlemen, we're all brothers under the skin. But we didn't help you in three hundred and fifty years. Why should we start helping you now?"

I couldn't believe my ears. Despite his being a good public speaker, I at first thought the words had come out of his mouth wrong. Inmates began booing and throwing rocks at him. I grabbed his shoulders and said, "Joey, you better rephrase that fucking statement you just made."

He smiled at me, and I still didn't get it.

"What the fuck you pulling?" I asked. "Who the fuck do you think you are?"

He kept smiling, and then I caught on to his angle. Aware that the hacks and the police were carefully monitoring our speeches, Joey had seized the opportunity to buy himself some insurance by letting the people with the guns and the power know he stood on their side. Actually, he wasn't on anybody's side but his own.

With his jeering audience getting noisier, Gallo grabbed the microphone again. "No, no, no," he said, "you don't understand. All I wanted to say is that *my crew of guys* can't help you."

"Fuck you, Gallo!" someone shouted. I almost regretted my speech about not hurting other inmates.

"You're The Criminal!" another guy yelled. That's what they began calling him, from that day on, The Criminal.

Thomas Johnson calmed down the crowd, and we didn't see any more of Joey. He just vanished. At the end of eight intense hours—

filled with negotiations, heated discussions among prisoners, fear of an armed attack—we returned to our cells after reluctantly agreeing to wait and find out if the authorities would come to grips with the grievances.

Nothing changed. Prison administrators ignored or forgot about the rotten conditions as soon as the turmoil subsided and the headlines disappeared.

But the inmates couldn't forget, or ignore, and less than a year later, with some of the same men participating, Attica exploded—with forty-three lives lost—and the whole world watched.

Chapter 12

THE PIERRE HOTEL ROBBERY

THE AUTHORITIES SCATTERED MOST OF THE AUBURN RIOTERS to different prisons in an attempt to buy some calm. But this divide-and-conquer scheme backfired. Separating the "trouble-makers" just gave them a broader base for agitating.

Joey and I ended up at Dannemora, the penal system's "hazardous-waste dump site." I was there less than a week before I cut two of Gallo's bodyguards across the knuckles with a swing razor. They had taken offense at remarks I made about their boss, and I showed them I didn't give a shit how they felt.

Joey and his crew came to my cell bearing a peace offering of boiled shrimp and chocolate-chip cookies. "Hey, Greek," Gallo said, "come on, shake my hand. I don't want no problems with you."

I hesitated.

A Lucchese wiseguy who had a cell near mine took me aside and whispered, "Listen, Greek, shake the guy's hand. When these blacks see us, they got to see us united. We need to keep everything in the family."

So I shook Joey's hand. After he and his men left, I swallowed my craving for seafood and flushed his gifts down the toilet. I didn't employ food tasters.

At Dannemora Joey continued to be obsessed with establishing his own crime family, which he could only accomplish by warring with the Colombo crew. He asked me time and again to join him, but I wouldn't make a commitment. I figured there was too much bad blood between us and, besides, I didn't think he could win.

Joey and I came out of prison about the same time. He hit the streets in May 1971, with less than a year to live.

He cut quite a swath in the months he had left. On June 28, 1971, one of Joey's recruits, a half-crazed twenty-four-year-old black man named Jerome Johnson, trained by members of Joey's crew at an upstate farm and acting on orders passed down by Joey, put two bullets in the head of Joseph Colombo, godfather of the crime family named for him. The shooting took place at 11:45 A.M. in Columbus Circle just before the start of a massive Italian-American civil rights rally organized by Colombo.

After undergoing five hours of brain surgery, the godfather survived for almost seven years, but only as a vegetable. Jerome Johnson lived just long enough to put him in that state. Gallo had stationed hitters to keep an eye on Johnson, and one of them shot him dead during the panic that ensued when Colombo went down.

Bosses of the other New York crime families knew who stood behind the killing, but they had mixed emotions. They hated the publicity the Italian-American Civil Rights League generated, and believed Colombo had changed from a crime boss to a media hound. The last thing these dons wanted was attention, and Colombo's theatrics had brought them plenty of that. He had even convinced the producers of *The Godfather* movie to delete any references to the Mafia from the film, a publicity stunt scorned by the bosses and applauded by Italian-Americans—the overwhelming majority of whom were decent people fed up with their ethnic backgrounds being associated with vicious mobsters. Colombo, loving the attention his sham civil rights organization brought, had also picketed the FBI's offices in New York, a move guaranteed to bring heat from a pissed-off Bureau.

On the other hand, how could these crime family titans look away from an attack on one of their own? Had *they* sanctioned it, the shooting would have been okay. And what would this man known as "Crazy Joey" do next? He had already recruited scores of blacks into his circle and was teaching them the secrets of successful organized crime management. Perhaps these blacks could emerge as a much more dangerous foe than the government ever had been.

The Mafia Commission delayed a decision on Joey Gallo's fate, but not for long.

While all this was occurring, I made a stab at going straight. I didn't even want to think about returning to prison, told Rocky Moro how I felt, and he set me up at a pretzel stand on 14th Street between Second and Third Avenues. It turned out to be a bad move for me.

I just wasn't cut out to be a vendor. Each morning hundreds of kids poured out of the subway, swiped pretzels, candy apples, and peanuts, and hightailed it down the street. I admired their spunk and lacked the heart to chase them and retrieve the merchandise. Besides, the cops surely would have hung a menacing charge on me if I'd guarded the stand too diligently and strong-armed any of the youngsters.

This was the second time I tried to go legit. In 1965, I'd called my brother Jimmy, who lived in East Orange, New Jersey, and owned a second home on the shore. We had seen each other only a couple of times since our separation in Louisiana, but when I asked if he had any work for me, he said, "Sure, come on over."

Jimmy stood 6'3", had jet black hair, and resembled George Hamilton. I could see this very nice, quiet guy wanted to help but clearly felt uncomfortable with me. And I with him. He was a hard-working successful businessman—owned two gas stations, a lumberyard, and a roofing company—who had never done an illegal act in his life. Very straight. A solid citizen.

Jimmy gave me a place to stay and a full-time job pumping gas in Newark, with the promise of advancement if I kept out of trouble.

This I achieved—for three weeks—but the work was deadly dull and my brother and I had nothing in common.

When I shook Jimmy's hand and told him I was going back to New York City, I know he was relieved. I've never seen Jimmy again, though I hear he has continued to prosper.

When I got out of the pretzel business and resumed cracking heads for Rocky Moro, Joey Gallo was becoming a figure to be reckoned with in chic society, a must on certain guest lists. Members of the "in" crowd wanted him at their dinner parties, hung on his every remark, fawned over him as if he were royalty. It started when actor Jerry Orbach played a role in the movie *The Gang That Couldn't Shoot Straight*, based on Jimmy Breslin's novel, supposedly depicting the character of Joey. After Gallo had dinner with Jerry Orbach and his wife Marta, she said Joey "absolutely" charmed her.

I believed it, but knowing him as I did, "conned" rather than "charmed" would have been a more accurate description. Joey immediately saw a benefit for himself and took advantage of it.

At the dinner, Mrs. Orbach said Joey asked whom she preferred, Sartre or Camus. Surprised by this unexpected erudition, she said, "I almost fell into my plate of spaghetti."

Marta Orbach called Joey "brilliant," which he was; and said he'd gone "straight," which he hadn't.

Through the Orbachs Joey made other friends: actress Joan Hackett, who loved it when he called her a "broad"; comedian David Steinberg; and the writer Peter Stone. As the *New York Times* said, "it seemed that he had at last decided to trade his life as a Mafioso for the life of glitter and glamour and opening nights. From the 'Crazy Joey' of the police blotters, he became the 'Joey' of the Broadway guests lists."

Marta Orbach and Joey started collaborating on a movie script, "a comedy about prison life," and on his memoirs, a book for Viking Press. Joey was somewhat serious about both projects, figuring to make a lot of money without ever having to tell the real down-and-dirty truth.

I saw Joey on 14th Street in 1971. He secretly owned several nightclubs on Eighth Avenue and a pair of sweatshops in the garment district where forty to fifty girls made material for suits. He ran dice and card games, and engaged in his old standby, extortion. Joey was at his best squeezing businessmen, selling them "protection." It didn't matter to him if a pool-hall operator or car dealer had already paid for protection from a different crime family; the individual who resisted could expect a beating or his windows broken or his establishment burned to the ground—eventually, if he continued to withhold payment, all of the above.

What could a businessman do? Prior to the rally in Columbus Circle, Colombo associates told Brooklyn storekeepers to close up for the day and attend the demonstration. Joey's soldiers warned them to stay open and not participate. That's what is called being between a rock and a hard place.

When I saw Joey on 14th Street he needed money. Carlo Gambino, at this time the boss of bosses, would also have said *he* "needed money," but that was only because Gambino never thought his pockets were full enough. Joey required cash to get back into shylocking and bookmaking, and to obtain these funds he had become one of the largest cocaine distributors in the suburbs. Before his death, he branched into trafficking heroin.

Joey was also using people like Lucky, a black he'd befriended in prison, to open up gambling houses for blacks. In addition, through his black associates, he ran rackets in Gary, Indiana; Cleveland; and Steubenville, Ohio.

"Greek, I want you to come with me," he said that day on 14th Street.

"I like my independence," I said.

"Well, how about going to see Lucky?"

"I might do that."

Lucky, a black numbers man for Joey in Harlem, was already becoming an organized-crime power in his own right. I thought I might do some work for him and still keep my distance from Gallo, who wasn't heading anywhere except the cemetery.

I did work a job for Lucky. Together we used baseball bats on a rival numbers man, putting him in the hospital. This led to two $5,000 hits I performed for a big-time black pusher looking to eliminate competition. Under the guise of meeting in a restaurant to purchase cocaine, I walked in and shot my two targets before they could react. A "good" hit. Whenever possible, I preferred to just go and do it. Wile E. Coyote methods—the real complicated stuff—were for other guys, though when I had to, I could play peel-the-onion (treachery, plots beneath plots) as well as anybody.

I also found employment during this time as a collector for a pair of Jewish shylocks. It paid $500 a week, and I only got called in as a last resort. Once these loan sharks wanted me to hit a guy's wife while he watched. That way, the husband would be alive to pay up. I refused. I never hit women or children.

Anyway, much of my time was spent collecting money for Rocky Moro, or scaring off guys who infringed on his territory. Among these rivals was Dominick LaMonica, who surprised me by saying he'd like to meet with Moro.

When I went to Rocky about the proposition, he said, "Yeah, I'll talk to LaMonica. Have him come to the warehouse on Worth Street."

Dominick LaMonica told me, "Fine, I'll go down there. We'll talk."

So I took Dominick and his associate, Patsy Russo, to the warehouse. As soon as we walked in, three guys stepped out and put shotguns to their heads. Red Kelly, New York's most feared enforcer, rumbled through a door carrying a baseball bat, and LaMonica and Russo turned white. The shotguns might have been Moro's way of conducting a meet, but Red Kelly gripping a bat meant only one thing.

They tied Dominick's arms to a chair and handcuffed Patsy Russo to another chair in the middle of the warehouse. First they broke Dominick's legs, then his arms, and finally they worked on his head. LaMonica screamed like crazy but nobody except the terrified Russo and their abductors could hear. Moro and his brother beat Dominick to death with a baseball bat. They took about thirty minutes to kill him, doing it real slow. Then Red

Kelly went over to Patsy Russo and took his time pounding the life out of him.

When the bloody, mangled remains of Dominick and Patsy were cut loose from the chairs and fell in dead heaps on the warehouse floor, Moro gave orders to slash open their stomachs—so the bodies wouldn't float—and dump them in the Hudson River.

Rocky Moro knew word would reach the street about what had happened, and he wanted it known what poachers on his turf could expect.

When I told Joey Gallo I didn't want to be around him, he said, "Okay, I understand." But he didn't. My negative feelings toward him outweighed the positives. I was one of the few who knew that twice he had been busted by the cops for rape and sodomy.

Not long after our conversation on 14th Street, Joey sent one of his bodyguards, Bobby Bongiovi, to tell me he wanted a meet. I refused, believing Gallo might snatch me, shoot me, or hit me in the head because of what happened upstate. Besides, at this time I carried a pistol as seldom as possible to avoid being tagged with another parole violation.

Early in November 1971, a few days before my thirty-third birthday, I sat with Sammy "the Arab" Nalo in Port Said, a popular Middle-Eastern nightclub on 28th Street between Seventh and Eighth Avenues. I had no idea I was about to receive the biggest opportunity of my life, the best shot I'd ever get at making the Big Score. At Nalo's request, I had come in the afternoon when the place was quiet so we could talk. He had a piece of Port Said, which each night featured singers and belly dancers imported from Egypt; great complimentary appetizers—Greek and Turkish meatballs, stuffed grape leaves, antipasto; an excellent list of entrées headed by rack of lamb; and an all-star cast of customers ranging from the celebrated to the notorious. Weekend evenings Colombo and Genovese wiseguys packed the seventy-odd tables set in front of a bandstand, enjoying the smoky atmosphere, beautiful women, and their favorite activity, plotting crimes.

Fat Tony Salerno frequented Port Said. A nondrinker, he sipped Turkish coffee and greeted lines of criminal sycophants. Port Said's clientele also included a glittering array of celebrities. At various times I saw Telly Savalas enjoying the floor show, and Anthony Quinn, Peter Falk, and Martha Raye.

"Greek," Nalo said, "I got something coming up."

"What is it?"

Sammy fidgeted with his glass of ouzo, an anise-flavored Greek liqueur. The Arab (he hated the name) was a sinister-looking little guy who never smiled. He stood only 5'5", had dark, deep-set eyes, hairy arms and chest, and a permanent five o'clock shadow; he was totally bald. Born in Detroit to Iraqi emigrants, Nalo matured into perhaps the most accomplished stickup man of his time.

"I can't tell you what it is right now," he said. "But I need to know if you want in."

"Of course. I'm ready to go."

I knew anything Sammy Nalo cooked up would be big. He and his partner Bobby Comfort from Rochester, New York, had stolen $1 million in jewelry and cash from the Sherry Netherland Hotel and made major scores at the Regency, Drake, Carlyle, and St. Regis. Nalo was the true genius behind these stickups, though gutsy Bobby Comfort was no slouch in the brains department. Comfort, whose suburban Rochester neighbors thought worked as a traveling salesman, was one of the world's great jewel thieves. Like Nalo, Comfort was a friend of mine. He, I, and Joe Sullivan had been teammates on the same prison football team.

Nalo and Comfort. They would have been brilliant together as generals, plotting surgically delicate military operations. Their philosophy: plan everything meticulously, then get in, do the job, and get out.

I figured the job would be a big one, but had no idea it might end up filling my retirement fund. Sammy's keeping a tight lid on the location made sense. Surely others were involved, and he didn't want any of us giving the game away by talking.

It wasn't until December 30, in the back room at Port Said, belly dancers performing out front, that Nalo divulged the target

—the Pierre Hotel—and introduced me to the rest of the crew. Later Bobby Comfort collaborated with author Ira Berkow on a book I enjoyed—*The Man Who Robbed the Pierre*—which told the story of what *The Guinness Book of World Records* at one time listed as the largest hotel stickup in history. Comfort said that only five people took the Pierre hostage, naming himself, Sammy Nalo, and three gangsters he called City, Country, and Doc. He used aliases, he said, "to protect the guilty."

In matter of fact, five people could not have managed the complicated, dangerous Pierre stickup. Besides Comfort, Nalo, and myself, the following five others participated in the headliner robbery:

1. Bobby G, a French-Canadian mobster who dealt drugs for the Lucchese family. He stood 5'7" with a round face, dark eyes, and salt-and-pepper hair. Bobby's job at the Pierre would consist of prying open lock boxes maintained for guests in an open vault.
2. Ali-Ben, known as The Turk. A friend of Nalo's, Ali-Ben was a strong, wiry, black-haired hit man who worked primarily for the feared Albanian mob. His task was to ensure that no guests surprised us by coming down on the elevator.
3. Al Green. A tall black man from Harlem, Green was married to Ali-Ben's sister. During the heist, he would stand outside the Pierre's only open entrance, on 61st Street—the 62nd Street entrance was closed between 2:00 A.M. and 6:00 A.M.—as a lookout.
4. Petey, the jewel thief with whom I had pulled three hotel stickups in the mid-1960s, handled general surveillance of the lobby—detaining, handcuffing, and escorting hostages to a lobby alcove.
5. Al Visconti, a Lucchese associate who kept guard on our prisoners. Visconti, once recognized as the New York State Prison system's heavyweight boxing champion, resembled a larger version of Rocky Marciano, broken nose and all.

It was a truly multinational crew assembled in the back room at

Port Said: a French-Canadian, a Turk, a black, an Arab, a Greek-Sicilian, a part Irishman (Bobby Comfort), and two Italians.

"Are there any of you who can't get along with black guys?" Nalo asked, when we were all seated.

"I don't generally work with them," Petey said. "But I can take 'em or leave 'em."

Others answered in a similar vein. It was clear Nalo was referring to Al Green, whom he considered indispensable precisely because of his skin color. Nalo figured most chauffeurs were black—they aren't—and that's how Green would be dressed. Also, the chauffeur standing outside the Pierre had to be a tough guy, willing to draw down on anybody who looked suspicious. In this case, suspicious equalled police.

Satisfied with the responses, Nalo said, "This is going to be a big, big job."

Like a good actor, he let his words hang in the air. Then he popped up from the table where we sat, unfurled a huge blown-up map of the inside of a hotel, and thumbtacked it to the wall. On the map were X's, and each X had the name of one of us next to it.

"This is the Pierre Hotel," Nalo said, "and you're going to know it like the back of your hand before you ever go inside."

Light glistening off his bald head, dark glasses making his eyes unreadable, Nalo strutted like a little general in front of his map. He had a pointer, which he first tapped against the X's, reciting names and duties, repeating, always repeating, as if he spoke to kindergarten children. We sat enraptured, listening to a master. Music and laughter from the front drifted into the room, but the level of concentration was so high we barely noticed.

Nalo was Pavarotti talking opera, Nureyev on dance, and we strained not to miss a word. After he presented an overall view of the heist—this guy here, that guy there, repeating as he went—he stood over each conspirator, had him parrot what he'd been told, then fired questions in machine-gun fashion. What if the cops come? What if they're already there, waiting to ambush us? That was Nalo's biggest fear. He'd chosen us carefully, but the greatest danger was someone running his mouth, bragging in advance to a friend or girlfriend. Nalo didn't trust anybody, a quality everyone in the room appreciated.

Occasionally Bobby Comfort rose to speak. The Pierre robbery had been his idea, though the nitty-gritty details upon which success depended were provided by Nalo. Bobby told us how we were expected to dress and what weapons to carry. The last thing he wanted was any shooting, but he acknowledged that events might spin out of control and that it might come down to that.

We met again on New Year's Eve, a second five-hour session at Port Said. Nalo, using the pointer, intricately and repeatedly "walked us through" the robbery. He finished with a pep talk that would have made Knute Rockne proud, telling us we were the best, that he personally had selected us from a long list of people he trusted.

"How much you figure the take will be?" Ali-Ben wanted to know.

Nalo smiled. We wouldn't have been worth shit if we hadn't asked the question. "Millions," the bald man said.

"How many millions?"

"I don't fucking know. Five. Six."

We wanted to know about the split. Nalo said he couldn't tell yet, but that it would be fair. He said he and Comfort would take the largest portions—they had done the most work—and a slice had to be set aside for a wiseguy-owned limousine company in Brooklyn that would provide transportation that would never be traced back to us.

Nalo had a good reputation in the underworld, and we accepted what he proposed. We knew of no instance of his stiffing anyone, which in this case would have been a very dangerous thing for him to do, given the crew he'd hired. The same held true for Bobby Comfort, a guy driven not by greed but by the same desire I nurtured—one substantial retirement score. He had a wife and daughter living with him in Rochester, and no yen to find legitimate work.

••••

We came in two cars. Occupants of the first vehicle, including myself, arrived at 3:50 A.M. on January 2, 1972, and checked to make sure all was calm. Ten minutes later Al Green, dressed in a chauffeur's uniform, wheeled a black Cadillac limousine up to the 61st Street entrance. Bobby G, with Petey and Al Visconti, got out and told the security guard, "Reservations—Dr. Foster's party." After a call to the registration desk confirmed that a Dr. Foster (Bobby Comfort) had indeed paid for a room, the guard unlocked the door. A moment later he was looking down the barrel of Al Visconti's gun as seven of us fanned through the hotel, taking it prisoner. Al Green remained on watch outside.

The date and time of the robbery were perfect. Most guests were soundly sleeping off hangovers acquired at New Year's Eve extravaganzas, which they had attended decked out in their finest jewels—fabulous treasures now being kept in safe-deposit boxes downstairs until more secure bank vaults reopened at 9:00 this morning. Best of all, because of the holiday, the hotel operated with a skeleton crew, including guards, whom we quickly rounded up.

The Pierre Hotel was the crème de la crème of New York hostelries. Princess Diane von Furstenberg often stayed there, as did Maria Callas, Aristotle Onassis, Merle Oberon, Prince Philip, Mrs. DeWitt Wallace (half-owner of *Reader's Digest*), Robert J. Kleberg, Jr. (owner of the King Ranch), Lady Sarah Churchill, Kirk Douglas, and even President Richard Nixon. Jewels and money were stored in lock boxes in a big open vault behind the cashier's desk, and after we collected security guards, elevator operators, cleaning men, a bellboy, and the desk clerk, Comfort and Bobby G, with Sammy Nalo bagging, began smashing open the boxes, a difficult task.

Bobby Comfort pulled double duty at the Pierre. He pried and hammered open money boxes, and occasionally made a tour of the first floor to see that everything was all right. Sammy Nalo threw valuables into suitcases we had brought. Holding a .32 automatic and packing a .38 snubnose under my tux jacket, I guarded the 61st Street entrance and handcuffed and led anyone who came in to Al Visconti, who was in charge of hostages. Al then brought the hostages to a large alcove near the registration desk, where he had them lie facedown on the floor.

The number of hostages steadily grew—ultimately totaling nineteen—but we had brought along plenty of handcuffs, three dozen pairs.

One guest arrived at the 61st Street entrance about 4:45 A.M. I opened the door, my back to him, then turned slowly around, shoving the .38 in his face. "Step right in, sir," I said.

"Wh-what's going on?" he stuttered.

"Sir," I said, "you have my solemn promise you won't be hurt if you just do what you're told." I marched him to the alcove and Al Visconti stationed him with the others facedown on the floor.

Most of us wore disguises and tuxedos. Sammy Nalo sported a huge wig, a fake nose, and eyeglasses. Of course we all used gloves and carried guns, though it would have taken an extreme circumstance for anyone to open fire. Not only would shooting in this luxury palace assure that the wrath of God (actually, the state) would come down on our heads, but it would mean an end to the robbery. Comfort and Nalo, as I said, carefully chose the crew to exclude hotheads and guys prone to panic.

Boxes weren't broken into randomly. Nalo forced the hotel auditor to provide the index cards that matched boxes to depositors. A guest named Elmer Shmergel, for example, might be richer than a Saudi prince, but if his name didn't ring a bell his valuables were left untouched. Harold Uris (real estate), Tom Yawkey (owner of the Boston Red Sox), and Calliope Kulukundis (the Greek billionaire) had recognizable names and paid for their fame.

Each time Bobby Comfort made his occasional rounds, we couldn't miss the look of near ecstasy on his face, nor did he try to hide it. He moved in a thief's heaven, and his face glowed like the jewels strewn across the vault floor.

"Big?" I said, smiling.

"The biggest," he said with a huge grin.

If the rich are genteel, then maybe it rubbed off on us. We didn't handcuff a guy who looked sick, as if he might pass out from fright. We called people "sir" and "madame," and never raised our voices.

We were a tough fucking crew, but no less solicitous than room-service waiters—if our arresting of guests and staff can be ignored.

The clock moved slowly, though it's supposed to race through a good time. I guess the enjoyable part came later, remembering this moment when everything was just right. In the hotel, I didn't let myself think of the money or jewels, but instead kept totally focused. I operated the same way on hits: there'd be time to celebrate afterward.

During our 2½-hour occupation of the Pierre, Bobby G, Nalo, and Comfort managed to break into about one-quarter of the 208 lock boxes in the vault. It began to seem like we had been inside forever, that surely the cops, or someone, would arrive at any moment.

Staying longer than safety dictated, though we never would have been able to live with ourselves if we had left early, Bobby Comfort at 6:15 A.M. addressed the hostages in a clear steady voice: "We're leaving here in fifteen minutes. I want all of you to remember that nobody was hurt. We never intended to hurt you. If you think about becoming a star witness, about identifying anyone you happened to see, you'd better reconsider. Don't help the police in any way. If you do, your wives, your kids, your mothers—anything in the world you value—will never be safe again. I'll come back or send somebody back. If you put us in prison, you'll get what's coming to you. If you don't, you've got nothing to worry about. I hope you understand."

Departing with a touch of class, Comfort gave a $20 bill to each hotel employee we had detained, and we left at 6:30, just ahead of the hotel's incoming 7:00 A.M. shift.

We knew at the time we were scoring big—heaps of jewelry, piles of money, stuffed into three large suitcases—but not until the tally at Sammy Nalo's apartment in the Bronx and another he rented in Manhattan did we realize how big. Newspaper accounts estimated the total at $10 million, but we figured it was closer to $24 million: $11 million in cash, $13 million in jewelry—a mind-boggling score.

Our numbers were more accurate than those bandied about by the police and media. I believe many of the guests were afraid to reveal the true amount of their losses. How could they explain all that cash? Better just to swallow the loss than pique the interest of IRS.

Previously, on October 11, 1970, Bobby Comfort and Sammy Nalo had stuck up Sophia Loren in her Manhattan Hampshire House apartment for what she reported as a $600,000 loss. However, Sammy said her jewelry had been worth more than $2 million on the retail market; if Ms. Loren deliberately understated its value, several obvious reasons jump to mind.

Sammy Nalo gave each of us $50,000 in Port Said the evening of January 2, promising me $750,000 more in a year, saying we had to sit on the rest of the loot until the heat cooled. He had taken a third of what we had stolen, and other thirds were in the hands of Bobby Comfort and Ali-Ben.

The press coverage was enormous, front-page headlines worldwide, and I enjoyed noting that totally absent was the outrage newspapers usually convey when a robbery occurs. *New York Post* columnist Pete Hamill wrote:

> The holdup at the Hotel Pierre was beautiful. Nobody got hurt. The prewar amenities were scrupulously observed. The robbers got away with something like $4 million, or maybe more, and when it was over everybody in New York felt better, except the people who got robbed.
>
> In a time when junkies hit old ladies in elevators for $14-and-change or come in the back window looking for the silverware you got one piece at a time at the RKO Prospect in 1951, something this well-organized, so minimally violent, and so grand in scale could only be applauded.

Hamill hit the nail on the head when he called the operation "well-organized." He would have understood why if he'd known the months of planning Nalo and Comfort had put into it, if he'd known the quality of this carefully selected crew, and especially if he'd been a fly on the wall when that bold, strutting little general ran it all down in Port Said's back room.

The holdup itself might have been "beautiful," but in less than a week everything turned to shit, including my dreams of a Florida retirement. Nalo went to the Lucchese crime family, specifically "Tony Ducks" Corallo, who demanded an outrageous 33 percent to move the jewelry. Nalo got so hot about Corallo's requiring such a large cut of the loot that he transported much of it to a friend's house in Michigan.

Bobby Comfort had returned from Rochester to help Nalo fence the jewels—Nalo owed a bundle to bookmakers who threatened to break his legs—and a snitch got Comfort busted in the Royal Manhattan Hotel. He described the scene in *The Man Who Robbed the Pierre*:

> "Where is everything?" one guy asks me. I tell him, "I don't know what you're talkin' about."
>
> "In that case," he says, "you're no use to us." He calls to another guy, "Hey, open the fuckin' window for this guy."
>
> The cop opens the window wide and the cold air blasts in the room, and then they drag me to the window. What the hell is this? Then they lift me up—holy shit!—and they throw me out! But they were gripping me by the ankles. I'm flapping out the window. I'm terrified. I pissed so fast it shot out like a bullet. It must have flown straight past my face because I never remembered getting wet.
>
> I'm looking straight down, I see people and cars. Everything is swirling. I'm in a state of shock, I'm choking, I can't breathe, I'm scared stiff. One of the cops at the window ledge hollered at me, "Start talkin'." Talk? I felt like my vocal cords were falling out of my mouth. I'm struggling to get some words out. I squeaked, "Talk about what?" He says, "You know what, just start talkin' about your robberies and when you lie, we're droppin' you."

They didn't drop him, and of course Comfort refused to talk. Even in his book, this stand-up heist artist never revealed who accompanied him and Sammy Nalo.

Nalo was also arrested (both he and Comfort ultimately received four-year sentences), and shortly afterward an individual in Michigan got scared and turned over $750,000 in jewels that Sammy had given him to hold. The cops never learned that millions more in cash and jewels got expropriated by another of Nalo's friends, who absconded to Mexico with the booty.

Ali-Ben and his brother-in-law Al Green read about the stolen-property recovery in Michigan, figured Nalo had tried to stiff them, and fled to Europe with the third they held. They lived it up on the Continent for years.

Bobby Comfort proved no more reliable than Ali-Ben, Al Green, or Sammy Nalo. All had been part of a perfect heist, but couldn't handle the aftermath. Comfort, meaning well, fenced jewels to members of the Rochester Mafia, who said, "Why the fuck should we give this guy anything?" They kept the loot and, when Bobby tried to get some of it back, almost killed him.

I wanted the $750,000 I'd been promised, and was enraged that $50,000 seemed to be all I would receive from history's most lucrative hotel robbery. Ultimately, over a period of time, I received a total of $175,000, the same as Bobby G and Al Visconti. Petey did a little better: $250,000. Ali-Ben and Al Green pissed away most of the cash in Europe. Bobby Comfort ended up with $1.5 million, less than he deserved, and Nalo got the jewels his friends hadn't stolen.

I chiefly blamed Sammy Nalo for the rip-off and vowed to kill him (someone beat me to it in 1988). I also was hot with Ali-Ben and Al Green, though I knew they hadn't cheated anyone until Nalo cheated them. Comfort, I figured, had merely been duped by rougher sorts.

I did indeed put bullets in the heads of two of the Pierre Hotel's robbers—Ali-Ben and Al Green—but that didn't occur until 1981. In 1972 I pondered bitterly how things *could* have worked out, and I hoped this wouldn't be my last grab for the brass ring.

Chapter 13

THE JOEY GALLO MURDER

ONE OF GANGDOM'S MOST FAMOUS MURDERS REMAINS THAT OF Joey Gallo, a crime for which no one was ever tried, that for twenty years has gone unsolved.

Until now.

My friend Sonny Pinto, who squeezed the fatal bullets into Joey's body, told me the whole story, and so did others—chief among these, "Pete the Greek" Diapoulos—who were there when the killing happened.

Joey Gallo got iced on April 7, 1972, while celebrating his forty-third birthday at Umberto's Clam House on Mulberry Street in Little Italy, a hangout for Colombo and Genovese crime family members. Umberto's was operated by Matthew "Matty the Horse" Ianiello. Ianiello served as Fat Tony's main man for peep shows, pornographic photos, dirty movies, prostitution, and highly lucrative bust-out joints—bars that featured girls persuading johns to buy them $3.50 drinks. The split on a glass of colored water was 50¢ for the girl, $3 for the house. Matty the Horse fronted seventy to eighty of these bust-out joints for Fat Tony in Queens, Brooklyn, Manhattan, and New Jersey. Funzi Tieri (the nominal boss), Fat Tony (Tieri's peer), and Chin Gigante divvied up the profits.

Joey and his group had celebrated at the Copacabana before heading to Umberto's. Accompanying him were his main bodyguard, a friend of mine named Pete the Greek Diapoulos; Diapoulos's girlfriend, Edith Russo; Joey's wife of three weeks, Sina—they had been married in an elaborate ceremony in Jerry Orbach's brownstone; Sina's ten-year-old daughter, Lisa; and Joey's sister, Carmella Fiorello.

Inside Umberto's, Joey and Pete the Greek sat with their backs to the door—not a usual gangster position. Perhaps they felt safe with the women and child along.

Joey knew he flirted with death at Umberto's, but he went there to demonstrate that he still got respect. It was also a matter of machismo, to make it known that no one could tell him where to go. Indeed, when he entered the restaurant the staff gave him red-carpet treatment because they all knew Crazy Joe Gallo lived up to his name. I saw him fight guys eight or nine inches taller than himself—big blacks and Puerto Ricans who kicked the shit out of him or piped him—but he never backed down. Joey was always into something, playing mind games and pitting one person against another. A guy born to cause havoc who got caught up in the middle.

The word was out that Carlo Gambino, Fat Tony, and Junior Persico had issued contracts on Gallo's life. In reality, these Mafia powerhouses feared the small army of blacks Gallo had gathered around him, though the reason they fabricated for the contracts was "revenge for Joe Colombo's shooting." They didn't care about Joe Colombo—in fact, they were happy he was out of the picture—but they would not admit their feared visions of organized blacks. "Kill Gallo where you find him" was the order.

When Gallo entered Umberto's, a piece-of-shit rat named Fat Joey Luparelli went to deliver the news to a group of wiseguys at a nearby social club. This social club was a place where wiseguys who didn't wake up till midnight spent their time plotting crimes, drinking, playing cards, and bullshitting.

Joe Yacovelli, a Colombo captain, addressed the other people in the club. "*That guy*," Joe Yak said, his voice thick with menace. "He's at Umberto's. Celebrating his birthday. With a bunch of people."

The club fell silent.

"Junior and Fat Tony want him dead. *Now*." Joe Yak could have played the Voice of Doom. "You hear me? They want him whacked. And we can't fuck up. We've got to kill this cocksucker."

Fat Joey Luparelli, Sonny Pinto, and Philly Gambino—the latter two Colombo men—listened to Yacovelli's instructions: "Joey, you block off that one-way street going toward Umberto's. Philly, Sonny and I will ride with you. Park right off the front entrance of the joint, away from the corner where they can't see you. That way, when it's finished, we can scoot right out of there. Philly, you're the lookout. Don't let nobody near us. You know the drill. Me and Sonny are goin' in."

Pinto told me he liked that part. "Fuck the lookout shit," he said.

It took fifteen minutes to prepare and get there. They carried .38 specials and a 9-millimeter semiautomatic. This group, except for Joe Luparelli, belonged to the Hammer & Nails crew, a group as hard as the name implied.

Sonny Pinto worked like Mad Dog Joe Sullivan, the most efficient killer I ever met. Sonny would race right in hitting everything in sight, and rush right out. No hesitation at all. When he came out of that car, he was going in *now*, to kill or be killed.

I knew Sonny from when I'd been an orderly at the Sing Sing death house where he'd awaited execution, and I understand how he felt that night: adrenaline pumping furiously, almost visibly, through his system, his mind focused totally on the kill.

Sonny was a good-looking guy, wavy, wiry hair—similar to Johnny Stomp, Lana Turner's old boyfriend, or Jeff Chandler. The girls liked him. At this time he was about forty years old, and he wore open-neck silk shirts and gold necklaces, pointed-toe featherweight shoes, and silk socks. He boasted that everything, even his underwear, was monogrammed. He had a pale face and dark eyes that could turn scary—a macho guy, like Gallo, living in a macho world.

Joe Yacovelli was the opposite of handsome. A casual observer would have judged him a nothing, a zero, and couldn't have been more wrong. He had a hook nose and bubble eyes, and wiseguys thought he more resembled a chestnut vendor than a crime boss. But that's precisely what he was, a captain in the Colombo family, and as such he was in charge of the Gallo hit. "Don't kill the women," he told Sonny Pinto. "Whack anybody who gets in the way, but don't touch the girls. That's disrespectful."

Pinto knew these orders were partly bullshit, that hitting Joey in front of his wife, sister, and stepdaughter was very disrespectful. The real story was that Joe Yak wanted to cover his own ass. He realized there would be heat from whacking Joey in a restaurant backed by Fat Tony Salerno, but he knew it would be a lot worse if a woman or kid died. Fat Tony wanted Gallo dead so much that he would let it happen in Umberto's, but he would be very angry if Yacovelli didn't exercise some damage control. "I fuckin' told you to kill Gallo," Joe Yak could imagine Fat Tony screaming, "not his fucking wife, his sister, and that little girl. Jesus Christ! Look at the heat you dumb cocksuckers brought down on us!"

Still, as Pinto later told me, "We was going to kill that motherfucker wherever we saw him, even if he was eating with the chief of police. That cocksucker would have gone, and so would the chief. Fuckin' Fat Tony can do his own hits if he don't like it!"

Of course, *nobody* called Tony "Fat Tony" to his face, but it was okay if he didn't hear you.

Except for Luparelli, the guys who went after Joey comprised a bad, bad crew, one that Junior Persico used to accompany on his hits. Junior, the de facto boss of the Colombo crime family, even though he was serving time when Joey got iced, would have loved having been along to kill Gallo personally.

Sonny Pinto charged into Umberto's. Pete the Greek went for his pistol but, before he could get it out, Sonny headed straight at Joey, who started to stand up. Pete and Gallo, caught by surprise, were too late. Pinto hissed, "Die, motherfucker, die!" and then let Joey have it.

Sonny kicked Pete the Greek's chair over, toppling the table. As Pete's chair pitched backward, his ass and feet shot up in the air. Sonny shot Pete once, in the hip.

While Pinto did the shooting, Yacovelli stood guard, holding cooks, waiters, and customers at bay. Mainly this was a precaution, because onlookers instinctively dive for cover when the fireworks start. Coming into Umberto's right on Sonny Pinto's heels, Yak shouted, "Everybody get down, motherfuckers! We'll kill you!" Then, even as the bullets were being fired, he couldn't resist saying, "Last for you, Joey."

Sonny and Joe Yak ran out to the waiting car, glancing back at an apparition they couldn't believe: Joey Gallo, shot three times, staggered after them, slipping and sliding on his own blood, blood everywhere, weaving along a floor littered with salad, spaghetti, and clam sauce. "You cocksuckers!" he managed to say. "I'll kill you!"

But they had killed *him*. He stumbled into the middle of the street, collapsed and died. It was 5:30 A.M.

The burly Pete the Greek, shot in the hip, got off the restaurant floor, grabbed Matty the Horse, slammed him against the wall, and held a pistol to his head. Pete, a loyal stand-up guy who'd treated Joey like a brother, knew the score. "You motherfucker," he growled at Ianiello. "You had everything to do with this!"

The terrified Matty said "No Pete! I swear! Nothing!"

Matty the Horse's word didn't count for crap with Pete Diapoulos, but then Fat Tony's henchman said something that made sense: "There's people here, Greek. If you whack me you'll be put away."

Pete, about to squeeze the trigger, heard police sirens approaching—the cops, who didn't hear the gunfire, were alerted by Joey's sister Carmella screaming as she crouched over his body—and thought, *The guy is right. If I shoot this punk, I'll go to jail.* Diapoulos put the gun down, too numb to realize he had been shot, walked outside to Joey's body, and started crying.

Diapoulos knew very well that Sonny Pinto and Joe Yacovelli

had killed Joey Gallo, but he wouldn't testify against them. He figured, probably correctly, that Joey wouldn't have wanted anyone ratting.

At Gallo's burial, Carmella cried and wailed: "Joey! The streets will run red with blood!"

Sure enough, they did. And *that's* what Joey would have wanted. What he wouldn't have liked was that *his* soldiers shed most of the blood. Of his entire crew, the only one who really continued to carve a niche in Mafia circles was his brother Albert, known as Kid Blast, who joined the Genovese crime family.

Unbelievably, the only person who went to jail because of Joey's murder was Pete Diapoulos. He was tried and convicted for illegal possession of a firearm, the pistol he pulled on Matty the Horse. The chief witness against him was the half-insane rat, Joe Luparelli, who said he had fingered Joey Gallo to Yacovelli, Pinto, and Gambino. Despite Luparelli claiming he could identify the hitters who went inside Umberto's, they were never charged. Luparelli owed money to the wiseguys, was scared shitless of them, and would never have had the guts to testify.

I spent some time with Pete Diapoulos on Rikers Island while he served that one-year sentence for the firearms violation. I liked this tough guy who kept his word. He had jet black hair, an olive complexion, and looked more like an Arab than a Greek. He was a fistfighter, very good with his hands.

Pete related a partial story of the Gallo hit to the police, but refused to testify. He would only go so far being a rat. No courtrooms for him. Pete didn't fear wiseguys, he didn't fear anybody, but he had rules to live by—not turning in gangsters being one of them. Besides, why bother? He had a good plan to start a new life.

Pete the Greek Diapoulos ended up better off than most who associate with the Mafia. He wrote a book about Joey Gallo with author Steve Linakis (a cousin of Maria Callas) titled *The Sixth Family,* and with money he had squirreled away moved to Greece.

Bobby Bongiovi, another of Joey's bodyguards, had been with his boss at the Copacabana the night Joey was killed, but not at Umberto's. Bobby had left the group to take a girl home, felt terrible about Joey's murder, and blamed himself. He thought he could have prevented it had he been present, a dubious speculation given the fury of Sonny Pinto when he roared into that restaurant. Anyway, after almost a year of grieving and drinking, Bongiovi on March 11, 1973, went to one of Matty the Horse's places, the Broadway Pub.

"I want to see him," Bobby told one of the barmaids. He carried a paper sack in his hand.

"You mean Sam?" the barmaid said. "He's in the back."

Bongiovi ordered a drink, took a couple of swallows, and called Wuyak over to him. "You Sammy Wuyak?" he asked.

"Who are you?"

"I'm a friend of Matty the Horse."

"He just left here."

"Where did he go?"

"He doesn't tell me those things."

"I've got a package for him."

"Oh. Okay." Wuyak, the night manager, wanting privacy, suggested they go to the washroom.

In the bag Bongiovi had a pistol.

Sam Wuyak was no more than a worker trying to make a living—he'd never been in trouble in his life.

"Where can I find the Horse?" Bongiovi demanded when they reached the rest room.

Wuyak looked at a man transformed. Angry, filled with grief, guilt, and rage, Bongiovi pointed the pistol at the night manager's head.

"I don't know where he is. Please. Believe me. Matty doesn't tell me anything."

"If I can't get your boss," Bongiovi said, "then, my friend, *you* got to go." Bobby shot Wuyak twice in the head and left the bar.

The cops were called, and the barmaid, just like a trained detective, held the drink glass so she wouldn't smudge the fingerprints.

Bobby Bongiovi's murder case was adjudicated in record time. Less than two months after the killing he was convicted of homicide; he received a life sentence. The evidence had been conclusive: his fingerprints on the glass and testimony of two barmaids. It marked the first time in more than *twelve years* in New York City that a mob figure had been tried for murder.

Bobby Bongiovi is still in prison. He could have been released a couple of times, but he's more afraid of being on the street, where he'd be killed, than he is of doing time.

I think Bobby realizes that Joey wasn't worth it, and certainly Bongiovi wasn't the first person the little bastard fooled. Bob Dylan composed a song—"Joey"—about Joe Gallo. Joan Hackett called him "the brightest person I've ever known."

I'll say this: Joey Gallo was a oner. He kept a lion named Cleo in his apartment to scare loan-shark victims into paying. A restaurateur he wanted to extort money from asked if he could have time to think it over. "Sure," Joey said. "You can have three months in the hospital on me." Unpredictable, exciting, deadly, Joey Gallo embodied just one part of an almost otherworldly allure I couldn't resist.

A few months before the Pierre Hotel stickup, a numbers runner for Spanish Raymond Marquez introduced me to his twenty-three-year-old niece, Beth Rivera.* She was 5'4", about 115 pounds, and had dark hair and striking emerald green eyes. A real beauty, and intelligent, too. She spoke three languages besides English (Greek, Italian, and Spanish) had just graduated from City College, and intended to be a teacher.

Since going AWOL way back in the 1950s, I'd had my share of sweethearts, harlots, and brief affairs—mostly one-night stands. Nothing serious. I enjoyed my freedom too much to become entangled in a steady relationship; I also reasoned that because of my profession it could only turn into a disaster for the woman.

Prison gates had transformed into revolving doors for me—a price I obviously was willing to pay for the highs I experienced

*This name has been changed

when free—but this mode of living constituted a terrible basis on which to build a lasting friendship or marriage. I saw many inmates drive themselves crazy worrying about their wives and families, and for them each day behind bars became an agonizing torment. I didn't need that; neither did any woman. Resigned to bachelorhood, I was surprised the way things progressed with Beth.

I was captivated with her beauty, personality, and especially her brains—I loved being around smart people of both sexes—and, perhaps sad to say, her weakness was a fascination with gangsters. She worshiped her uncle and enjoyed mingling with his associates. There are plenty of women like this who read about crimes or hang out with lawbreakers to experience danger vicariously. Criminals often have an almost visible aura of evil about them, but just as the devil can attract, so can they. I avoided mob groupies, but I had never met one with all the attributes rolled into this charming package named Beth.

"How about going to Port Said with me tomorrow night?" I said after her uncle introduced us and courteously disappeared.

"Let's see *The Fantasticks* instead," she suggested.

"What's that?"

"A sweet, nostalgic musical."

And that's how it started, at a little playhouse in Greenwich Village.

On future dates we toured the Metropolitan Museum, strolled the stone paths of the Cloisters, compared our interpretations of paintings at art shows in Central Park and Fifth Avenue. We took fishing trips to Long Island and the Hamptons, read books to each other, and held hands on quiet country walks.

In March 1972, Beth moved into my four-room 15th Street apartment that featured four color TVs—"Three of these have to go," she quickly decided—a Tiffany lamp, expensive Oriental rugs, an antique white walnut sleigh bed, a hand-carved dining-room suite, and a five-piece grouping of valuable oil paintings. My tastefully arranged, impressive residence had all the trappings of many sessions and much money spent on the head decorating consultant at Sloan's department store. I didn't bother to inform my new live-in companion that I had furnished it from top to bottom with swag—suitable pieces I had "selected" from a host of hijackings and burglaries, or paid next to nothing for to a fence.

After Beth moved in, the apartment, which had formerly served as a convenient place to hang my hat between jobs, became a love nest I hated to leave: rainy afternoons with her voluptuous body between the sheets next to mine; candlelight dinners (my mouth watered for hours while she prepared paella, "the house specialty"); and long intellectually challenging conversations about our mutual and exclusive interests. The women I had previously dated hadn't been a great deal brighter than most of my illiterate hoodlum friends.

Beth and I couldn't spend enough time with each other, at home or when we went out. Attending cultural events was a joy, and Beth's gangster fixation made her always game to accompany me in wiseguy bars and nightclubs. She even wanted to go with me inside the social clubs, but those were strictly male enclaves: absolutely no women allowed.

My romance with Beth was the first true love I had experienced, but not my closest brush with matrimony. During one of my prison hitches, wiseguys arranged a marriage for me. The idea was to have the "wife"—with unlimited, unquestioned visiting privileges—deliver messages from the outside and take mine back on a regular basis. At the very last minute, a preacher standing by, the plan was abandoned.

By the summer of '72, Beth was hearing wedding bells, and I wasn't exactly opposed to the idea. "When are you going to marry me, Tony?" she asked, using one of my street names, one night after dinner in the apartment.

"Soon as I make enough money," I said, my brain suddenly turning murderous with the memory of the blown fortune from the Pierre Hotel.

"Forget about that big score. Together we have enough to open a boutique that will provide a comfortable living. Tony, keep going like you are, and you'll end up dead on the street, shot down like a dog. I don't want that to happen. I love you."

"I love you too, baby. Don't worry about me. I'm always careful."

"I know about the people you associate with. They'll kill you whenever it suits their purposes."

"Just wait a little while, Beth. I'll hit a big one. Buy us a nice home. We'll live like human beings. Have a houseful of kids."

The last entry in this pipe dream appealed to her. Coming from a large family and having baby-sat cousins and neighborhood tykes as a teenager, my lover was well prepared for motherhood and eager to bear my children.

As Beth and I loved into the autumn, she gave up the boutique notion and began teaching at a nearby high school. I had watched her communicate easily with kids in the park and knew her natural winning way with them would make for a rewarding career, which it did. In compliance with her work schedule, and to give us maximum time together, I tapered off my criminal activities, though I still kept a cash flow by doing odd jobs. Mostly I delivered drugs to Harlem for Philly Rags and two New Jersey drug dealers, Alphonse "Funzi" Sisca and Arnold Squitieri.

Before Beth, I had kept my nose to the grindstone, like an up-and-coming politician, making contacts at all hours and expanding my operation mainly through referrals. I hung out in bars with wiseguys, visited their social clubs, called around to various underbosses to see if they had work for me. I was always available.

After Beth, I reduced the constant hustle, let people come to me, and waited for jobs to fall into my lap.

One did. Philly Rags called me at home, arranged a meet, and said he wanted me to hurt a black guy who refused to pay for a half-kilo of heroin. On November 21, 1972, carrying a pistol and a baseball bat, I cornered my quarry on 22nd Street and started pounding him with the bat. A cop appeared out of nowhere, got the draw on me, and carted me off to jail.

Beth visited the next day. "I'll wait for you, Tony. When you get out we'll be married and start a new life together."

I didn't say anything to disillusion her, but I had seen enough guys in the stir lose women who'd also pledged undying faithfulness to know that Beth's romantic scenario was unlikely.

They charged me with first-degree assault and possession of a dangerous weapon, but the black guy was a reluctant witness. Three days after the event I copped a plea of guilty to menacing and the judge gave me seven months.

Chapter 14

EXTORTION IN NEW JERSEY

SING SING HAD UNDERGONE A SEA CHANGE WHEN I ARRIVED early in 1973 after a brief stopover on Rikers Island. Previously the authorities had ruled the institution with an iron hand, but now convicts who knew the ropes and had money (I qualified eminently on both counts) could get away with or buy almost anything. Alcohol and drugs were as plentiful as cigarettes; in fact, the market was wide open.

In the past, correction officers had enforced regulations too strictly and too violently, but after the Auburn and Attica riots, they switched course 180 degrees. Why risk prisoners disrupting routine with complaints filed by an ever-growing battery of liberal New York City lawyers? Besides, there was something (bribes) in it for them.

No signs advertised SEX FOR SALE, but it was. An empty room, often in the hospital, was the normal meeting place. White New York City hippie girls, riding serious guilt trips, brought their message of love to inmates, usually blacks, and ended up in private rooms with these prisoners, who paid guards $50 to leave them alone for a few hours. Often these highly idealistic girls—bent on helping to free a "victim of the system"—wound up victimized themselves, putty in the convict's hands.

"You care about me, don't you?" the inmate would ask the flower child.

"Of course I do. That's why I'm here."

"I have other needs besides legal. Physical needs. Do you understand?"

"I think so. But, but I can't . . . "

"Why not? Ask yourself honestly. Isn't the real reason because I'm black?"

"No! No, it's not that!"

And so it went. I had to hand it to some of those blacks: they were smooth. While we paid other women for sex, they scored for nothing with love children who believed they were conveying some kind of revolutionary message. A lot of the blacks, and most of the whites, didn't give a fuck about politics, but they talked a good game when it might lead to pussy.

I had a blast during this brief stay at Sing Sing, maintaining a party atmosphere in my cell, staying drunk four and five days a week. I feasted on fine food brought in from the best outside restaurants. Steak. Champagne. Shrimp. It seemed the *majority* of Sing Sing hacks were corrupt, and for a price they would smuggle in even the most exotic orders.

I delivered mail, hung around the chaplain's office, and partied with the usual crew of guys in a locker-room atmosphere of macho fellowship. Philly Gambino was in for a parole violation; Hank Dusablon was still doing time for those murders; and Pierre Hotel participant Al Visconti was there, convicted for a different robbery. Visconti later made the Inmate Hall of Fame with the smoothest kind of escape imaginable. He had a friend draw up a phony writ of habeas corpus, and the authorities opened the gates and sent him on his way.

My sentence was almost like a vacation under the circumstances, and I enjoyed having inmates coming to me for advice and protection. On the street I got accorded a high degree of respect, but behind bars I took on almost the stature of godfather.

Beth Rivera wrote four or five times a week, but visited only once. Even this was unexpected, since I had asked her to stay away. Still, it was good to see her, and good to feel her warm soft body after a $50 bill palmed to a guard opened up a private room for us in the hospital section.

As we were making love, I feared Beth's departure would cause me a great sense of longing. But it didn't. While I gallantly told myself, like I had so many times, that a serious give-and-take love affair with a woman would be no good for *her* (and who can deny this?), the truth was I wanted complete independence, as a person and as a criminal, and I believed marriage would slow me down. No psychiatrist ever explained the deeper meaning of my avoidance of lasting relationships with women, and I never spent much time analyzing it. I hung out mostly with men, I suppose, because I was more comfortable in their no-strings-attached company.

Beth continued to reside in my 15th Street apartment and wrote constantly about how we would get away and begin a new life when I was released. I had serious doubts about the viability of this program, though I was still obsessed with a retirement score, so I stalled by saying we needed more money. I realized I liked my life, and now even prison didn't seem so bad. *Nobody* fucked with me any more; I started to think of the guards as room-service waiters; and getting drunk with various wiseguys wasn't much different in jail than in one of their social clubs. In addition, Jerry Rosenberg was with me whenever I needed to talk to someone. Little Jerry the Jew was fun, forever stirring things up, playing practical jokes, filing lawsuits, and getting under the skins of pompous wiseguys. He had a little boy's zest for life and never-faltering optimism that if he just kept trying he'd beat his murder conviction.

My sentence was only seven months, but I had enough salted away to last a lifetime in the joint. After all, I wouldn't be renting any limousines or dressing to the nines to impress somebody. The free spending inside was purely for self-gratification. I felt secure still having a good amount from the Pierre heist, plus extra cash saved from other jobs, about $200,000 in all. A revolving-door convict like myself needed to make certain he had funds to last through the jail time. It's heartbreaking to see an inmate, particularly one hooked on nicotine, without a penny in his commissary; but most prisoners are broke, and so are their friends and families.

While life was sweet at Sing Sing for me and other jail-wise convicts, it was no picnic for the majority. Often illiterate and frequently violent, these inmates, helped not at all by Auburn or Attica, were doomed to suffer every indignity the penal system could inflict. Even guards with time *only* for wallet-fattening prisoners would have let up on any inmate who had the spiritual wherewithal to call the ACLU, but few mustered the initiative.

Actually, for those who knew the ins and outs, prison conditions improved throughout the 1970s, right up until Ronald Reagan took the presidential oath of office (Jimmy Carter would have won a landslide among inmates, *if* they could have voted). With Reagan it was downhill again, a steady unchecked slide into today's terrible overcrowding and violence.

I was released in June 1973 and moved back with Beth. She had just completed her teaching year and suggested a Puerto Rican vacation, but I said I needed to get cracking on that retirement nut. In truth, I surely would have realized more success and more freedom on the outside if I had spent time using my head instead of my boundless, shotgun-style energy.

At first I split my time between managing dice games that John Sullivan fronted for Fat Tony Salerno in a Manhattan hotel and extorting businesses in Wildwood, New Jersey, and on the Atlantic City boardwalk. The latter activity began after a friend introduced me to Gary Garafola, an associate of Philadelphia godfather Angelo Bruno (in reality Bruno's family was merely an extension of Fat Tony's Genovese outfit).

Garafola told me he was tired of most of the money he extorted ending up in the pockets of the greedy, stay-at-home godfather, and he posed a dangerous but potentially profitable scheme: we would bleed New Jersey businesses located in Bruno territory, enterprises the Philadelphia boss had thus far ignored.

Gary Garafola was a tough guy, someone who wouldn't choke

in a tight spot. He shot and killed Frankie DePaula, a light-heavyweight contender who had fought champion Bob Foster for the title, when he learned DePaula intended to testify against him in a hijacking case.

The shakedown we worked out was simple and irresistible. Entering a jewelry store, I would walk behind the counter and say, "I want these watches for my kid." The owner would start coming unglued as I put his merchandise in my pocket.

"Hey, how ya doin'?" Garafola would say to him.

"What's . . . He has to pay for . . . "

"No, Pops," Garafola would interrupt. "*You* gotta pay *us* five hundred dollars a week."

"I can't . . . "

"Open your ears, motherfucker, and shut your mouth. I'm offering you a good fucking deal. We're not gonna spank you too hard, like someone else would. You've heard of Angelo Bruno? Sure you have, you miserable old piece of shit. Well, some of Bruno's legbreakers will be callin' on you in a few fucking days to demand a thousand a week. We'll protect you from Bruno, keep his apes away from you, and we'll only charge half what he would."

If the businessman refused to pay, which seldom happened, we wrecked his place. Usually it didn't go that far, but if he kept being a hardhead, we'd cuff him around a few times and before daylight the next morning hurl a bucket of sand through the front window of his shop.

After giving him enough time to find out how helpless the cops were (we always had airtight alibis), we would return and talk sense to him. "Cocksucker, we told you to do yourself a favor and pay the money. You should have paid. Now, you asshole, it's going to cost a thousand dollars just to replace that window. You want us to break that window every night? You think the cops will put a man full-time outside your store?"

He knew they wouldn't. And he knew we'd keep coming back. By this time he needed just a slight nudge. "You call the cops again, motherfucker, and we'll break every bone in your body. We'll bust your head with a baseball bat. Your fucking brains will be part of the wallpaper. Get smart, cocksucker: pay the five hundred dollars a week. It's less than Angelo Bruno's gonna want, and maybe even less than your fucking life is worth."

The jeweler inevitably paid, but we wouldn't be done with him. Garafola and I would "encourage" him to call shop-owner friends of his and explain the benefits of *their* paying $500. "I'm telling you," he would say, "these Mafiosos want five hundred dollars a week, and this Bruno person will demand a thousand. So you give them five hundred. They're good guys. They'll keep Bruno away from us. I'll tell you the truth, we can't run any business without them involved."

He gave only the facts—except for being mistaken about our Mafia membership and adding that "good guys" reference—they *couldn't* operate their stores without paying us.

Should a merchant make another attempt at rebellion and complain to the cops again, a fire would burn down a section of his store and he would see the light. Each week, regular as clockwork, Gary and I made our rounds collecting the money.

I found it interesting how our influence, the influence of any Mafia-type character, corrupted even the victims. A businessman would work up his courage and ask, "You guys probably know a lot of people, right?"

"You can believe that," I said.

"I was wondering . . . "

"What, Artie? What you wanna know?"

"My wife's birthday is coming up. I . . . "

"You want a nice present for your wife?"

"Yes, but . . . " He was afraid, not sure what our reaction would be.

"What kind of present, Artie?"

"I was thinking about a fur coat."

"Fur coat! Can we get him a fur coat, Gary?"

"Yeah," my partner said.

"You want a nice fur coat, right?" I said.

"Yes. If it's not too much trouble."

"Trouble? We like you, Artie. We're helpin' you against Angelo

Bruno, ain't we? That's what we enjoy most, helpin' you. What kind of coat you want?"

"Could you get a full-length ranch mink?"

We could have gotten him anything, from a stolen carton of cigarettes to a top-of-the-line yacht. The mink he wanted retailed for $5,000, we picked it up for $500, and sold it to him for $2,000. Everyone was happy.

And Artie had been corrupted.

We brought out the worst in everybody. People we extorted purchased cars from us, furniture, boats. Grocers bought meat; convenience-store owners ordered cigarettes; and jewelers acquired diamonds from us much cheaper than they could through their regular wholesalers.

We learned secrets about our victims that even their priest or rabbi didn't suspect. Several times we were asked to commit murder—usually by an old coot who dreamed of collecting a bundle on a heavily insured wife to finance fun and frolic under tropical palms with his young, perky mistress.

We never took any of these contracts. I had committed numerous murders and never been busted for one (all it took was one), and I steered clear of these surefire recipes for getting caught. Even a poor homicide detective knows that the most obvious suspect is the victim's mate, and slightly aggressive interrogation would have elicited a sobbing confession from any one of these out-of-their-element storekeepers.

Gary and I expanded our protection racket, shaking down a construction-company owner (did he want his building-in-progress torched?), and half-a-dozen nightclubs. From extortion alone we cleared $10,000 a week, a gravy train we should have known would derail.

Angelo Bruno got wind of our activities and dispatched some muscle to talk to us. When we met the gorilla in a roadside bar, he immediately growled, "Angelo wants to know what the fuck you're doing."

"Tell Angelo to fuck himself," I bluffed.

The ape looked at me with widening eyes. "You a crazy man?" he asked. "You want a bullet in the head?"

"Look," Garafola said, "tell your boss we got some good hitters here."

The guy took our message to the godfather, who didn't buy any of it. He sent his man back to tell us, "Get the fuck out of New Jersey," and that's what we did.

I stole indirectly from Fat Tony Salerno not only in New Jersey by operating in territory he "owned" through Angelo Bruno, but also from the dice games I ran under his auspices at the Wilson Hotel. When a gambler beat the odds and won big, I telephoned his description to confederates waiting at a phone on the corner. They would stick him up soon as he came outside, making it unlikely he'd try his luck at the Wilson again.

The games themselves, which included blackjack, lasted nonstop from Friday night until Monday morning and were, like most Mafia games, scrupulously honest. The odds favoring the house were enough to guarantee Fat Tony would win. Actors and stagehands liked to play, as did waiters, garment-industry executives, second-story men, bank robbers, lawyers, motion-picture moguls, Wall Street stockbrokers, and always plenty of wiseguys.

Food was provided free, and so was the smoky, tense atmosphere gamblers love. Guys would come in with a toothpick (a few hundred dollars) expecting to build it into a lumber company, and inevitably lose it all. Seeing it from the house's end—the winning end—never stopped me from trying to beat the horses. Gamblers don't learn: later, John Gotti made millions on his bookmaking operations, but lost millions betting his own selections.

We didn't use chips at the Wilson Hotel; everything was cash. I frisked each customer for weapons when he came in, and had the authority to loan up to $100,000 at shylock rates to any bettor Tony Salerno deemed creditworthy.

The tables had a per-bet $500 limit, and the house netted $30,000 a weekend. This doesn't compare to the $1.3 million the

Trump Castle wins daily, but it was nothing to sniff at. Besides, Fat Tony had a couple dozen similar operations spread around the city, and the $30,000 was over and above what we paid vice cops to look the other way. Often these detectives insisted on playing; and when they lost, they expected to be reimbursed.

Beth and I continued to live together, but she began to doubt that I *could* settle down. I kept professing that it would be just a few more years of bringing in this kind of money and we'd retire on Easy Street.

Actually, I wondered if I'd ever get out. I had started using cocaine, the current drug of choice among wiseguys, and lost heavily at the tracks, extravagances that made serious saving difficult. Rather than taking stock of my predicament, I increased my criminal activity, fronting a pair of dirty bookstores on 42nd Street for Fat Tony Salerno and delivering dope to Harlem for Arnold Squitieri. Often I didn't bother to come home at night.

Maybe I was hyperactive, committing all these crimes. But I was, after all, a *criminal,* and I know I enjoyed always being on the go. Besides, I continued to tell myself that I'd stop when I hit a million—I congratulated myself on finally settling upon this nice, round figure. Bitterness still ate at me when I dwelt on the Pierre Hotel aftermath. Fucking Sammy Nalo, I thought, was lucky to be in prison.

In any case, much of the heroin I delivered came from the Pleasant Avenue section of East Harlem. Six months earlier, in April 1973, federal agents and city detectives had busted eighty-six important drug dealers and runners, including such former associates of mine as Ernie Boy Abbamonte (later a Gambino family insider), Gennaro Zanfardino, and Herbie Sperling.

Police called it the "largest crackdown in history," but in reality other underworld figures merely stepped into the void. When I stopped by Pleasant Avenue (a six-block street between FDR Drive and First Avenue) in the autumn of '73, little had changed. Residents still bagged heroin and addicted themselves on dust inside their shabby tenement apartments. Doors and windows were shut to prevent the slightest of breezes from blowing this commodity more precious than gold onto the floor, underneath furniture, or even into the street.

Pleasant Avenue was safe to walk along. Muggers bold enough to assault citizens on Fifth Avenue or Park knew better than to ply their trade here. The avenue's ordinary residents weren't about to complain about the drug dealing: like later-day Colombian peasants, their livelihood depended on narcotics.

My frequent trips to Harlem brought me into contact with one of the country's largest dope dealers, a black man named Nicky Barnes. This 5'5" flashy dresser employed some 200 black hoodlums and had much of the Harlem drug trade tied up. A few years later, on December 12, 1977, *Time* magazine called him "a legend of defiance and success [to blacks]."

Barnes, for years, was always being arrested—bribery, dope peddling—but until 1978 had only served one short sentence for a narcotics violation. He owned four Mercedes, two Citröen-Maseratis, and three hundred custom-tailored suits, and he hung around with powerful politicians and big-time entertainers. To numerous poor black youngsters, he stood out as a shining symbol of success, a man to be emulated. Unlike the stereotype of a dandified black gangster talking ghetto jive, Nicky was quiet, thoughtful, composed. He considered himself a businessman.

Nicky Barnes learned criminal organization from Joey Gallo while the two served time together. Gallo intended to recruit black gangsters into a criminal family, headed by himself, that would overwhelm the Italians. But when Sonny Pinto took care of Joey, Barnes utilized what he had learned to recruit his own soldiers, form his own organization. And he remembered well the Gallo Golden Rule: *Get others to handle the stuff for you, never let anything be traced to you.* That's why the police had so much trouble making charges stick.

Barnes was, alternately, a wild spender and the most stingy of businessmen. The young women who cut and bagged his heroin had to work buck naked, lest they try to steal some of the powder.

They were forced to wear surgical masks, not to prevent addiction but so they wouldn't feed their habits for free by deliberately inhaling the drug.

Barnes owned gas stations, travel agencies, nightclubs, and entire housing projects. He was rich as Fat Tony Salerno or Carlo Gambino—I'm talking tens of millions of dollars—but one thing kept him from being as powerful: he couldn't develop a direct source for drugs and had to deal with the Italians to obtain his junk.

I spent several nights hopping from nightclub to nightclub with Nicky. He took me to a place he co-owned that catered to black gangsters and featured beautiful Cuban waitresses and a high-stakes dice game in the back. Nicky was always "giving" me girls, and often I accepted.

I went to Sugar Ray Robinson's Harlem bar on Seventh Avenue with Nicky. A jazz band and floor show provided the entertainment in an atmosphere of blue mirrors and subdued lights. Robinson himself came to our table, wearing a white-on-white dress shirt, brown silk slacks, and a Panama hat. Very respectful to Nicky, Robinson did most of the talking, going a mile a minute, and I couldn't follow most of it. He kept his head down, never looking in our eyes.

I also went to Wilt the Stilt's with Nicky. Owned by Wilt Chamberlain, this Harlem watering hole always had a number of adventurous young white women hoping to strike up an affair with a gangster or an athlete. From a money standpoint, a gangster would have been the better choice. One night with a hoodlum might be rewarded with a big diamond. The athletes usually figured they were doing the girls a favor.

The floor show at Wilt the Stilt's was superior to what I had seen at Robinson's joint. Maybe Sugar Ray didn't want to shell out for headliners. Whatever, Chamberlain hired great entertainers, singers, and comedians, most of whom I judged much more talented than their highly paid white counterparts performing on national television.

My frenetic criminal life during this period extended to dealing counterfeit money. I could buy $1,000 in very good quality $20 bills for $65, and almost immediately resell them for $120. I employed four junkies full-time as "money changers." They would take a short cab ride, pay the hack with a bogus bill, collect change, and start the cycle again. Profits mounted into the thousands each day.

I also put two people on the road constantly passing phony bills at bars, department stores, and convenience stores in New Jersey and Pennsylvania.

My entrepreneurship gave me a slight taste of how the godfathers made their fortunes. No matter how hard an individual worked—and none in my profession ranked more active than I—he could only earn so much. What Junior Persico discovered early on, that large sums of money were accumulated by taking advantage of other people's labor, represented a concept that came to me very late. My venture into passing counterfeit money—had I been able to continue—could have earned me a larger return (for less work) than all my other butt-my-head-against-the-wall enterprises.

During this ultra-active time in my life, I not only murdered Buster DellaValle, but two other drug dealers who had fallen into disfavor with the Genovese family. Whenever I was on the outside, I made sure to keep myself in the contract-killing business. It was what had earned my reputation, set me apart from thousands of other eager criminals, opened so many doors for me, and what I did best.

This stint on the streets ended a day after the second anniversary of the Pierre Hotel robbery. On January 3, 1974, while trying to rob a drug dealer of his dope and cash—what would have been a considerable haul—I was captured by a police stakeout team that had been shadowing the dealer. Since I was carrying a gun, the charge was forcible theft with a deadly weapon, and despite a major effort by John Sullivan to obtain a lenient sentence, the judge gave me thirty to sixty months.

Beth visited me before I pleaded guilty. This former gangster groupie, now a dedicated and respected school teacher, said she couldn't take any more of my craziness and didn't want to see me again. I agreed this was the right thing.

I knew something decent had been removed from my life. In

truth, I still think about her, and another of those paths not taken. I don't know if it ever could have worked out. Nor did I know that the thirty- to sixty-month sentence—which with good time could be considerably shorter—would turn into seven-and-a-half long years.

Chapter 15

THE CONTRACT ON HOFFA

IT HAPPENED IN SEPTEMBER 1973, SEVERAL WEEKS AFTER THE Buster DellaValle hit. John Sullivan, driving his Mercedes, picked me up in front of the Wilson Hotel where he and I ran the dice games on two separate floors. John had said Fat Tony Salerno wanted to meet me.

What could this be about? Salerno, coboss of the Genovese family with Funzi Tieri, wouldn't want to chew the fat about how I whacked DellaValle, ask my advice on the stock market (he had a vast concealed portfolio), or recommend that I buy a car from his dealer instead of Carlo Gambino's.

No, this meeting would be strictly business. The Genovese family had long been awash in money, and Salerno kept his eyes on everything: heroin and cocaine, prostitution, bookmaking, shylocking, massage parlors, bust-out joints, discos, girlie magazines, dirty movies, peep shows, gay pornography, and cigarette machines (Fat Tony once bragged he got fifty cents for every pack of cigarettes sold in Manhattan vending machines). The Genovese family owns movie houses. They controlled the giant ultralucrative New York Coliseum. It is surely the most powerful force in the Teamsters union and on the docks, from which its soldiers daily steal vast stores of merchandise. This mighty organization could shut down the docks on command, or through its Teamsters' influence cripple the nation's transportation. It even owns gum machines in the subway, hot dog vendors on the street.

Then and now, the Genovese crime family vies with the Gambinos for supremacy in a classic struggle between money and muscle. The truly colossal Gambinos have the manpower (about 2,000 soldiers), but the Genoveses are much richer.

I itched with curiosity about the purpose of the meeting with Salerno. Naturally, the sober Sullivan, attentively peering through the Mercedes' windshield at traffic, offered no clues at all.

John double-parked on First Avenue between 115th and 116th Streets, right in front of Fat Tony's social club—this is called getting off on the wrong foot. "Move that fucking car," Salerno told Sullivan when he learned its location. Fat Tony suspected FBI agents concealed themselves outside, feverishly jotting down license numbers of vehicles stopping at the club. But unless the feds were asleep at the switch, John's plates had already been duly noted.

The social club, the hub around which the Genovese family's criminal life revolved, was an inauspicious red brick building with the windows painted black. An inscription on one of the windows read, "Club."

We opened an unlocked door and walked inside. The man guarding the entrance, one of Fat Tony's cousins, recognized John and nodded.

It was 3:00 P.M., sleeping time for mobsters, and only seven or eight regulars sat on wood chairs at flimsy card tables clustered in the plain, uncarpeted room. On two of the folding chairs with padded red vinyl seats that horseshoed the room on three sides sat a pair of blue-suited businessmen, eyes downcast, staring at briefcases clutched in their laps. In the back, in a makeshift kitchen area sparsely furnished with a refrigerator and coffee urns, I spotted Fat Tony turning from his espresso machine and heading toward us. We met him halfway.

"How ya doin'?" he said to John.

"Good, Tony. Good."

"This the Greek?" The squat, dumpy godfather—5'7", 220 pounds—looked me over head to foot.

"This is him," Sullivan said.

Suddenly Salerno grabbed me, hugged me, and kissed me on each cheek. I was relieved that he made the gesture twice. Just one kiss, in his circle, meant death.

"I heard a lot of good stories about you," he said. His gruff voice, accustomed to command, vibrated authority. "Too bad you're only half Italian," he said, laughing, "or I'd 'make' you right here and now."

Salerno led us down a corridor off the kitchen to his private office. It, too, had no carpet, only functional pieces of mismatched furniture, and bare walls, except for one picture, a prominently positioned portrait of FDR. No frills for this Mafia don who was rumored to be among the 300 richest people in America. A Castro Convertible sofa he slept on hugged one wall, and a door at the back led into a small yard where he occasionally retreated from the pressures of running his massive crime machine.

"Take a load off," Fat Tony said, and John and I settled onto plain wood chairs across a coffee table from Salerno, who lit a huge, noxious cigar and stared at me benevolently through a cloud of blue smoke.

I knew quite a lot about Fat Tony Salerno and didn't doubt the familiarity cut both ways. In fact, he employed me. The ownership of the two pornographic bookstores I ran could ultimately be traced to him; ditto the dice games.

Fat Tony had scrambled to the top over piles of bodies, many of whom he had personally killed for Vito Genovese. Now, at age sixty-two, in a more sedentary life-style and obviously unwilling to defy the laws of gravity with a strenuous exercise regime that would have tightened the paunch hanging over his belt, Fat Tony still displayed beefy arms and shoulders. He had eyes that could implant fear in the fearless, bushy John L. Lewis-type eyebrows, a little hook nose, and a balding head of gray hair. He wore a white shirt with long sleeves rolled up to his elbows, enormously baggy pants three decades out of style, and ancient featherweight shoes.

Salerno leaned over the table, cigar stuck in the side of his mouth, his thin wet lips smiling, but not his eyes, and I knew from his first utterance that I had a major problem. Each word he spoke sent tiny pellets of spit from his mouth to my face. With his face no more than six inches from mine, I had no way to avoid the missiles without showing weakness, the character trait he despised most.

"Want something to drink?" Salerno asked.

"No," I said.

"I could send out for a drink." I had heard alcohol wasn't kept in the club, a place reserved for business of the most sober kind.

"No. Thank you."

"How about espresso? I was making some when you got here."

"Fine."

The godfather disappeared through the corridor, returning a minute later with steaming cups for John and me. Sullivan hadn't said a word in his absence.

This powerful gangster (ranked second only to Carlo Gambino in the Mafia, a position some wiseguys thought was too low) enjoyed boasting how far he'd come on a third-grade education. Being a crude man didn't make Fat Tony short on brains, however. He was a whiz with numbers, able to astound associates by calculating complicated equations in his head with computer speed, and a voracious reader of newspapers, particularly the *New York Times* and the *Wall Street Journal.*

Salerno was a walking sports encyclopedia. Far exceeding a fan's memorization of batting averages, earned-run averages, and win-loss records, he kept abreast of possible game-determining developments like which athlete was injured and unlikely to play, or which team was rocked by internal dissension. Insiders constantly funneled information to him, and he backed choices with money straight from his pocket, betting as much as $100,000 on a single contest. He never wagered with Genovese bookmakers—the equivalent of winning or losing his own money—a practice to which John Gotti later fell victim. Unlike Gotti, Salerno was a shrewd gambler, and wiseguys dreamed of receiving tips from him.

Fat Tony fixed numerous prize fights and an occasional horse race, but he found that being privy to events other people rigged was much more lucrative. Organized-crime figures from coast to coast curried favors from him, and shared the lowdown about upcoming ring "tank" jobs or harness-horse and thoroughbred "boat races." A few times, I knew, he had passed winners along to John Sullivan.

Peppering me with spit, his fat face so close I couldn't lift the espresso cup to my lips, this head of the Genovese organization talked to me in a manner I supposed represented his idea of a friendly discourse.

"Where you living?"

"Fifteenth Street."

"Who you hanging out with?"

"Philly Rags. The General. That crew."

"You see The General often?"

"Yeah."

"What you think of him?"

Jesus Christ. What was I expected to say to this? Most wiseguys would have stalled, stammered, and hoped to learn what *Fat Tony* thought of The General before giving an answer—an assessment I also wanted to hear. But since I had no idea where he was coming from, I just thought *fuck it* and told him the truth.

"Yeah?" he said. I was afraid that big cigar angling from his mouth might swerve and burn me. I wished he would get to the point of the meeting.

Instead he wanted to know about guys in his family that I'd done time with. What do you think of this guy? What do you think of that guy? No matter how I replied, his face registered neither approval nor objection. Then, "I heard you had some trouble with Nunzio."

Was this why I'd been summoned? For an old fight with a wiseguy?

"Nothing big," I answered carefully.

Fat Tony switched to another subject: "What's your opinion of Matty the Horse?"

"I never met him."

Surprise lifted the bushy eyebrows. Salerno leaned back a few inches and grew silent. He looked down at his hands, edged closer, and stared straight into my eyes.

I'll never forget what next came out of Fat Tony's mouth: "Greek, I need you and John for a very important job that's coming up very shortly." He didn't go into details—like mentioning who, where, or when. It has to be bigger than DellaValle, I thought. He'd let John Sullivan judge my competence for that one. For this, he sized me up in person.

The skin twitched around Tony's eyes. No more bullshit about my character analysis of his friends. "This is a *very big job*," he repeated. "There can't be no fuckups. You and John will be sharing something between one-hundred-thousand and two-hundred-thousand dollars."

Salerno never once asked if I'd take the job. He was accustomed to telling people, not asking. Regardless of how I felt, whom he wanted hit, or where he wanted it done, I had no intention of turning him down. I took pride in my standing in organized crime, which I'd earned by the murders I'd committed—any piece of shit could pass counterfeit money or scare defenseless businessmen into paying extortion. And if my ego needed confirmation that I'd been successful, here it was, coming from one of the world's premier mobsters. For this "very important job" Salerno could have chosen from a thousand killers.

Fat Tony stood up from his chair and I from mine. He reached inside his baggy pants and pulled out the biggest roll of hundreds I'd ever seen, peeled off $5,000, and handed it to me. I thanked him. Then he kissed me again—twice—and walked us through the corridor into the main room of the social club.

The two blue-suited businessmen with briefcases had been joined by three more. They started to rise from their chairs, but Salerno shook his head, an inflexible smile on his face, and they eased back onto their seats. He would see them, in time, and they would wait until he was ready.

"You need to lose some weight," I teased Salerno as John and I headed out to First Avenue.

"You need to gain some," Fat Tony shot back. "I don't like thin guys." I looked at him closely and detected a grin. "Stuff yourself with pasta," he said. "Put some meat on those bones."

Nobody ever accused John Sullivan of being a blabbermouth. Grim and humorless, with a voice gangster-film casting directors would love, he kept many secrets. He disseminated information CIA fashion, strictly need-to-know, and he never got embarrassed by leaks. That's why I was surprised, as we drove away from the social club, when he asked, "You know who Tony was talking about?"

I didn't have an inkling.

"Jimmy Hoffa."

Usually I did the talking but, driving back downtown in his Mercedes, John Sullivan related the reasons for the murder contract on Hoffa. They started with Tony Provenzano, Tony Pro, who ran the Teamsters Local 560 in Union City, New Jersey, was a strong union delegate, and was also a captain in the Genovese family. Tony Pro had done time in Lewisburg Penitentiary with Jimmy Hoffa. During a discussion in the yard, Provenzano told Hoffa to forget his dreams about running the Teamsters when he got out. "We got our man in there right now," he said, referring to mob flunkie Frank Fitzsimmons.

Hoffa, half a tough guy, smacked Tony Pro in the eye, right in front of a bunch of inmates. Mafioso consider it a mortal sin for anyone, especially an outsider, to hit or "disrespect" a made guy, much less a crime-family captain. Then Hoffa screwed up worse by lipping off to Tony Pro: "Before I lose the union, cocksucker, I'll go to the grand jury" concerning the involvement of Provenzano and Fat Tony with the Teamsters. Hoffa threatened to snitch about being forced to provide money from union funds so organized crime could buy businesses and expand criminal enterprises: for example, Rancho La Costa Country Club, the 5,600-acre resort in

Carlsbad, California, funded by a $93,700,000 loan that syndicate boss Moe Dalitz obtained from the Teamsters.

A prisoner who witnessed the Hoffa-Provenzano fight saw Tony Pro come toward Hoffa and shout, "If you don't get out of my shit and back off of me, you'll end up like Castellito. They won't find so much as a fingernail of yours."

In 1970, when Tony Pro emerged from Lewisburg, he had an additional reason for wanting to keep Hoffa out of power. Under Fitzsimmons, local Teamster officials had been given more power, which meant Provenzano had a license to steal by making private deals with trucking companies that sought to cheat on the national freight contract.

Tony Provenzano's brother Nunzio, also a member of the Genovese family, relayed news of the confrontation to Fat Tony. The godfather, clearly the single most influential, behind-the-scenes force in the Teamsters, didn't care that Hoffa had smacked Tony Pro, but he did want the pliable Fitzsimmons kept in office. What really drew his attention was the talk about grand juries.

"At first," John Sullivan told me, "Salerno didn't do nothing. But he sure kept a close fucking eye on Hoffa's activities. Hoffa's still making noise about getting his job back, and then exposing the under-the-table deals. He ain't gonna get his job back, and the only place he can go with his information is to the feds. No way can Fat Tony risk this guy turning canary."

"Has Fat Tony consulted the other families?" I asked.

"No. He decided it himself."

"Something this big, I thought he'd have to get an okay."

"He don't bother with that Commission shit. Fat Tony don't need no permission."

As a matter of fact, that's why Salerno had reached beyond the typical wiseguy hitters to independents like Sullivan and me. If anything went wrong, an Irishman and a Greek couldn't easily be tied to the Italians.

In retrospect, having read everything I could about the labor leader, I believe it was inevitable that Jimmy Hoffa would have met his end at the hands of one gangster or another. Early on, as a teenage labor organizer, this tough, 5'5", husky little upstart learned that large companies never hesitated to employ underworld muscle to smash picket lines, and Hoffa began to draw union supporters from the same criminal pool. Maybe he thought he could use these gangsters and then distance himself from them, but it never works that way.

At age twenty-three Hoffa married Josephine Poszywak, and they produced two children, James P., Jr., now a Detroit attorney, and Barbara Ann Crancer, now living in the suburbs of St. Louis, also a lawyer.

People close to Jimmy Hoffa knew of a third child in his life, though those who thought he had adopted little Chuckie O'Brien were wrong. After O'Brien's father died in a union-related incident, Hoffa felt sorry for and helped support the boy and his mother, and did indeed treat him like "a son of mine."

O'Brien, forty years old at the time I met Fat Tony Salerno, would soon reward the man he called "Dad" by supporting Frank Fitzsimmons. Worse, he became a Judas.

Much of Jimmy Hoffa's popularity came from rank-and-file union members who believed the tough-talking labor leader stood foursquare with them against trucking-company bosses. If he associated with mobsters and employed goons, so what? The owners had too long had these people on *their* payroll, plus the cops to smash picket lines. By the mid-1950s, Hoffa had risen to the presidency of the nation's largest Teamster local, 299 in Detroit.

Jimmy Hoffa was elected president of the International Brotherhood of Teamsters on October 4, 1957, and two months later the union was expelled from AFL-CIO membership because, Hoffa claimed, of machinations originating with Robert Kennedy. These two would battle each other until Kennedy's assassination in June 1968.

Robert Kennedy said he was outraged by Hoffa's undeniable connections to the Mafia, charges that rang hollow in the ears of the labor leader, who knew full well the fortune-making connections of Bobby's father Joseph to top gangsters, including bootlegging partners Owney Madden and Frank Costello during the prohibition era. Hoffa later learned that Robert Kennedy's brother, John, had shared a girlfriend named Judith Campbell with Chicago mob boss Sam Giancana, and that the Kennedys had sanctioned a CIA arrangement with Mafia bosses Johnny Roselli and Sam Giancana to assassinate Fidel Castro. Plus, Hoffa certainly became aware of Robert Kennedy's affair with Marilyn Monroe, whose mob-connected close friend Frank Sinatra once told Eddie Fisher, "I'd rather be a don of the Mafia than President of the United States."

Like father, like son, Jimmy Hoffa figured, knowing Joe Kennedy had indulged in extramarital affairs with Gloria Swanson and Marion Davies, among others. Once Frank Sinatra brought a pair of women with him to Hyannisport, and a Kennedy servant stumbled on Joe as he fondled the breasts of one of them. The servant apologized, stammering that he had been shining Kennedy's riding boots. "My riding boots!" Joe Kennedy exclaimed. "Just in time!"

Franklin D. Roosevelt, Jr., called Joe Kennedy "one of the most evil, disgusting men I have ever known." Harry S Truman said he was "as big a crook as we've got anywhere in this country."

And indeed, the Kennedys undoubtedly practiced a double standard where the mob was concerned. "They used [Sinatra] to help them raise money," said Boston Mafioso Vinnie Teresa. "Then they turn around and say they're great fighters against corruption. They criticize other people for being with mob guys. They're hypocrites."

No, Hoffa did not believe the Kennedys were outraged by his association with mobsters. He believed instead that the Kennedys were antilabor and eager to weaken powerful unions they could not control. Indeed, during Hoffa's presidency, the Teamsters grew from 800,000 members to more than 2,000,000, making it the world's largest labor organization.

Another key figure in the plot to kill Jimmy Hoffa, along with Chuckie O'Brien, Tony Provenzano, and Fat Tony Salerno, was a captain in the Detroit Mafia, Anthony "Tony Jack" Giacalone. Hoffa trusted Giacalone, his "rabbi," the mob contact who in theory was supposed to protect the Teamster leader. Instead Giacalone delivered Hoffa to his killers.

Giacalone, known in Detroit as "King of the Streets," made his reputation as a fierce loan-shark collector for Michigan godfather Joe Zerilli. He branched into bookmaking and numbers and by 1969 had chalked up fifteen arrests, including felonious assault, armed robbery, and rape.

The higher Giacalone rose in the Mafia, the more his image improved. He became Jimmy Hoffa's closest mob confidant—and super-rich from selling Teamster favors. Giacalone acquired a mansion in Grosse Pointe, a penthouse condominium in Miami Beach, and membership in the exclusive Doral Country Club. The flashy Tony Jack sported dark glasses, silk suits, and a $20,000 ring. In a city dominated by automobile moguls, many considered him one of the community's two or three most powerful men.

He was "Mr. Giacalone" to the Motor City elite.

As plans for the Hoffa murder were playing out, few people referred to Giacalone as King of the Streets. The new inductee into Michigan high society was now an "investor" or a "socialite."

Giacalone's carefully constructed facade would be stripped away once federal investigators began collecting suspects in Jimmy Hoffa's murder. Not only would Tony Jack be exposed to his fancy friends as a sinister gangster, but it would be revealed that this "second or third" most powerful man in Detroit wasn't even his own boss. The real strings of power were manipulated by a short, fat, sloppy godfather who controlled a fabulous fortune and slept in a back room in East Harlem.

Chapter 16

THE JIMMY HOFFA MURDER

THE DISAPPEARANCE, I.E., MURDER OF JAMES RIDDLE HOFFA ranks right near the top of America's great unsolved crimes: maybe even first for individuals who accept the conclusion of the Warren Report, which names Lee Harvey Oswald as the sole assassin of President John Kennedy.

Kennedy and Hoffa. They were linked in life and still are in death by most people, who do not believe their killers—or the reasons for the killings—have ever been discovered. Maybe the Kennedy case will forever remain a mystery. But not Hoffa.

In 1985 the deputy chief of the Organized Crime Section of the Justice Department, Paul Coffey, talked about Jimmy Hoffa with a *Los Angeles Times* reporter. "I believe we are going to solve this case by accident," Coffey said. "Someday, when the people are real old and in prison, and there is no real fear anymore, someone will tell us what happened. There is a lot of institutional memory in the Mob, so we could still solve this case ten or fifteen years from now."

It won't take "ten or fifteen years." I know the whole story because I was there. I'm going to relate who else took part, and why, in the mind of the Mafia, the murder was necessary. I should add that I come forward so the truth doesn't die with me, and because I have nothing, absolutely nothing, left to lose.

After the meeting with Fat Tony Salerno, during which he approved me for the assassination team, two events seemed to take me out of the Jimmy Hoffa hit: the 2½-to-5 years I received for forcible theft with a deadly weapon, and a much more serious December 1974 indictment for murder in the prison stabbing of a Dannemora inmate.

In early December 1974, jailhouse lawyer Jerry Rosenberg subpoenaed me to Manhattan to testify in one of his many lawsuits. While housed at the federal institution at West Street, I was visited by John Sullivan and Jimmy Coonan, the latter having been added to the Hoffa hit team.

Fat Tony wasn't screwing around. The cold fearless Coonan was perfect for the Hoffa contract. I had accompanied him to that 46th Street rooftop when he tried to kill Mickey Spillane, had grown close to him in prison where I watched him mature, and most recently had been purchasing counterfeit money from his Irish associates. Coonan had experience chopping up bodies, a qualification Fat Tony deemed necessary.

I knew I would soon be returned to Dannemora, and I'd passed the word along to John Sullivan that furloughs could be purchased. The cost for three days on the outside was $3,500, and the money needed to be passed to a major New Jersey drug dealer who had been buying furloughs for himself.

It turned out Fat Tony loved the idea. He knew a great alibi when he saw one. How could I be on the outside committing a murder when I was locked down at Dannemora?

At the meeting with Coonan and John Sullivan, we discussed also purchasing a furlough for Joe Sullivan, who was also serving time at Dannemora. Mad Dog would have loved to come along, but even he agreed it was too risky. As the only person ever to escape from Attica, he was under constant surveillance by administrators.

"When's this gonna happen, John?" I asked.

"Damned if I know," he answered. "Tony's watchin' and waitin'. There are details he needs to arrange."

I figured it wasn't definite yet, that Salerno still was unsure which direction Hoffa was headed. Meanwhile, he had a deadly crew assembled, just in case.

I could tell John Sullivan wanted to get started. An old-time hit man himself—a man who loved killing—he increasingly had assumed the role of middleman, accepting contracts and farming them out to people he trusted. Still, John missed the excitement, the thrill of murder, and he looked forward with keen anticipation to what he hoped would be his date in Detroit.

Many months went by. While I prepared to fight that murder charge, Fat Tony grew ever more alarmed about the activities of Jimmy Hoffa. The former union leader was a vocal, active officer in the National Association for Justice, a prisoners' rights organization, and his pronouncements rang with a reformer's zeal. Salerno knew that a guy who called for change in one area—prisons—might branch into others.

Fat Tony's worst fear came true: charismatic Hoffa campaigned energetically to regain the union presidency, hammering home a "throw the Mob out" platform. The union was the goose laying the Genovese organization's golden eggs, as *Time* magazine later pointed out: "Leading the family's extortion list is the International Brotherhood of Teamsters."

At the time of his death, Hoffa had just finished cooperating with author Oscar Fraley on a book. Fraley wrote about Hoffa's "warlike charges against those he accused of bilking him out of the Teamster leadership, a firecracker recitation of frauds, kickbacks, and complicity with the underworld. Point by point, he ticked them off on thick, square fingers that could double into fists like mauls. And there would be more, 'many more,' he said, when he got those hands on the Teamster pension-fund books."

As Fraley pointed out, and as Tony Salerno knew, "You had to believe him. As one old-line trucking company owner told me: 'To the Teamster, Jimmy was God. They knew he was always fighting for them, physically if necessary. And I'll tell you another thing. His word was as good as gold; a handshake was better than a bale of legal papers drawn up by a battery of lawyers.'"

Fat Tony knew what rode on the outcome of the battle over control of the union, and this godfather, who ordered the deaths of small-time drug dealers for *mistakenly* infringing on his territory, didn't intend to permit Hoffa to cut the flow of his family's greatest source of income. Teamster money had built and/or bought the Desert Inn; the Fremont; Caesar's Palace; Circus Circus; the Dunes; and the Stardust.

Fat Tony feared three potential outcomes: (1) the stoppage of cash flowing to Genovese coffers should a crusading Hoffa regain the union presidency; (2) the exposure by Hoffa of vast amounts of money the crime family had ripped off from Teamster pension funds; and (3) a blizzard of indictments when the full extent of the pillage became known.

Rumors out of Washington, D.C., made matters even more urgent. Fat Tony's grapevine told him that President Gerald Ford was considering the removal of a restriction from Hoffa's parole agreement that barred him from running for union office until 1980. Hoffa figured to win any *honest* Teamster election, and maybe a militant rank and file would demand one.

All this was too much for Fat Tony. Previously he could at any time have called off the hit—he didn't even have to cancel, just never mention it again to John Sullivan—but now, in early 1975, he took steps that made his decision irreversible.

Both John Sullivan and Jimmy Coonan told me what happened next. Salerno contacted Anthony "Tony Jack" Giacalone, Hoffa's rabbi, who had grown rich in Detroit as the man to see if someone sought a Teamster loan. Chuckie O'Brien's deceased mother had been Giacalone's girlfriend, and Chuckie called the mobster "Uncle Tony."

Fat Tony began by telling Giacalone to "stay away" from Hoffa, meaning not help the ex-union leader in any way. Then Salerno ordered the Detroit gangster to contact Chuckie O'Brien.

Briefly Giacalone tried to play the role of rabbi. He advised Fat

Tony to "ease off of Hoffa. He's a scared rabbit, and once you've scared somebody, they're going to run to the feds on you."

Fat Tony didn't want to hear this, and that's when he stopped pulling punches. "He's not running no place, because he's going to be dead," Salerno said bluntly. "And if you get involved, *you're* going to be dead."

Giacalone ranked as a big noise in Detroit, but a nullity, a cipher in organized-crime circles when compared to Salerno. I'm sure Mafia big shots in other parts of the country are capable of busting hell wide open on their own turfs, but they have to obey when orders come from New York. A provincial godfather is to a Big Apple godfather as a branch manager is to a corporate board chairman.

Salerno instructed Giacalone to set up a meeting with Hoffa, and suggested that he use Chuckie O'Brien as the bait.

At first Chuckie O'Brien balked. He didn't want to be part of a murder, especially one as big as this. Maybe he even still felt a trace of loyalty to his benefactor, without whose help and influence he would have been nothing. Whatever, he hemmed and hawed.

Then "Uncle Tony" Giacalone told him Salerno had offered a bundle of cash and an unofficial (not on the books) position as a union boss: literally, Fat Tony offered to take care of him financially for the rest of his life.

Still O'Brien wavered, but he had to accept when the Genovese godfather, through Giacalone, *un*sweetened the pot: "If he don't do it," Salerno told Tony Jack, "or if he decides to tip his father off, we'll kill him, his father, and his whole family."

What could Chuckie O'Brien do? Fat Tony was a strong man; O'Brien was weak. Tony Jack met with O'Brien again, threatening him with stories, all true, about what would happen to anyone foolish enough to defy the head of the Genoveses. O'Brien, thoroughly frightened, agreed to help turn his "father" over to executioners, and thus Salerno had recruited an individual essential to his plan, someone who held Hoffa's trust.

Giacalone contacted Jimmy Hoffa and made arrangements for a

phantom sitdown, which Tony Jack said would include himself and Tony Provenzano, "to talk everything over and make amends for what occurred in Lewisburg."

Of course, Giacalone and Provenzano had no intention of being anywhere near Hoffa when the hit came down. While the union leader was being snatched, Tony Pro had numerous witnesses to swear that he was playing cards in Union City, New Jersey; and Tony Jack was seen at Detroit's Southfield Athletic Club by so many people that an FBI memo read, "almost everyone interviewed at the SAC complex revealed that Giacalone definitely appeared to be establishing an alibi, inasmuch as he made himself very visible, which is not his normal style."

Using the Jersey drug dealer, Fat Tony funneled $3,500 to the right contact at the prison to get my furlough arranged. I would leave on July 29 and have to return on August 1. On the appointed day I was picked up in Plattsburgh, New York, by John Sullivan, Jimmy Coonan, Salvatore (Sally Bugs) Briguglio, and a guy from Union City, New Jersey, who served as Bugs's driver.

Everyone was tense. On edge. I knew Sullivan and Coonan didn't trust Sally Bugs. Part of the tension stemmed from going on a major hit, where a screwup meant the end of everything for all involved, but another part came from fear of the mob's infamous Machiavellian motives. Could this whole Hoffa thing be a ruse to kill *us?* Did Sally Bugs and his boss, Tony Pro, really want Hoffa dead? Or would they intervene and whack us? Gangsters who don't think in these terms won't last long.

The driver dropped us at the Buffalo airport, and we flew, under assumed names, to Detroit. From there Bugs drove us to a safe house in suburban Mount Clemens, where Tony Provenzano waited.

Tony Pro told us what he wanted done. He gave John Sullivan $25,000 in cash, and promised $175,000 more when the job was done. Pro said Hoffa was getting ready to rat on him and the Teamsters.

We spent the night at the Mount Clemens home. Provenzano

cooked spaghetti and scungilli (conch), and it was so hot it almost burned a hole in my mouth. "Who the hell you looking to kill," I asked, "Hoffa or me?" Pro didn't think it was funny. I wasn't laughing either. When Pro was out of earshot, Coonan called him "a little fag" and "a stool pigeon," and although John Sullivan agreed with the sentiments, he played the role of peacemaker. Coonan was ready to kill Pro and Bugs and forget the whole thing.

That night Coonan, Sullivan, and I played cutthroat pinochle, $100 a game. I won $1,000 from Sullivan, which he has never paid. Many years later he told Joe Sullivan he forgot. Yeah.

We slept in shifts. Sullivan and I went to sleep first, with Coonan standing guard. Bugs stood guard while Pro slept.

The next morning Provenzano and Briguglio left to pick up Chuckie O'Brien. Pro said he wouldn't be coming back, which suited us fine. Fat Tony had made sure the house in Mount Clemens contained everything we needed: a pair of .22s with screw-on silencers, two P.P. .38s, plastic bags, surgical masks, and a chainsaw. Coonan and I would be the shooters. We chose the .22s. John Sullivan, using a .38, was to shoot Sally Bugs or Chuckie O'Brien if either made even the slightest false move.

At 2:30 P.M. on July 30, Sally Briguglio and Chuckie O'Brien met Hoffa in the parking lot of Machus Red Fox restaurant, seven miles northwest of Detroit on Telegraph Road in Bloomfield Township. Hoffa had left his Lake Orion cottage at 1:15 P.M., having told his wife Josephine that he intended to meet "Tony Jack and a couple of other guys." On his calendar he had written: "T.J.—2 P.M.—Red Fox."

At 1:30 P.M. Hoffa stopped at Airport Service Lines, owned by Louis Linteau, the former president of Pontiac Teamsters Local 614. Linteau, described by the FBI as "a notorious con man," was away at lunch, but an employee remembered Hoffa saying he had hoped Linteau would accompany him to his meeting with Giacalone. When the FBI questioned Linteau, he told them Hoffa had informed him on July 26 that he'd be sitting down with Giacalone and probably Tony Pro.

Hoffa grew suspicious at the Red Fox when his friend Tony Jack wasn't with Chuckie O'Brien. Instead there was Sally Bugs, a captain in the Genovese family.

O'Brien had been recruited for just such a purpose. He reassured Hoffa and gave him a phone number where he could reach Giacalone. Over the phone Giacalone told Hoffa to go with his "son" and Sally to a "nice" home in Mount Clemens where he and Tony Pro would be waiting for the sitdown that "should iron out all our differences."

O'Brien told Hoffa he had checked out the house and it was safe. Indeed, Hoffa knew the area, tracts of pleasant suburban homes, a place even he didn't associate with murder.

Hoffa sat in the front seat of the car and Sally Bugs drove. Hoffa knew Bugs as a business agent for Tony Pro's Local 560, and maybe even that he had several murders to his credit. A compact 5'7", he had about him the studious look of a college professor.

Chuckie O'Brien rode in the rear. He was too frightened to drive, but his "father" didn't know that. Plus, Hoffa wanted someone he could trust sitting behind him. He knew all about getting hit in the back of the head, and if Bugs had to be along, the driver's seat was the best place for him.

They rode in silence, Hoffa with one eye on the road, one on Briguglio. On several occasions Bugs thought he was about to say something, but each time the moment passed. Later, Bugs said Hoffa uttered just one word on the entire trip, which would make it his last. When Sally said, "Almost there," as they neared the safe house, the former Teamster president replied, "Good."

Meanwhile, at the Mount Clemens house, Sullivan, Coonan, and I had positioned ourselves in the kitchen adjacent to the living room, which was just to the left of anyone entering the front door.

We weren't concerned about Hoffa's rough-guy reputation. We had dealt with vicious hoods way out of Hoffa's league, and, besides, we weren't going to fool around. Just shoot him and get it over with.

Still, we understood the magnitude of the hit, that probably for us it would never get bigger than this, and the realization helped totally focus our minds. Coonan and I gripped the silencer-equipped .22 pistols; they were loaded with extra dumdum bullets, which explode on impact.

Sullivan wasn't a talkative man and Coonan and I respected that, so mainly we waited in silence. Coonan occasionally paced; Sullivan sat on a stool and stared at the floor; I stood near the stove, running the projected action over and over again in my mind. We intended to move as soon as the front door closed. We knew the hit would happen quickly, and we were dead ready.

When Jimmy Hoffa walked into the house, turned left, and started to sit down, Coonan and I burst out of the kitchen, followed closely by John Sullivan. I pumped two slugs into Hoffa's forehead, the noise like two whispers—*Ssssst! Ssssst!*—and the former union leader bucked backward. Then Coonan fired, and Hoffa slumped to the floor, settling sideways half-on, half-off an easy chair.

The Teamster boss died instantly. The deadly couple of seconds had to have been a blur to him. I don't think his brain had time even to register that he was under attack. Like most murder victims, his eyes remained open in death, and none of us moved to close them.

Instead Chuckie O'Brien started to cry. Loud, wrenching sobs. Sally Bugs talked to him, tried to calm him down. O'Brien bent over, convulsed, turned away from his "father," and collapsed on the floor.

Coonan, Sullivan, and I paid no attention. The muscular Coonan got his arms under Hoffa and carried the body down to the basement. Sullivan and I trailed him, urging him not to hurry. Coonan laid Hoffa on a large table underneath a bright lightbulb. As in an operating room, all the paraphernalia was ready: surgeon's smocks, surgical rubber gloves, goggles, electric saw, meat cleaver to sever tendons, black plastic garbage bags, and precut sections of rope. We stripped the body and deposited the clothes in a bag; then I cranked up the chainsaw and cut the head off. I took out a pocketknife, snipped off a lock of Hoffa's hair, and gave it to Coonan, who put it in his pocket.

Coonan and I did the cutting and he and Sullivan double-bagged each body part, carefully tying the bags. Sullivan first put the head into a nearby meat freezer. Next Coonan cut off both arms and sawed each in half. The three of us were awash in blood. I amputated one leg, chopped it apart at the knee using the cleaver, and then did the same to the other leg. Sullivan and Coonan deposited these in the freezer. Finally we sawed the torso, the only part of Hoffa remaining on the table, into three parts, and they were packed away with the rest. The ghoulish Coonan, especially, loved this work. Given his druthers, he would have done the cutting with a *knife*.

We washed the tools, cleaned up the basement, took showers, and returned to the living room. Sally Bugs was still trying to comfort an ashen-faced, almost catatonic Chuckie O'Brien; it had been forty-five minutes since Coonan had carried the body to the basement.

Sally Bugs went out to a pay phone and called Giacalone. "The job's done," he said. "These guys want their money."

"I'll have someone bring it over right away," Tony Jack said. That was the deal. The payoff had to be made immediately after the hit. After that, as per the agreement, the three of us were to take the body to Central Sanitation Services at 8215 Moran Street in Hamtramck, Michigan, a garbage disposal company owned by two alleged underworld figures named Raffael Quasarano and Peter Vitale, where it would be crushed into old cars.

Bugs drove from the phone booth to a deli and brought back Pepsis and big meatball heroes, smothered in mozzarella cheese and tomato sauce. The sandwiches bore a resemblance to what we had just cut and bagged; everyone except Chuckie O'Brien dug in. He said he couldn't get anything down, so Coonan, who had worked up a hearty appetite, ate his sandwich. Some mobster (I can't remember who) once said the toughest guys weren't those who could kill and retain complete composure; real tough guys, he said, enjoyed a good meal afterward. Coonan was definitely a tough guy.

Chuckie O'Brien recovered enough to know that he wanted out of the murder house, and we let him go. He drove away in the car that had delivered Hoffa to his killers. The rest of us were to leave with Giacalone's man, who duly arrived with a suitcase stuffed with money. But a heated argument ensued before a count could even be made. "Tony Jack wants you to dump the body someplace else," the bagman said.

"That wasn't part of the deal," John Sullivan said.

"Well, it's what Tony Jack wants."

What happened, I later learned, was that Giacalone and Tony Pro had argued over how the body would be disposed. Tony Jack had become very scared, and he didn't want anything else happening that could tie him to the killing—like the body being discovered at a place associated with him.

"Can we take the parts to one of his other places?" Sullivan asked the bagman.

"He didn't say nothing about that. He said for you guys to take care of it."

Coonan was steaming, and I wasn't too happy either. Sullivan persuaded Sally Bugs to call Giacalone. "These guys," Bugs said, "want to know if they can take the body parts to one of your other places."

"Jesus Christ, no."

"They want to talk to you."

"I don't want to talk to them. I don't want to get no conspiracy. I don't know John Sullivan, I don't know Jimmy Coonan or Tony the Greek, and they can't use my places. They handled the body; let them handle the burial."

It was quite a mess, caused by Giacalone's panic. He had earlier suggested that Central Sanitation Services would be available, but that if something went wrong there he would guide us to a river where the parts could be scattered. That bit about the river was why the body got chopped up in the first place.

The FBI later followed up a lead that suggested Hoffa's body had in reality been disposed of at Central Sanitation Services. A Bureau affidavit read: "Informant 1 has advised FBI agents, as recently as August 7, 1975, that he has personal knowledge, obtained directly from persons present, that at least ten murder victims have been disposed of by Quasarano and Vitale through and by the facilities described herein. Quasarano and Vitale own and operate Central Sanitation Services, on which premises are located an extremely large shredder, compactor, and incinerator . . . utilized commercially . . . for the destruction of . . . refuse. Informant 1 has related that these facilities are also utilized by Quasarano and Vitale for the total destruction of the bodies of murder victims in extremely important syndicate murders. Informant 1 has advised that he believes Hoffa to be a victim of such a murder and Hoffa's body to be totally destroyed by means of the aforesaid facilities. . . . "

What happened was that not only Giacalone had become scared, but Quasarano and Vitale as well. They backed away from accepting Hoffa's body, probably a wise decision in view of that informant with access to their innermost secrets.

We pondered what to do. "Is this house really safe?" Sullivan asked Sally Bugs.

"Yeah, as far as I know."

"Tony Jack," said Giacalone's bagman, "don't want the body left here."

I said, "Let's leave it right here in the freezer."

"That's right," said Jimmy Coonan. "It's Tony Jack's problem now. We're leaving the body right here, and youse guys can take care of it. That's the deal."

In 1976 I was housed at the Metropolitan Correctional Center at 150 Park Row, where the feds had moved the old West Street prison, and Coonan and Sullivan paid me a visit. As usual, they horsed around, joked, and winked. Suddenly, Coonan tossed a clear plastic coin case containing that lock of Hoffa's hair onto the table. "It's my good-luck charm," he said.

Maybe it was. He had many more murders in his future and more than a decade of high-rolling before the government finally put him away.

Earlier, just a few days after the murder, New York undercover cops spotted Russell Bufalino, a Genovese underboss, dining with Tony Provenzano and Sally Bugs at the Vesuvio Restaurant in

Manhattan. Bugs, though the cops didn't know it, was telling Bufalino and Tony Pro about what had come down in Mount Clemens.

There were several afternotes to the Hoffa murder. Chuckie O'Brien, Anthony Giacalone, and Tony Pro all took the Fifth Amendment when testifying before a Detroit grand jury investigating the "disappearance."

O'Brien ended up convicted of extortion in an unrelated matter, but this was a mere annoyance compared to the constant fear he has lived in every day and every night since the murder. The chance always exists that he may yet be indicted for his "dad's" murder, and he does not have the constitution necessary to serve long hard time.

I saw Chuckie O'Brien under fire and do not consider him a real killer. Fat Tony presented him with a terrible choice—Hoffa *or* you and your family—and Chuckie did what I believe most people would. An example of how frightened he is: when informed that Tony Provenzano was looking for him at the 1976 Teamsters convention in Las Vegas, O'Brien spent two days hiding under a friend's bed.

Tony Jack Giacalone received a ten-year sentence for tax evasion.

Tony Pro received a life sentence in 1978 for the 1961 murder of Anthony Castellito, a Teamster official who made the mistake of considering running against Provenzano for the presidency of Local 560. Tony Pro died in jail in 1988.

In December 1975, Mad Dog Joe Sullivan and a Gambino associate named Augie Manori drove a truckload of oil drums from Michigan to New Jersey. One of the drums contained the jumbled pieces of the man who once had fought for the rights of the nation's truckers.

Fat Tony had tired of arguing with Tony Jack about who would dispose of the body, and took care of the matter himself. Hoffa's remains were transported to the Meadowlands, where wiseguy construction crews were doing work on Giants Stadium. The plastic bags were buried in cement.

In September 1981, Joe Sullivan and I went to a Giants football game. Joe pointed to the spot where he had buried the body and said, "You think Jimmy's watching the game? Hey, Jimmy, this touchdown is for you!"

After I had turned rat and joined the Witness Protection Program, the FBI came to me and said they had learned from a "solid source" that John Sullivan, Joe Sullivan, and I had been part of the plot against Hoffa. I gave them bits and pieces of the story, relating some of the events described in this chapter and the previous one. They gave me a lie-detector test and asked me point-blank if I'd had anything to do with the Hoffa killing. I told them "yes"—and passed the test with flying colors. I didn't tell them everything I have here, and I have never revealed the actual location of Hoffa's body, because I wanted in return a promise from them: a reduction in my sentence. I found their refusal to be very curious. The feds had waived off nine murders for Jimmy "The Weasel" Frattiano, and his information counted strictly as penny ante compared to mine.

Consider this: about the only thing those agents didn't ask was whether I had been present at the time of the killing. Yet this was an obvious query, given all the right-on-the-money information I had. I believe they were afraid to ask that question, or to press the matter, because my answer might have ruined other law-enforcement careers. I was supposed to have been securely locked up at the time Hoffa got hit.

The FBI knew, but couldn't prove (or maybe they didn't want to prove), that prison officials at several institutions had been selling furloughs during these years, and crime bosses, wiseguys, and inmates who knew the ropes were purchasing them and going outside the walls to commit crimes. Little danger existed that the prisoner would simply refuse to return. That would have enraged the godfathers, who counted on this system for themselves and guaranteed a major contract on the head of anyone foolish enough to make a run for permanent freedom.

If a prisoner paid enough, he could be away for as long as two weeks. Usually the furloughs lasted from one to four days. Maybe a guy wanted to see his family. Party. Do a job. I committed *nine murders* while outside on various furloughs.

Lawyers and police seldom ask a question if they suspect they might not like the answer. My handlers knew the selling of furloughs to Mafioso and other violent criminals would have inflamed the public.

Jerry Rosenberg and the well-known mob attorney Gino Gallina represented me in the murder I committed at Dannemora (see next chapter), and Gallina, a former prosecutor, handled another case for me in 1977. Which brings up how I was able to pay this crooked lawyer. For the Hoffa hit I received $60,000; Coonan and John Sullivan each got $55,000; and Joe Sullivan got $30,000 for burying the body. I'd instructed John Sullivan to leave my share with Fat Tony, and it was the godfather who passed along $20,000 of this to Gallina.

Anyway, I soon became suspicious of Gallina when, during his many visits, he kept asking about the Jimmy Hoffa murder. My doubts were confirmed when Fat Tony Salerno passed along word that Gallina, trying to buy his way out of a cocaine bust, had allowed himself to be wired up by the FBI to obtain information on mob activities. Gallina was not only testifying to a New Jersey grand jury, but he had told the feds he could find out who hit Hoffa.

I don't think he could have done it, though besides myself he represented Tony Pro and Sally Bugs. Salerno ordered Gallina's murder, and in November 1977, Joe Sullivan and I shot and killed him in Greenwich Village.

On March 21, 1978, Sally Bugs was shot dead outside a Mulberry Street restaurant in Little Italy, not far from where Joey Gallo had been gunned down. The rumor was that Bugs had been negotiating with the FBI to trade information on the Hoffa hit for immunity in the 1961 Anthony Castellito murder, the crime for which Tony Pro earned a life sentence.

Which leaves just a few others to update. Jimmy Coonan is serving a 75-year sentence for a RICO conviction (the federal Racketeer Influenced and Corrupt Organizations statute). Joe Sullivan is doing 75 to life for murder. Fat Tony collected 100 years in his RICO trial and died in prison in 1992.

John Sullivan was the only winner. Seeing he couldn't outgun Coonan in their on-and-off war to control the West Side, Sullivan retired as a rich man—and a smart one—to the good life in Florida.

How powerful a force was Fat Tony in the Teamsters? James Neff, in his book *Mobbed Up*, told about John "Peanuts" Tronolone, a Cleveland crime boss, informing Jackie Presser (a FBI snitch) that Presser would be the new head of the Teamsters: "'You got the support of all the families on the East Coast. You're gonna be the next president.'"

Tronolone continued: "'There's gonna be some requests from the families, and you're gonna have to do some favors. All requests will come through me. I know Maishe [Rockman] used to screen 'em for you. Now that you're gonna be president, you have to deal with a family guy about family business.' He said that Fat Tony Salerno would have final approval on all deals."

Finally, me. When I came out of prison in 1981, Joe Sullivan told me, "Listen, we got to kill this Augie Manori, because he was instrumental in burying the body."

Joe and I shot Augie in the head with a 9-millimeter semiautomatic, cut open his stomach, wrapped him in a rug, and dumped him in the Hudson River.

As we were drinking together later that night, Joe started laughing. "You know," he said, "I didn't really kill Manori because I thought he would talk. I believe he's been fooling around with my wife."

Gail Sullivan and Augie Manori had once been married. If Sullivan's suspicions were correct, and they probably weren't, Manori had done a very foolish thing calling on his former spouse.

Chapter 17

THE RICHIE BILELLO MURDER

I HAD REENTERED THE PRISON SYSTEM ON JANUARY 3, 1974, FOLlowing that arrest for forcible theft with a deadly weapon, and I didn't officially come out again until August 24, 1981—seven years, eight months, and twenty-one days later. Nonetheless, this relatively long stretch of confinement encompassed a significantly active period of my criminal life. It began with a murder.

His name was Richie Bilello, a real nasty son of a bitch, and I'm proud I killed him. Originally imprisoned for homicide, Bilello had grabbed a young man who made the mistake of double-parking in front of his diner, taken him inside his store, and forced the kid to suck his prick. After ejaculating into his victim's throat, Bilello asked, "Who's your God?"

"You are," the trembling youngster replied.

"Right," said the sick pervert, and shot the kneeling victim in the head.

Bilello's behavior was disgraceful during the riot at Attica. Rather than join other inmates who were trying to improve prison conditions, Richie acted out his own agenda, which included sticking his cock into the mouth of a hostage guard. Bilello became the first prisoner convicted for crimes committed during the rebellion.

The man was strictly bad news. A burly 250-pound, forty-four-year-old sadist, he raped inmate after inmate at Dannemora in 1974. In addition, as an associate of the Lucchese family, he knew many of the organization's secrets, which he busily shared with authorities. He was ratting on Paulie Vario, the Lucchese captain made famous in the movie *Goodfellas*, plus Jimmy Burke (played in the same movie by Robert DeNiro), who made his mark masterminding the $8 million Lufthansa heist in 1978.

Normally, I would have had nothing to do with Richie Bilello, who was as far removed from my circle of friends as anyone could get. But then, in October 1974, he became my problem—more accurately, I *made* him my problem.

Word reached Joe Sullivan and me about Bilello loudly proclaiming that Jerry Rosenberg had been a rat at Attica. This was ludicrous. Rosenberg, one of the heroes of the rebellion, had nearly gotten killed there, and for more than a decade he had consistently been a champion of inmate rights. In other words, the polar opposite of Richie Bilello, who really was a snitch.

Younger inmates didn't know Jerry's history. Likely some hothead, stupid enough to believe loudmouth Bilello, would think he'd be doing the right thing by shanking Rosenberg.

No one knew this better than Jerry the Jew, who told me he'd have to go after Bilello. He'd have done it, too, though he couldn't fight at all. "That's suicide, Jerry," I said. "Let me see what I can do."

Joe Sullivan and I confronted Bilello in his cell. "Motherfucker," I said, "what's this lying bullshit you're telling about Jerry?"

"It's the fucking truth. He's a rat. A lowlife stool pigeon."

"You ever say that again, I'll tear your fucking head off your shoulders."

"Yeah? You and who else?"

"I'll kill this cocksucker now," Joe Sullivan said, starting to step around me.

"I don't want no problem with you," Bilello said quickly.

"You want trouble with the Greek," Sullivan said. "The Greek is me."

From that point on, the only question was *how* I would kill the piece of shit. I worked in the print shop, across the hall from the office of Bilello's counselor, and waited for Richie to be called in for a session on October 28. When I saw him sitting on a bench outside the counselor's office, I came out of the print shop and settled down next to him. Acting friendly, under the pretense of making peace, I gave him a cup of coffee. That occupied one of his hands. When he asked if I wanted a Pall Mall and extended the pack of cigarettes with his other hand, I said, "Yes, thank you," and drove a knife into his chest.

He shrieked, then, "No! No! Please, God!"

I hit him with the knife twice more, again in the chest and once in the throat, and left him collapsed and bleeding on the floor. Unfortunately, before I could get back inside the print shop, an inmate walking up the stairs spotted me.

An Irish mobster in the print shop cleaned up the knife and threw it out a window (there would be no way to trace the weapon to me), and we returned to our workstations. Moments later a guard came into the shop, looked around, clamped his eyes on me, and said, "You, come out in the hall and help get this guy onto a stretcher."

Bilello was still conscious as we carried him to the elevator and, incredibly, he gurgled to the guard, "I want to see my lawyer. I'm going to sue this fucking prison."

"Who did this to you?" the guard asked.

"Tony," he said, a rat to the end.

"Tony who?"

No answer; Bilello had passed out. Arriving goon-squad reinforcements relieved me of stretcher duty, and I returned to the print shop. A few minutes later a pair of guards were in my face with the very frightened eyewitness.

"You Tony?" one of the hacks asked.

"My name is Donald."

They locked me down in the hole. In fact, they locked the

whole prison down. Ignoring pleas made over the public address system, not a single inmate was willing to donate a drop of blood to help save Richard Bilello. He died in the prison hospital five hours after I stabbed him.

The authorities had me pretty much dead to rights, though—thanks to that witness, whom they immediately separated from the rest of the population, plus Bilello's partial deathbed identification.

FBI agents visited me three days later in solitary and offered immunity for the murder if I would snitch on Jerry Rosenberg by saying he was involved in a bunch of illegal activities in prison. Jesus Christ, I'd just killed a rat. Where were these guys coming from? I told them to go to hell.

Although I heard that a Clinton County district attorney said, "A statue should be erected" to the guy who got rid of Bilello, the state was nevertheless determined to prosecute.

Paulie Vario was so delighted with the Bilello murder that he put $500 on the prison books for me. He also helped arrange for high-powered Gino Gallina to represent me, but I insisted Gallina be co-counsel with Jerry Rosenberg. I don't know of another instance where the beneficiary of a murder represented the defendant.

My reason for using Rosenberg had nothing to do with playing a prank on the system. The Jew was more skilled than most outside lawyers, and he worked tirelessly even for inmates who weren't his friends. He and Gallina began to prepare a vigorous defense.

In the end we decided it made sense to plea-bargain the Bilello killing. The state had threatened to ask for the maximum, believing it could prove the killing premeditated (which it was). In exchange for a 6½- to 13-year sentence, I pleaded guilty in February 1975 to murder. Rosenberg felt bad about the sentence—I'd done the killing for him—and I wasn't too happy about it either.

Why the fuck was it always me? I asked myself. Why did I have to be the one avenging some wrong? A thousand guys had good reason to eliminate Richie Bilello, and somebody would have, if I hadn't gotten him first. I spent many long nights calculating how dearly I paid for the prison reputation I treasured.

I was warehoused much of 1975 at the Federal House of Detention in Manhattan, on hold to testify in a lawsuit brought by Jerry the Jew. I purchased four furloughs during this time, using two of them to commit stickups and two to commit murders. Furloughs were being sold almost as freely as Met souvenirs in Shea Stadium.

Back at Dannemora in September, I met Willie Boy Johnson and John Gotti, the latter a man who started out fearing me, then using me, and finally wanting me dead.

I liked Willie Boy better. A huge former prizefighter, he was an easygoing, likable half-Native American whom Gotti treated like shit. Willie Boy was doing time for armed robbery, and he spent most of it running errands for his boss. He was so pleasant, so willing to please, no one suspected Willie Boy lived a double existence as an FBI informant. For more than fifteen years he was the government's eyes and ears on Gotti, and when this information became public, I still don't think anyone really hated him. I know he was the only rat I can't bring myself to despise, and that includes the loathing I direct on myself. In any case, that's how popular Willie Boy was. Even Gotti was more saddened than angry when he learned he had a snitch in his midst, but not sad enough to stop himself from having nineteen bullets pumped into Willie Boy on August 29, 1988.

Each did what he had to. Gotti couldn't let an informer live. Willie Boy must have known what was coming, but he never bothered to move away from his neighborhood. I believe I understand how much he must have disliked himself, how he probably welcomed the bullets when they came.

I think there were two reasons Willie Boy snitched: he resented his demeaning subject-to-monarch relationship with Gotti, and his cozy deal with the FBI allowed him to commit numerous crimes without fear of prosecution. The authorities weren't going to throw him in jail and lose their best pipeline into the activities of the Gambino family. He provided them with too much accurate information on the largest Mafia family in the world. The Gambinos control unions; they are major loan sharks, bookmakers, hijackers, and extortionists; and they own hundreds of restaurants and bars. Their biggest source of income, of course, is drug sales.

Willie Boy ratted, albeit selectively, on many of these operations, and he even got away with murder. On March 18, 1980, one of Gotti's Howard Beach neighbors, John Favara, was driving home from work, a blinding sun in his eyes, when Gotti's favorite child, twelve-year-old Frank, suddenly sped in front of Favara's car on a minibike. The youngster died immediately in the collision.

Gotti and his wife Victoria were inconsolable. Frank had been a good student, a good kid, the one who'd take over the legitimate empire his father intended to bequeath. For months Victoria dressed in black, and Gotti, usually outgoing and effervescent, became withdrawn and more. The couple turned part of their home into a shrine for the dead boy.

"The driver of the car that killed Frank Gotti will be eliminated," portended an unidentified woman who called the 106th Precinct.

"That kind of stuff only happens in movies," Favara said to a detective relaying the threat.

Favara didn't understand that many gangsters steal an identity from movie characters or notorious criminals of yesteryear. Like a kid might try to imitate a role model athlete, Gotti wanted to be known as Al Capone II.

The accident hadn't been Favara's fault, but the future godfather had him kidnapped and murdered. I've heard he was tortured by Gotti himself, and that the abductors were Tony Roach Rampino, Funzi Tarricone, and FBI snitch Willie Boy Johnson.

Gotti landed in Dannemora, after going through the reception center at Green Haven, for the May 22, 1973, killing of James McBratney in Snoope's Bar & Grill on Staten Island. The McBratney contract had been issued by Carlo Gambino, who believed McBratney was part of a team that kidnapped and murdered his nephew Emanuel Gambino. McBratney hadn't done it, but Carlo *thought* him responsible, and nothing else mattered. Nor did anything count to Gotti except currying favor with Gambino, and in this he succeeded. He won his "wings"—got made—by helping to whack McBratney.

Angelo Ruggiero, who told John to look me up at Dannemora, was with Gotti at Snoope's, but the guy who actually shot McBratney was Ralph Galione. Witnesses identified Galione and Ruggiero but not Gotti, who didn't know he had been turned in by Willie Boy Johnson.

I noticed when I first shook hands with John in the Dannemora yard that his skin was smooth as a baby's ass. At this time he was thin, with an olive complexion, piercing dark eyes, and a full head of black hair, which made him look more Puerto Rican or South American than Italian.

That first day Gotti wore a gray sweatshirt, green prison pants, and expensive, very conspicuous dress shoes. "The alligators have got to go," I told him. "Get yourself some sneakers."

"I don't like tennis shoes," he said. "They make my feet flat."

"This place is like a giant sports complex," I explained. "Most of the guys are into one game or another. And the ones who don't play sit around on the courts like old men, scratching their balls and telling war stories. You can't do time in dress shoes. After it rains the yard is ankle-deep in mud."

But in what I would learn was typical know-it-all John Gotti behavior, he stuck with the fancy footware, the first of a dozen pairs I watched him ruin.

After we walked the yard and I got a feel for him, I invited Gotti to join "my" court—the most prestigious in the joint, including Joe Sullivan, Jerry Rosenberg, Jackie Coonan, Bobby Bongiovi, and Philly Rastelli—and he accepted. We did a lot of cooking there, played endless hours of cards, and exchanged mobster stories.

Gotti, even then, long before he became godfather, was very arrogant. Loud and abusive. He treated Willie Boy like a slave: get me a soda, fetch my mail, deliver this message. His language was filthy. Even when being polite around tough guys, Gotti couldn't talk without using obscenities. Often when he spoke he put his hands together, as if praying, and gestured expressively. He actually had a fairly generous nature, which later set him apart from the other, greedy godfathers, and his obviously rehearsed bravado imparted a certain appeal.

At this time I was serious about handball and played to win. Gotti insisted I should take him as my partner.

"You a good player?" I asked.

"The fuckin' best," he replied.

"You sure?"

"I've played a lot. Never lost a match."

So we scheduled a game together. He showed up in those ridiculous alligator shoes and got hot when I again suggested he switch to sneakers. "This is how I play, goddamit!" he said.

Well, he was just terrible: no coordination, two left feet, hands like boards. After we lost the first few points I said, "You're not playin' too good. In fact, you stink."

Gotti spun around, his dark eyes flashing, and said, "Don't you yell at me, motherfucker!"

He thought I'd "disrespected" him in front of a crowd of guys watching the game. So I didn't say anything for the rest of the match, which we lost because he was so clumsy in those slick-bottomed alligator shoes.

Later he visited my cell, huffing and puffing about my disrespect. I got in his face. "You told me you were good at handball," I said. "You're the worst fucking player I ever saw. You told me you never lost; I don't think you ever won."

"I *always* fuckin' won!"

Joe Sullivan intervened just before fists flew, and when Gotti left I said to Joe, "Never fucking lost, my ass!"

But it turned out Gotti had told the truth. The guys he'd played had all lost, on purpose, because they were afraid to beat him. I thought it a serious deficiency that he wasn't aware of why he always won. Petty as a game of handball might sound, it typified Gotti: in no area of life did he want to be surrounded by people stronger than himself.

According to prison rules, inmates were allowed to have a maximum of five cartons of cigarettes. Gotti—who smoked only cigars—kept five cigarette cartons in his cell at all times and about forty more on hold with other prisoners. In the joint smokes are money, and one day when Gotti paid a black kid cigarettes to clean his cell (an action reminiscent of Joey Gallo), I upbraided him about it: "You think you're King Farouk? People in here don't care who the fuck you are."

Indeed at this time he wasn't much, just incredibly ambitious. "Somebody might stick a knife in your back if you go around acting superior," I continued. "Your cell is your home. Take some pride in it. Clean your cell yourself. Put your hands in the shit bowl and wash it like everybody else does. This way you show equality."

I could tell from his expression that my advice wasn't pleasing him. "I'm telling you for your own good. In prison there are no servants. Each con pulls his own weight."

Gotti read books on philosophy and the Catholic religion. "I want to acquire knowledge," he told me, "so I can hold my own with educated, intelligent people." His goal was to make a lot of quick money illegally and get richer by investing it in legitimate businesses. He made a big show bad-mouthing junkies and drug dealers, but surely he knew that most of his friends were dope peddlers.

Gotti showered a lot, always keeping himself very clean. At times he could be kind and good-hearted, but he had a tough-guy complex that required him to curse and scream. He feared Joe Sullivan and me (we had committed many murders—he had done perhaps three) and a number of other people at Dannemora. Always belligerent, he would back off when someone stood up to him. (Since he didn't like backing off, he later lined his inner circle with yes-men and flunkies. His present-day Gambino operation is long on muscle and short on brains, a commodity the Genovese family has in abundance.)

One of the toughest guys at Dannemora was Nicky G, an enforcer and weightlifter who stood 5'9" and weighed 245 pounds. Nicky wasn't *quite* as mean as Red Kelly or Harold Konigsberg (a 300-pound enforcer for Tony Provenzano), but only the insane dared mess with him. Enter Gotti, who stole some steaks from

Nicky. Gotti then went to his cell, cooked one of the steaks, and ate it alone. A number of convicts didn't like him because he was one-way like that. Anyway, Nicky asked me to get his T-bones back, because he didn't want to pursue the matter violently, the only approach he understood.

I went to Gotti and suggested he return the meat, and he said, "Hey, fuck that guy. Those steaks are mine."

"You oughta give them back," I said. "Nicky's no punk."

"Tell him I ate 'em all."

When I relayed the news to Nicky, he reacted predictably: "I'll break his fuckin' neck."

A few days later Nicky confronted John in lower F Block where all of us were locked. "How the fuck do you get off stealing my fucking steaks?" Nicky asked.

Gotti, despite my warnings, was surprised by Nicky's fury. He was also scared, but tried to save face in front of a crowd of cons, including me and Joe Sullivan.

"Maybe," Nicky growled, "I should just knife your ass, but I'm gonna give you a fair chance. You want to be a tough guy, well, I'll treat you like one. Throw your hands up and let's get this shit on."

Gotti desperately wanted out of the situation and quickly glanced around, searching for help, but nobody moved, not even his flunkies. Nicky poked him lightly in the stomach, backing the future Mafia don off a few inches. "Come on, you fucking punk, fight!" Nicky told him in a voice filled with menace. "You want to be tough, I'll show you tough."

The thoroughly frightened Gotti took a swing at Nicky. Then Nicky just crushed him, delivering two pile-driver left hooks to his right eye, knocking him back against the bars of a cell. Then he hit him again with a right hand that could have gone through a brick wall. Gotti sagged and went limp, out cold.

Like I said, you didn't fuck with Nicky G. He bent down, took Gotti's head in his hands, and began pounding it against the floor. He would have killed him, and there never would have been a Dapper Don, if a bunch of us hadn't pulled him off. It took twenty minutes to revive Gotti, his right eye completely closed, his face a map of ugly black and purple lumps. For the next three weeks he mostly stayed by himself, always wearing sunglasses whenever he had to venture among the population.

Oddly enough, Gotti earned a lot of respect because of the incident with Nicky. Pathetic as a fighter, Gotti nevertheless had swung at Nicky, and that's what counted: standing up for yourself, not sniveling. Nobody expected Gotti to win the fight. Even Nicky, who never got his steaks back, expressed a grudging admiration. Few people dared even to throw weak slaps at this brawny brawler, a genuine prison terror.

I had no doubt Gotti's ego and massive ambition would carry him as far as luck allowed in the Mafia hierarchy. And after his release, he didn't forget the tough guys from prison. He employed Joe Sullivan, me, and others to help him kill his way to the top of the Gambino organization.

Gotti was another who discovered how to obtain furloughs, as described by John Cummings and Ernest Volkman in their book *Goombata*: "Several prison guards got three hundred dollars each to take Gotti on trips back to Queens for conjugal visits with his wife and to have supper in one of the Italian restaurants he favored. At the same time, it was arranged that a fellow hood Gotti met and befriended in prison, Arnold (Zeke) Squiteri, would be permitted similar visits to his home in the Bronx. Additionally, the guards were put up at a local motel with prostitutes to play with while Squiteri and his mob associates met elsewhere to discuss business. Since Squiteri was a heroin trafficker, those business conversations had to do with narcotics. . . . "

Gotti served less than two years for the McBratney killing, and he was released from Green Haven after a stopover at Auburn. He told me to look him up when I got out, and I said I would.

From Dannemora I went back to the Federal House of Detention in Manhattan.

Just as Gotti's furloughs had consisted of more than "conjugal visits with his wife" and "supper in Italian restaurants," my furloughs were money-making expeditions, mainly to finance my sky-high legal expenses. Flashy Gino Gallina with his glittering diamond rings and heavy gold necklaces didn't come cheap (he didn't come at all if he didn't get what he asked), nor did the attorney who represented me in a 1976 beef with the Internal Revenue Service. The year before at Dannemora I had been part of a wide-ranging fraud perpetrated by numerous inmates joined by a variety of respected citizens: two education-department employees, two correction officers, a lawyer, and a Catholic priest.

Walter Sher, a jewel thief in for a 1962 murder (his conviction was overturned in 1980), was the acknowledged mastermind of the scheme, and for a time it was wildly successful. We obtained blank employer and employee tax forms, picked a corporation out of the Yellow Pages, filled out the papers, and mailed them to the IRS for refunds. My job was going from prisoner to prisoner and learning their Social Security numbers and other related data.

Before the scam was uncovered and mushroomed into a scandal that garnered headlines nationwide, we ripped off a fortune. Half the money went to the inmates, half to the plotters. Many of the conspirators pleaded guilty and received jail terms, but some of us opted for a trial and were found not guilty. The prosecutor knew of my involvement, but since I had never signed anything and he couldn't produce a paper trail, the jury refused to convict.

I committed two more murders in 1976—and almost got killed myself.

It happened in December at Auburn. A good friend came to me complaining that he had been beaten out of a half-kilo of heroin by "Peanuts," a 5'5", 200-pound former dope dealer for Joey Gallo. My friend offered to pay me if I could scare the money out of Peanuts, and I agreed to try. Guards were watching when I finally managed to approach him, and he told me to fuck myself.

Feigning illness, I got myself admitted to the prison hospital where Peanuts worked. It was the only way to spend meaningful time with him, and I figured a beating would be all that was required. Before this could occur, however, he sneaked into my hospital room while I slept and drove a knife into my chest.

The blade missed my heart by less than an inch. I spent three weeks in intensive care, and another three weeks in the hospital before returning to the general population.

I didn't tell who stabbed me (had a guard stuck the shiv in me, I wouldn't have talked), nor did I ever exact revenge on Peanuts. Prison authorities knew who did it—they probably thought "Peanuts" deserved a statue—and they tucked him away so securely I couldn't find him.

Joe Sullivan, who had been released from Dannemora in December 1975, visited me religiously twice a week during the long stretches I was locked in Manhattan. I was his father confessor and best friend, maybe his only one, and he had a need to talk about his killings. One day he might cry, the next he'd be laughing, full of fun, relating his latest "environmental cleanup." More than once he visited me on West Street and gave me details of a murder before the news had even appeared in the paper or on TV.

One such homicide occurred on August 20, 1976, when he eliminated Eddie Cummiskey, who was second in savagery only to Jimmy Coonan among the Westies. Joe rode up to a Hell's Kitchen tavern on a bicycle (the cops still wrongly believe the killer came in a car), calmly walked into the Sunbrite Bar, and put a bullet into the back of Cummiskey's head from point-blank range—a murder committed for Fat Tony Salerno.

Taking the contract on the dangerous Cummiskey was all in a day's work for Joe. It meant nothing to Mad Dog that his victim was practically a legend. A little guy, Cummiskey once got into a beef and slugged a burly bartender. It didn't hurt the man at all. "You punch like a little girl," the bartender taunted.

Cummiskey, his feelings hurt, produced a .38. "Oh yeah? Well do I shoot like a little girl?" He fired three shots, and for the bartender lying dead on the floor it was a rhetorical question.

It was Cummiskey, widely feared in Hell's Kitchen, who taught Jimmy Coonan how to dismember a body with a knife. (Cummiskey's training came from work as a butcher.)

Joe would have whacked John Gotti if the mood had moved him, even though Gotti once *gave* him $75,000. He liked Mad Dog, but the gift also served to keep Sullivan around him, committing murders the future don deemed necessary. Joe would kill *anybody*, except his wife, Gail.

Sullivan used money he made from his hits to buy a house for himself and Gail in Richmond Hills, on the border of Brooklyn and Queens. I visited his home many times. Gail stayed on there until 1990 with the two children, comfortable with her large backyard and solid wood-and-brick home.

Even Sully occasionally became glutted with blood and violence, and then he'd take Gail to Europe for a vacation. They visited the mainland, loving the food and the culture, and also toured Ireland, where Joe made friends with members of the IRA. In the end, with the law closing in, he almost went to live in Ireland, where he would have been safe, but it didn't happen.

In 1976, Joe still had many crimes and murders to go. Amazingly, he hadn't hit full stride yet and, it must be said, neither had I.

Chapter 18

MURDER ON FURLOUGH

UNDERWORLD FIGURES SAID THEY DID ME A FAVOR BY ASSIGNING me outside jobs while I served my sentence; and I, in need of money, agreed. Still, these wiseguys had ulterior motives for making the offers. By contracting someone with an "I was behind bars when it happened" alibi, they bought an added edge against a prime worry: having blame traced back to them. In the event the truth about a certain crime was discovered, authorities might elect to overlook it rather than court a scandal guaranteed to ruin careers. How safe and/or duped would the public feel, knowing that killers could leave jail on furloughs to commit more murders?

For the 1977 Gino Gallina hit I wore a jogging suit and covered my face with black makeup. Joe Sullivan came dressed as a priest.

Usually I had no animosity toward a victim—I considered myself a professional doing my job—but Gallina I genuinely disliked. Talking out of both sides of his mouth as a rat was bad enough, but it galled me to see him strutting around in those $2,000 English suits that *my* money bought. It was ludicrous. I had to kill people so I could pay him to defend me against a previous murder. Moreover, I felt Jerry Rosenberg (who didn't charge a dime) had been more aggressive and effective on my behalf during the Bilello plea-bargain negotiations. Gallina, like many lawyers, was more dedicated to collecting fees than working to earn them.

Time magazine, November 21, 1977, wrote about the Gallina murder, hitting the mark squarely when it revealed the reason:

> Like the Mounties, the Mafia always seems to get its man. Unlike Canada's national police, however, organized crime always has murder on its mind. FBI and other Justice Department officials are now contemplating the disturbing fact that no protection—not even the supposed secrecy of grand jury proceedings—is a barrier to Mob hit men when they set out to protect *omerta,* the curtain of silence around Mafia affairs.
>
> Gino Gallina, 42, a handsome former Manhattan assistant district attorney who became a lawyer for the Mob, was gunned down in gangland style on a Greenwich Village street. Seven bullets riddled Gallina, and he died 90 minutes later.
>
> At the time, Gallina was a key witness before a Newark grand jury, testifying, among other things, on Mafia executions by a special hit squad armed with silencer-equipped .22-cal. automatic pistols. The ".22-cal. hitters" have claimed at least 20 victims in the past two years, including six FBI informants and potential witnesses. Though Attorney Gallina, who had defended major crime figures—notably members of the East Coast Genovese Mafia family—was killed by .38-cal. bullets, he was undoubtedly the 21st victim. Federal officials blame his slaying on a leak from the grand jury; leaks from secret Government files and sealed court records have led to the deaths of the other informants.
>
> Gallina's closed-door testimony concerned four top Genovese family gangsters: New Jersey's Vincent Gigante, John DiGilio, Salvatore Briguglio and Tommy Principe. The FBI considers all four to be prime suspects in ordering .22-cal. murders. Gallina told the grand jury how the Genovese leaders moved racket money into real estate in upstate New York.
>
> More than that, while singing to the jurors, Gallina also told

> federal officials that he could identify the killers of Teamster Boss Jimmy Hoffa. Missing for two years, Hoffa presumably was rubbed out by members of the Genovese family for disrupting lucrative deals it had developed with the Teamsters since 1967. Gallina informed the Feds that he had hidden a tape-recorded account of the killing that included the voices of mobsters who had a hand in it. He said Hoffa's body could be found from information on the tape.
>
> The problem now—besides plugging the leaks and protecting informers—is finding the tape. After Gallina's murder, investigators drew a blank in looking for the probable hiding place: a safe-deposit box he had rented under a fake name.

I don't believe there was any tape recording. Gallina had been wired up by the FBI to try to record information, but the people who knew weren't going to confide in him. Sally Bugs, who was killed not long after the Gallina murder, was trying to cut his own deal with the FBI (why help Gallina?) and, besides, Bugs didn't know where the body had been buried.

Fat Tony wouldn't have confided family business even to a priest in the confessional, and certainly not to Gino Gallina, a snitch whose killing Salerno ordered. John Sullivan was one of the most closemouthed gangsters I ever knew, and I knew a lot of them. Jimmy Coonan? Forget it. This savage man of the streets had only contempt for Gallina, a smooth-talking, soft-handed dandy. The Detroit connections? As far as I can tell, Giacalone and O'Brien had no reason to know Gallina even existed. Joe Sullivan? Joe also had a deep distrust of Gallina and no reason to tell him anything. When Mad Dog felt the need to confide in someone, he came to me.

There was nothing complex about buying a furlough. The drill was very simple. I had to notify, a week in advance, the official who sold the furloughs, and make the payment at that time. When the appointed hour arrived, the official called me (or whomever) out of my cell and took me down to Receiving. There I was given a street suit, and the clerk was notified that I had an approved leave. The clerk wouldn't know any better and wouldn't challange a high-ranking superior. The official would thereupon walk me onto the street and wish me a good time.

Getting back in was just as easy. I would report to Visitor's Reception, usually before 4:00 P.M., in time to be taken upstairs for the evening head count.

Whacking Gallina put me in need of a new lawyer, so Joe Sullivan introduced me to his mouthpiece, former U.S. Attorney General Ramsey Clark. The opposite of Gallina, Clark was deeply idealistic, a fighter for causes. A handsome 6'3", 190 pounds, he was Joe's good friend (Joe named a son Ramsey after him), and he recognized much good in Sully—it existed, though many will laugh.

I talked to Ramsey Clark a number of times, eliciting his advice but never formally retaining him. In the 1980s, when told I had become an informant, he said, "The Greek was about the last person anyone thought would rat."

During 1977, buying furloughs, I also killed two drug dealers and made several large heroin deliveries into Harlem. Except for these excursions to the outside, however, life had become harder for me. *Getting* to a position of respect and leadership in prison had been more enjoyable (at least in retrospect) than *being* there. The stark realities were bars and locks and somebody else telling me what to do. I spent many nights regretting that Richie Bilello murder; I'd paid a big price for respect.

Although I committed two more murders in 1978, I had to experience most other criminal activities vicariously through Joe Sullivan. He continued to visit me regularly, often accompanied by his wife, Gail. I appreciated their coming. They were good friends.

Joe told me about winning a shoot-out on Ninth Avenue against a cop killer named Tom the Greek. *This* Greek had been involved with Jimmy Coonan and several others in a Staten Island jewel heist, and then had absconded with the loot—half of which he gave to Gambino godfather Paul Castellano to buy protection.

Coonan was the wrong guy to cheat. He gave the contract to Joe, who located Tom the Greek, tracked his movements, and learned he regularly entered a Ninth Avenue building at a certain hour. On the selected day, Joe, wearing a disguise, rode a motorcycle past the Greek, then dismounted and charged his quarry on foot. Tom saw him coming, bubbles of foam about his mouth, and opened fire. Joe hit the pavement, aimed, and Tom the Greek would steal no more.

A highlight for me in 1978 was meeting, through Harold Konigsberg, the great heavyweight champion Joe Louis. The Brown Bomber visited Harold at MCC, and the mob strong-arm man introduced us. I asked for Louis's autograph, and he gave it to me.

I spent most of 1979 at the Eastern Correctional Facility at Napanoch, 120 miles north of New York City, a medium-maximum-security prison that the authorities tried to run like a college. Napanoch's main building resembled a Gothic castle with English-style guard towers. Built in 1900, Napanoch featured a lovely old church standing next to the ball field. Although the prison was old, it had an indoor track where I jogged, well-kept handball and basketball courts, and a let-live philosophy that made life bearable for inmates who didn't get out of line. Since I was shooting for parole, I was one of those inmates—most of the time.

Joe Sullivan's coming to see me, which couldn't have been convenient for him, gave me something to look forward to, and so did a few "conjugal" visits from women whom I paid guards to let me see.

A visit I didn't enjoy occurred when two FBI agents had me called out of my cell and seated in a vacant office. They wore typical G-man attire, gray suits and black wing-tip shoes. Without mincing words, one of them said, "We want to learn about your relationship with Joe Sullivan."

"He's a friend of mine."

"We have reason to believe he's been on fifty or sixty hits, and that you took part in some of them."

"That's bullshit."

"We know it for a fact." The G-man paused for a minute and then spread a cat-that-ate-the-canary smile across his face before asking, "When are you going in front of the parole board?"

"In eight months."

"We can arrange for you to be put on the street, *if* you'll give us information."

"I can't tell you nothing."

The FBI agent doing the talking got to the *real* point: "You don't need to inform on Joe Sullivan. Who we really want to hear about is Ramsey Clark."

"You've come to the wrong guy."

"Well what about Sullivan's hits?"

"I don't know nothing concerning that kind of shit."

"You're never going to make parole." He said it with such matter-of-fact authority I had to believe him.

"That's your opinion," I bluffed. "One thing's for damn sure: I'd rather stay here forever than fucking cooperate with you."

"Fine. Maybe we'll put your pal Joe Sullivan in here with you. He's violating *his* parole every time he visits this place."

They did try to go after Sully, but Ramsey Clark fought them off. I think the real reason the agents came to see me was part of a larger attempt to discredit the former U.S. Attorney General, whose politics the Bureau detested.

Several events occurred at Napanoch in 1980: my parole application, as predicted, got turned down—a devastating blow, even though I'd expected it; John Gotti sent a message to me that I should see him when I did get out—he had work for me; and I whiled away time by training the Napanoch boxing team. I was forty-one years old and not entirely comfortable with the perceptions the mostly younger prisoners had of me: a wise old head, albeit still nobody to cross.

Wise old head? I kept beating myself up over that fucking Bilello murder.

Floyd Patterson brought some of the fighters he managed to the prison, knowing they could gain valuable experience against genuine tough guys without having an official loss mar their records.

"How ya doin', Champ?" I greeted him.

"Looks like you got some strong competitors here," he said.

"You bet," I said, and one of my guys did beat one of his.

We had terrific matches at Napanoch, and the word spread. Sugar Ray Leonard and Roberto Duran came by to watch the fights.

Refusing to let the feds interrupt our friendship, Joe Sullivan still came to see me. One afternoon he related a story of Mafia treachery that to me best exemplifies the draconian plots-within-plots that typify life in the mob. Two murders, still unsolved, that Joe committed in furtherance of this treachery, proved to me once and for all that he was the outstanding contract killer of his generation.

The first hit was the headline-making killing of Philadelphia godfather Angelo Bruno, known as the Gentle Don (a misnomer). Bruno's consigliere, Antonio Caponigro, had sought out the Genovese family's Frank "Funzi" Tieri and asked permission to have his boss whacked. Tieri, who shared power with Fat Tony, told Caponigro to go ahead. The consigliere promised, in return, to hand over valuable Atlantic City gambling operations to Tieri. Mad Dog Joe Sullivan, recommended by Tieri, killed Angelo Bruno the night of March 21, 1980, emptying both barrels of a shotgun into his head from point-blank range as the godfather sat in a 1969 Chevrolet parked in front of his South Philadelphia home. Tieri had approved the Bruno murder ostensibly to obtain the bigger share of New Jersey gambling revenue, but why split it with Caponigro at all?

The overmatched, foolishly ambitious consigliere had a big surprise waiting for him. He came to New York for a meeting with Fat Tony, expecting to be christened the new Philadelphia godfather, and Salerno greeted and spoke briefly with him at his social club on 116th Street. After Fat Tony excused himself to "take a piss," actually to get out of range, Joe Sullivan materialized from hiding and riddled Caponigro with bullets.

Now the Genoveses had everything, just as Tieri had planned. Soon, because Tieri died about twelve months later of natural causes, all the gambling operations were in Fat Tony's hand.

This indeed was treachery: Caponigro betrayed Bruno; Tieri betrayed Caponigro; Tieri betrayed himself by dying; and even Fat Tony, with a 100-year RICO sentence waiting down the line, ended up with a handful of air. I saw Fat Tony in the late 1980s at MCC, an old, old man, a line of relatives waiting to visit him. Surely this most practical of gangsters realized that they queued not out of love, but greed—buzzards establishing a pecking order—for the vast fortune he could bequeath them. (Fat Tony died in prison on July 27, 1992.)

I've read numerous reports that Bruno's consigliere was savagely tortured and had money stuffed in his mouth and anus. I know Joe Sullivan never tortured anybody, and if the body was defiled, it was done by someone else and occurred after Caponigro's death. But what do the cops know? They never solved this case, nor the Bruno killing.

When Joe finished telling me about the Bruno and Caponigro hits, he said, "Greek, I'm really glad you and me have straightforward jobs. All we do is kill people; we don't have to get involved in all that bullshit family politics."

A few weeks later Joe came back and caught me on one of my rare paranoiac days. I asked him, "If somebody paid you, Sully, would you whack me?"

"Business is business," he said with a smile.

I didn't like his answer, and it must have shown on my face.

"Listen to me, brother Greek," he said. "No, I wouldn't kill you. You're my friend. Anybody who asks me to take you out, I whack him." Then Joe grew grave. "If it was flip-flopped, would you come after me?"

"Business is business," I said, making sure to smile.

At Napanoch I had long conversations with Harold (Kayo) Konigsberg, who had been convicted along with Tony Provenzano for the Anthony Castellito murder (both convictions were later reversed although Provenzano's was upheld on retrial). Konigsberg had excellent mob connections: Carmine Galante had been in his wedding party, and he had worked with Meyer Lansky. Numerous bodies were buried on this gangster's New Jersey chicken farm, a few of which the authorities dug up.

Life magazine, June 25, 1971, ran a lengthy article—"The Gorilla Cowed His Keepers"—about Kayo, describing "fists like sledgehammers and eyebrows that arch erratically over cold, sleepy eyes."

"He is a terrifying human being," *Life* decided, a fair enough assessment. "Those who know him best—lawmen, underworld associates, even his own lawyer—fear him most. 'Animal' is the word they use repeatedly to describe him."

Konigsberg was very proud of the *Life* story. He displayed it on a wall of his cell, and read it aloud to me. "Bastards don't know a hundredth of what went on, though," he said.

The FBI once ranked Kayo as the leading loan shark in the country. He enjoyed having late-paying clients, because it gave him the excuse to beat them with a lead-filled rubber hose, an exercise he loved, or dangle them out high-rise windows, which he found even more pleasurable. On these collections he was more fearsome than Red Kelly, because with Red someone else's money was at stake, while Konigsberg always recouped his own investments.

A lumbering, ugly giant, Kayo told me he had made several films of former heavyweight champion Joe Louis having sex with movie stars, and that he used this material to force Louis to make appearances at mob trials. Indeed, in 1957, when Jimmy Hoffa was being tried for bribery in a Washington, D.C., courtroom, the Brown Bomber showed up. In full view of the jurors (eight of the twelve were black), he wished the Teamster leader well.

Anyway, Konigsberg, like an earlier version of Chin Gigante, often faked insanity to beat court cases. He would show up for trial in a wheelchair, or on a stretcher, barefoot, his otherwise naked body wrapped in blankets, drool tracking down his chin. While his lawyer called him "obviously insane," Kayo would "flip into" a trance, motionless and staring straight ahead, whereupon the attorney would bemoan, "He's worse than insane—he's a vegetable."

Konigsberg wasn't insane at all, but he was a very vicious guy. He had many associates outside the prison, and they took pictures of the wives and children of guards, which he then showed to his keepers as a warning of what could happen if they messed with him.

Kayo spent time in many prisons (not as many as I, though; I believe, as will be demonstrated later, that I hold the world record) and authorities were always trying to send him somewhere else, make him some other warden's problem.

Konigsberg couldn't be controlled. He had well-paid lawyers to make sure guards would regret killing him, and no hack wanted to beat him or throw him into solitary because of fear of retaliation against the guard's family. Thus, the only hope was finding a prison foolish enough to take him.

I can't say I saw much good in Kayo. He knew a lot of mob stories, which I enjoyed hearing (it helped pass the time), so I hung around him, but compounding his overly brutal nature, he was also—when it suited him—a rat. Often he huddled with the feds, offering to give up this guy or that, if they'd just let him out.

The big event of 1981—the *only* event mattering to me—took place in June when, accompanied by my prison counselor, I again appeared in front of a parole-board officer to make my pitch for release.

The interview didn't begin encouragingly. "I don't think there's any hope for you, Mr. Frankos," said the parole-board member, a black woman in her sixties. "You're a bad apple."

"Why do you say that?" I tried to look hurt.

"There's nothing but violence on your record. You have no education. You . . . "

"I'm a high school graduate."

"No education *in here*. You never took advantage of any programs in here." She gave me a searching look. "How would *you* like to be killed at age forty-four?" She was referring to Richie Bilello.

"I'm sorry for what I done," I said, hoping my face reflected remorse. I'd been practicing for weeks. And I *was* sorry, not for killing him, but for getting caught, and for being so stupid.

"You're not sorry. But let me ask, why do you presume you deserve parole?"

"I done a lot of thinking these eight years. I feel bad about what I done. What I done to Mr. Bilello's family. I hope you'll give me a chance to make it up to them, and to make something of my own life too." These were words all parole officers want to hear.

"Do you have a job waiting for you?"

"Yes."

"What is this job?"

"I'd be working as a cook in a French restaurant on the East Side for a nice couple that's kindly giving me a chance." Actually, they were fronting the joint for Fat Tony. My job would be mostly no-show. The counselor, who was there to plead in my behalf, confirmed that I did indeed have employment waiting.

"Where do you intend to live, Mr. Frankos?"

"In Manhattan."

"Do you plan to go over to the West Side?" She was looking at a thick sheaf of papers, undoubtedly reports dealing in part with "known associates." Jimmy Coonan and the Sullivans, solid gold references with inmates, carried negative weight with this woman.

"No, ma'am," I answered. "I'm going to stay on the East Side. I'll keep my nose clean and work hard."

"Well, you *can't* go there [to the West Side] if we parole you. Which I don't think we will."

"I just want to work, make something of my life in the time I have left, do the right thing for myself." Again, code words: *do good for myself.* Parole-board members believe the key, the best motivation, is a selfish one. I had received this advice more than twenty years ago from veteran old-time inmates. Now I was the old-timer. I hoped it would work, it *had* to work, and I let myself think it might. It had been a couple of minutes since she'd called me a "bad apple."

"Have you seen a psychiatrist?"

"Yes, ma'am." I didn't add, *yeah, and what a crock of bullshit I fed him.*

"It's true," my counselor said, right on cue, confirming that I had consulted the prison shrink.

"I'll tell you what, Mr. Frankos," the parole-board officer said. "No decision will be made this instant. But if you do make parole and violate it, for any reason, you'll never get out of prison again, mark my words."

This was a hollow threat, but I attempted to look humble, worried, and thoughtful.

Three days later I received written notice that my release date was set for August 24. I screamed with joy, and everybody in the block knew what that meant. It sounded like all of them cheered, and late into the evening I heard shouts of encouragement, "Way to go, Greek!"

Chapter 19

MAD DOG SULLIVAN

A FOUR-ROOM APARTMENT (FULFILLING THE HOUSING PRECONdition of my parole), provided by the couple fronting my job at Fat Tony's restaurant, waited for me on East 53rd street near Second Avenue, but I didn't see the place until 5:00 A.M. on August 25, the day after I left Napanoch. I'd been picked up at the prison by four of Nicky Barnes's soldiers, driven to his nightclub in Harlem, and given a large "coming-out" party. I drank like the thirsty sailor on shore leave I once had been, gambled with Nicky's money in the club's back room, had sex with one of the half-dozen women he made available, and got pats on the back and congratulations on my release from guys I didn't even know. Clearly, Barnes intended to put me to work for him.

At 9:30 A.M., bleary-eyed from only 4½ hours sleep, I was awakened by a pounding on my apartment door. *What the fuck is this?* I thought, bumping my shin against a chair on the way to finding out.

It was Joe Sullivan, dressed in a hat and three-piece suit, a big shit-eating grin on his face. We grabbed and hugged each other in the hallway, and I said, "Come in and talk, my friend."

"That can wait," he said, waving toward the stairs. "I've got a package for you."

I heard three unmistakable light clicks of high heels on the floor, and out stepped a beautiful long-legged, smooth-skinned Latin woman wearing nothing but a black see-through peignoir cinched at the waist by a huge red shiny bow.

"Welcome home, Greek," Joe said. "She's all yours. I'll be back in an hour. There are a lot of people who'd like to see you, so make it fast."

It took willpower not to make it *too fast* with this foxy, curvaceous lady who performed some absolutely mind-blowing moves. We got it on twice, and she had left when Mad Dog returned after sixty minutes, as promised.

Once inside his white Cadillac, he said, "We got plenty of work to do. You'll be a millionaire, my friend, before this year is out."

These were words I wanted to hear. But I had intended to spend at least a week taking it easy, enjoying the outside after 7½ years in rathole prisons. *Ah, what the hell,* I thought, *I can adjust.* It was great sitting next to Sully. Where were we heading? It didn't matter. I was free, and adventure and money awaited.

We picked up John Sullivan, who was waiting for us on 59th Street at the New York Coliseum, which he managed for Fat Tony. Joe told me John had a matter to discuss privately with me, and that was okay with him. "Hope it's something good," he said.

It was all bad. After breakfast in a nice 49th Street eatery, where we relived old times, John Sullivan and I retreated to the toilet for a talk. He handed me an envelope containing $2,500—a "coming-home present" he said in that gruff voice—and got right down to business.

"I don't want you talking to Joe about this," he said.

"Okay," I promised. Maybe I'd tell him, maybe I wouldn't. But I didn't say this to John Sullivan.

"Fat Tony would like you to hit Jimmy Coonan," he said.

I tried to show no emotion, but my mind raced. I suspected right away it might be John Sullivan himself who wanted the boss of the Westies whacked. I guessed that he had never really accepted Coonan's beating him out of the Hell's Kitchen rackets. "Why Coonan?" I asked.

"Coonan is backed by Paulie Castellano," John said, referring to the Gambino godfather, "and Fat Tony is *our* man. This is a power move for control over the docks."

It could have been true. Salerno lusted for the waterfront profits, which he'd have if John Sullivan ran the show on the Upper West Side. Still, I wasn't sure how firmly Coonan stood in Castellano's corner; he'd work for anyone who would pay him. (The fact is Coonan would later be part of the murder squad that took Castellano out and put John Gotti in.) Most important, I didn't like that line about Fat Tony being "our man." My entire criminal life had been a struggle to avoid being some boss's bought-and-paid-for flunkie.

It had been a narrow path to tread, as this meeting showed. Sullivan wanted me to kill Coonan—God knows why, maybe it really was Fat Tony, but it could be for personal reasons or even a long-range scheme to eliminate everyone connected to the Hoffa murder. If so, that meant *my* turn was coming, and maybe John Sullivan's, too.

What the fuck to do? I liked Coonan, had done jobs for him. Now Fat Tony and John Sullivan, men I also liked and worked for, wanted me to kill him.

"Jesus Christ," I finally said to John, "I just got out of the joint. Coonan won't go out easy. Let me fucking think about it and get back to you."

John gave me one of his hard-guy looks. "Don't think too long," he said.

Joe and I dropped John back at the Coliseum, and then Joe parked in front of the first pay phone he found and called Jimmy Coonan, of all people, in New Jersey. While they talked, my brain threatened to short out from overload. Why did John Sullivan want Mad Dog kept in the dark about the Coonan hit? Or was this a test, and was Joe at this moment luring him to his death?

Coonan met us ninety minutes later at an upscale bar on 57th. Everything seemed on the up and up. We grabbed each other warmly, did a little circular dance, then sat down for some serious drinking. Coonan had brought a guy named Tommy Collins along with him. (Collins later ended up getting forty years in the same trial that put Coonan away.)

I could see that the Irish boss was doing just fine: confident, brash, and rolling in money. After a little bullshit about that rooftop shoot-out and the Auburn uprising, he sent Collins out "to see that guy on the corner." Collins returned a few minutes later with $3,000, still another "coming-out present." Why Coonan didn't just peel the money out of his pocket, I don't know.

Coonan was a regular chatterbox, telling Joe and me about all the work he wanted us to do. First there were garment district shakedowns, but there would be murders, too. He had all kinds of killings people wanted him to commit, and his own hitters were overextended. "The price of fame," I said.

My ears pricked when he told of having trouble with some of "the wops," but he said he could handle it. What he meant was he could handle it with help from me and Joe. I braced for something bizarre, like his saying he wanted John Sullivan whacked, but instead he talked about John Gotti and Paulie Castellano. Gotti, he said, was a "good wop." He did a lot of business with Gotti. Castellano was "a bad wop," no street smarts, too prudish (translation: he didn't want his people dealing drugs), too "upper-class snooty." This didn't sound like someone who—as John Sullivan averred—was "backed by Paulie Castellano." Increasingly I believed that whacking Coonan was John's idea, and we might not have backing from Fat Tony.

Coonan waxed so eloquent about the fine qualities of John Gotti that he insisted Joe and I call on him right away. "I know for a fact he wants to see you, and he'll be at the Ravenite now."

After a few more drinks Joe and I headed for Mulberry Street in Little Italy and the infamous Ravenite Social Club, a center for the Gambino family. Bleak and drab on the outside—no sign alerts passersby to this New York landmark—it had an utterly stark interior. The big front room, lit up bright as a movie set, had tables and chairs set about randomly, gray and white paint peeling from the walls, and no shadows for lurking gangsters. But gangsters were everywhere: mostly old-timers playing cards, camping out the way war veterans do at a VFW hall; and a few young up-and-comers, using the place to get their marching orders. The Ravenite, very loud, was no place for thinking, or for quiet sit-downs; wiseguys went elsewhere for that.

The overwhelming impression inside the Ravenite, however, was light, so bright that coming into the joint out of a dark night could temporarily blind a visitor. Not that many people visited this inner sanctum, which was for wiseguys only (unlike Fat Tony's club on 116th Street, where businessmen called to pay homage), with just a few trusted others—like Sully and me—allowed.

Gotti spotted us the moment we entered. He had been standing in the middle of the room with three of his crew, talking loudly and waving his arms, two traits I'd witnessed many times at Dannemora. He stopped in the middle of his sentence, literally ran at me with his arms open, hugged me, picked me off my feet, kissed me on both cheeks, and carried me the length and breadth of the big room. He was far too dramatic, too excessive, but his crew loved it, and I have to say I was caught up in the display.

When at last my feet touched the floor again, he scanned me up and down and said, "You're looking good. The same old handsome Greek." He hesitated. "But still not as handsome as me, my man." He roared with laughter, gave me another rib-crunching hug, and then one to Mad Dog. No doubt about it, the future godfather knew how to welcome people.

Gotti introduced us around, though we already knew most of these mobsters, and then took us to a nearby diner for strong espresso and serious talk. It was all one-sided. He never stopped talking, and we didn't interrupt.

The bottom line was he had towering ambitions—and a lot of young Turks who were fanatically loyal to him. He was headed for the top, and wanted to know if we were "with him."

With him? We weren't "with" anybody, but we didn't tell him that. We did say we were available for jobs. Gotti didn't push it, didn't bluster or threaten. He knew he dealt with two professional killers, and around gangsters like us he always backed away a little, tried diplomacy.

"Good," Gotti said, getting up to go. "You'll make a fucking ton of money with me. Call Angelo Ruggiero in the next few days. Everything's set up."

It was after 9:00 P.M. this August 25, 1981, when Joe Sullivan pointed his white Cadillac toward Richmond Hills. He had called ahead and told Gail to set an extra place at the dinner table for me.

Before we'd gone far, Sully pulled onto a dock and pointed down to the water. "Greek, you know what this is?"

"Of course. Unless they changed the name while I was in the joint, it's the Hudson River."

"This is one of my favorite graveyards. I've buried a lot of guys here—a few you knew; some that I didn't. Here is where I dump 'em, here is where they rest."

Back in the car, on the Westside Highway, he said, "Greek, I need you on some hits I have lined up. In fact, two guys got to go this week." He drove a little farther, then rapped the steering wheel with his fist and laughed. "See, you really are going to be a millionaire. Everybody wants you, including me."

Yeah. But so far the only one I knew I'd work with was Joe.

When we went in his house, Gail and I exchanged hugs and hellos, and she said, "Are you hungry?"

"You can ask that, knowing how many years it's been since I ate a real home-cooked meal?"

Finishing a delicious corned beef, Sully's favorite dish, he said, "Come downstairs, buddy, and let me show you the addition I built while you were away."

Hearing this from the average suburbanite, one would expect to see a cozy wood-paneled den or maybe a new pool table in a rec room. Not here. Ever the pro, Sullivan had installed a firing range in the cellar to practice shooting his 9-millimeter and Magnum into sandbag targets. As we fired a few rounds, it felt good to have a gun in my hand again.

After midnight, while he drove me back to my apartment, I said, "I appreciate you showing me around, Sully, but I'd really rather party for a few days, get my feet back on the ground before we plunge into a bunch of heavy shit." He, John Sullivan, Jimmy Coonan, and John Gotti were too much for anyone to handle in one day. Mad Dog said he understood. So I was surprised when he was at my door yelling at 9:30 A.M., August 26. "Get up, Greek! Get up! It's party time!"

And it was. Booze and dames, cocaine and gambling, great food and fancy nightclubs. We went until 4:00 A.M.—harder for him than me because he had that drive back and forth to Richmond Hills—and started again at 9:30 A.M.

After three straight days of alcohol and fleshpots, I said, "God-damn, Sully, going back to work will be easier on the body than this."

On August 30, ready for action, I called John Gotti's good friend Angelo Ruggiero. "Hey Greek," he said, "John wants to see you. Come on out to the club." This was the Bergin Hunt and Fish Club in Ozone Park, Queens, where Gotti conducted business.

A meet was set up three blocks from the Bergin, at my insistence. Joe Sullivan had told me an "army" of cops constantly watched this wiseguy hangout, and I didn't need a parole violation for consorting with known criminals.

Gotti was pacing on the street corner when I arrived, talking with Willie Boy Johnson and Angelo Ruggiero. I approached with my hand out, but he grabbed my shoulders and kissed me on each cheek. After handing me $3,500—"I'll get this late coming-home present out of the way first"—we talked for a few minutes about our time together at Dannemora. Like at the meet several days before, I didn't bring up the handball games or his knockout loss to Nicky G.

"Why don't you move out here?" Gotti asked.

"I got a place in Manhattan."

"Get another one. I want you near me."

I said I'd think it over. I didn't intend to work exclusively for him.

"Well, I'm glad you came out. I want you to meet Funzi and Arnold. They got a need for you."

He referred to Alphonse Sisca and Arnold Squitieri, two of his major drug-dealing associates. Squitieri, particularly, I'd known from before. He was an immaculate dresser who wore pounds of jewelry, had a passing resemblance to Warren Beatty, and was nicknamed The Gimp because of a club foot. Squitieri sold to Harlem blacks—he knew every important black dealer in the city—and made piles of money. He was a junkie in the mid-1950s who simply stopped using and started dealing.

Squitieri and his friend-since-childhood, Funzi Sisca, were in charge of Gotti's drug operation. Their dope came mainly from the Cotroni Gang in Montreal and other tight connections in Sicily, Syria, Afghanistan, and Turkey.

My first delivery wasn't for Squitieri and Sisca, however, but for Gotti himself. Transporting two pounds of pure heroin, I rode with one of his soldiers to a nightclub in Harlem. Our red Corvette was met by a BMW carrying a major dealer named Vince. "Greek!" he said, surprised to see me, "How ya' doing'?" We had done time together. "You working for Gotti?"

"Riding shotgun. It's a one-time deal."

"Let's get together later. We'll party."

"I'd like to Vince, but I can't," I said. Common sense dictated getting in and out of Harlem as quickly as possible. Aside from gangs always looking to rip off a white dealer, there were plenty of garden-variety muggers I didn't want to encounter. I suspected, correctly as it turned out, that Vince had posted snipers on nearby rooftops.

"You got the goods?" Vince asked Gotti's soldier.

"On the floor," he said. "If you got the money, we'll make the exchange."

Vince motioned to another black man who emerged from the BMW and handed me a brown paper bag stuffed with hundred-dollar bills. We turned over the heroin and drove away. Gotti had said not to stay and count, and we didn't.

I met Squitieri and Sisca a few days later. Although residents of New Jersey, they did business out of Astoria, Queens, and I took a second apartment out there to be around them.

Squitieri was a very generous guy. He could afford to be, of course, but so could other Mafiosi who'd try to beat friends out of a cup of coffee. Arnold paid $2,500 toward my apartment, took me on a shopping spree for clothes that set him back $10,000, and arranged a good deal for me on a 1977 white Cadillac. He did a lot of other arranging too: I got a driver's license (very illegally), a passport (in case I had to go overseas to pick up drugs), a fake birth certificate, a fake Social Security number, and *five* credit cards. He accomplished all this in one day!

My first job for him and Sisca involved riding shotgun with them up to the Canadian border to pick up thirty-five kilos of heroin from the Cotroni family, which ran the Montreal Mafia. Our contact, a very tough international drug dealer who enjoyed calling himself a "professional pharmacist," was largely responsible for making Montreal the most violent city in Canada. His soldiers delivered the drugs to us at a motel, and our return trip to New York City proved uneventful.

As I've said, Squitieri was no tightwad. He gave many an ex-con fresh out of prison a half kilo of heroin to "get you on your feet." Squitieri knew I already had strong connections in Harlem, and he helped me set up my own minibusiness by providing kilos of heroin on consignment.

Squitieri behaved like a real-life Santa Claus. He carried a thick wad of hundreds, peeling them off to down-and-out strangers he encountered on the street. The cops ultimately estimated his personal wealth at $10 million, though it was probably more. When he got arrested—a frequent occurrence—he always paid bail with cash. His wife simply dipped into one of his many safe-deposit boxes and came up with the money.

Squitieri and Gotti were a sight to behold at Aqueduct. Neither one of them could pick a winner, and their daily losses usually exceeded $30,000. On weekdays, when the track betting handle was smaller, their wagers alone could make a horse the favorite, and often the public got sucked into betting a loser by following the "smart" money appearing on the tote board. As for gambling, Gotti's money was never smart.

I could have worked twenty-four hours a day for Squitieri and Sisca, and never caught up with everything that needed doing. But I didn't let myself fall into that grind. I reserved at least half my time for Manhattan and hanging around Joe Sullivan. I tried to dodge John Sullivan—I didn't want anything to do with hitting Coonan—and though he knew how to get hold of me, he didn't.

A typical day for Mad Dog and me when we were both on the outside in 1981 started with his authoritative 9:30 A.M. wake-up knock on my apartment door.

While I showered and dressed, Joe phoned around, asking, in code, if there was "work" for us. Work meant a hit. During this regular routine, he checked, like a stockbroker calling clients, the Mafia social clubs first, then contacts with the Greek gangsters, Irish gangsters, Arab gangsters, Jewish gangsters, and the black mob in Harlem. Usually something popped up, also relayed in code, whereupon we drove to an agreed-upon spot and obtained the details.

If nothing did, we ate breakfast in a greasy spoon. "Don't worry," Joe would say. "I got another job I've just been postponing. You want in, buddy?"

"How much is my share?"

"I'll give you five thousand."

"Let's talk about it over a drink." He knew I'd accepted. I just wanted a drink.

We'd go to a bar. I'd have a Tom Collins; he'd sip white wine and give me the scoop. Sully always had a picture and the daily schedule of the intended victim. We would discuss every contingency—especially what we'd do in case of an unexpected intervention—then head out and take care of business.

When there wasn't a job, Joe drove us to various social clubs, just to keep our hands in the action, and we bullshitted, drank, gambled, and snorted with the wiseguys.

That's how we spent the afternoons, driving from one social club to another, getting high. We would enjoy a good dinner, maybe see Coonan at one of the dives he hung out in, then have a quick coke and sex party in some hooker's apartment. About 1:00 A.M. Joe would go home to Gail, and I'd hop from nightclub to nightclub until 3:00 A.M. I knew Sully would be back at my door at 9:30.

We never tired of each other's company or talking about sports, hits we did together, and guys we knew in prison. As multiple losers, our conversations often wandered to how bad it would be to get busted again. Sully would ask, "You still want to whack this guy?"

I would think it over. "Why the fuck not?"

Now and then we drank and relaxed at Joe's house in Richmond Hills. Sometimes we worked there too: like the time we killed and dismembered three hoods in his basement.

I received a contract from John Gotti to whack three unconnected karate experts for sticking up his loan sharks. These were tough, brainless cowboys who would happily have held up Paul Castellano or the chairman of the New York Stock Exchange. It didn't matter to them.

Joe lured each of them to his house with the same story: "As an intermediary for the Gambino family, I want to relay an offer from Gotti to let bygones be bygones if you'll agree to stay away from his loan sharks."

I doubt it even crossed the minds of these punks that Joe would be bold enough to ice them in his own home.

When we had the three in Sullivan's basement, we pulled pistols, sweet-talked them into lying on the floor with assurances that we only wanted to search them, and in less than two seconds shot each one in the back of the head.

That was the easy part, the killing. Next, donning goggles and gloves, we chainsawed the bodies into several dozen parts, then spent hours scrubbing and cleaning the basement, and, finally, transported the remains upstate for burial.

Joe and I enjoyed coming up with off-the-wall scores. We talked about kidnapping and ransoming Frank Sinatra's bodyguard, an overrated piece of shit named Jilly Rizzo who had much of the media convinced he was the toughest creature on two feet. "Wouldn't you love to make that arrogant bastard cry?" Sully asked me.

"Can't wait," I said. "Counting Sinatra's cash will feel pretty good too. Old Blue Eyes will pay through the ass to get him back."

But like other ideas, such as robbing cashier cages at Aqueduct, this one never got out of the bullshitting stage.

Much more serious was a contract Fat Tony Salerno gave Joe to murder Frank Sinatra. Salerno had heard that the crooner might be called in front of a grand jury and questioned about the bankruptcy of the Westchester Premier Theater. Sullivan hated Sinatra, and began researching how best to perform the hit. I think the man who escaped from Attica and killed godfather Angelo Bruno would have succeeded, but Fat Tony ultimately called off what would have been one of the most sensational murders in American history.

First-rate killers-for-hire are never short of work. When one or the other of us got too busy, Sully gave me some of his hits, and I handed him some of mine. I silenced a witness against a Queens drug dealer for him, and Joe whacked a black hoodlum for me.

We committed two killings the morning before going to that game in the Meadowlands where Mad Dog pointed out Hoffa's resting place, and another that night.

The murders became so surreal I once went with Sully on a double hit not knowing the names of the victims or why we were killing them.

My most out-of-character job began on October 11, 1981, when I "switched sides" and worked as a cop, sort of. I was hired directly by Fat Tony Salerno.

The day before, at Our Lady of Mount Carmel Convent on 116th Street, a nun had been beaten, raped and sodomized. Two attackers had shoved a broom up inside her, carved twenty-seven crosses on her rear and breasts with a sharpened nail file, then peed on her and shoved her down a flight of stairs.

Salerno was genuinely outraged. He hadn't always been Fat Tony, Mafia Kingpin—once he'd had a mother who loved him, nuns who taught him, Jesus Christ! what was it with these new animals, a *sister* of the Church, for Christ's sake—and he *suspended all but the most urgent Genovese family operations* so his soldiers could locate the perpetrators.

I was called to 116th Street and asked to join the search because of my familiarity with the area. Fat Tony said, "I'm offering a $25,000 reward for the filthy scumbags, dead or . . . dead." For two days I questioned a variety of lowlifes to learn the word on the street—the sick creeps were probably out bragging. Meanwhile, Salerno's minions, assisted by black drug dealers in Harlem, fanned through an ever-widening circle of neighborhoods. These dope peddlers, and Fat Tony himself, though shocked by the savage attack, capitalized on this opportunity to earn goodwill for themselves. The nun had been a particularly admirable individual, known for good works with children and the poor, and mobsters could expect many benefits if they brought the attackers to justice, particularly the ballooning realization that at crunch time criminals were more effective than police.

I would have bet on the Mafia against the cops—Fat Tony had very creative ways to extract information—but it was ultimately the work of an officer named Bo Dietl that led to collaring the perverts—one in Chicago and the other in New York. Their names were Harold Wells and Max Lindeman, and they should have counted themselves very fortunate that the police, not the Genoveses, caught them.

My life took a terrible change for the worse on October 15, 1981. As I entered Jilly's (a nightclub named for Sinatra's bodyguard) in midtown Manhattan to collect a debt, eight cops surrounded me and threw me to the sidewalk. They jammed shotguns to my head, handcuffed and shackled me, and carried me like a side of beef into a waiting limo (yes, a limo!), which took me to the precinct.

They took $2,300 out of my pocket, a $1,700 watch off my wrist, and a $4,000 pinkie ring.

I was put into a cell removed from other prisoners, and for the next few hours sat watching a parade of black detectives amble by the bars *to look at me*. I later learned the reason: they wanted to see the white hitter they'd been told had the balls to go into black neighborhoods and kill.

Ultimately I was driven out to Yonkers and handcuffed to a railing in the police station. It wasn't long before an assistant district attorney, wearing a friendly smile, came over to talk.

"How are you, Donald?"

"Who are you?"

"I'm Robert Neary." I'd heard of him. "Here's my card."

"I don't want your fucking card."

"Have you ever heard of Clarence Jones?"

"No."

Neary sighed. "All right, Mr. Frankos, you'll be our guest this morning. We'll take you to a lineup."

I was unable to contact the lawyer I wanted, and for the lineup I was represented by a public defender.

It turned out that a former basketball-star-turned-drug-dealer named Clarence Jones had been killed outside the door of his Bronx apartment on September 12, and the cops figured the killers were me and an ex-convict named Joe Kersch.

They had a witness. Jones's girlfriend had been with him when he got gunned down, and now she stood behind a one-way mirror and picked me out, a truly astounding feat. If I had done that hit, I would have been wearing so much makeup not even Joe Sullivan could have identified me.

But what kind of defense would this be? "Hey, she can't know it's me, because on all my other hits I wore great disguises."

How would the jury like that?

Or my lawyers could call Sid Cesspool and Ollie Outhouse to testify, "Yeah, the Greek was one of the best. Always wore disguises. His fuckin' mother wouldn't know him, not when he was out whackin' all those guys."

I knew as soon as I stepped out of the lineup that things didn't look good for me. I could see it in the faces of the cops. They were very serious this time. They considered me a menace and wanted me bad.

I got sent to Attica, where the prosecutor intended to keep me until the case came to trial. Joe Sullivan managed to contact me and passed along one of his most ingenious schemes. This was in March 1982, a few weeks after his own arrest for several homicides. Mad Dog suggested that at my trial he would confess to being the hitter: since he was indeed an infamous contract killer, the jury would have plenty of reasonable doubt. Then *I* would testify at *his* trials, taking credit for those murders.

It might have worked. Of course, I had alibis for Joe's homicides, and he had one for mine, so we would be acquitted even if the prosecutors got cute and decided to switch the indictments the way we switched the murders. The plan fell through when we realized that one of Joe's killings had occurred *after* I had been arrested.

Mad Dog had been hiding out for several months before they caught him, and his capture prompted a large one-word banner headline on the front page of the *New York Post:*

SEIZED!

Underneath the headline was a picture of Joe and a girlfriend posing as Bonnie and Clyde. The girlfriend was dressed as a flapper; Joe wore a 1920s hat, coat, vest, black shirt, and white tie. "I wanted to go down in a blaze of gunfire," the caption read, and I believed Sully had really said that.

The *Post's* front page graded as subdued when compared to the inside of the tabloid. Across an entire page screamed the headline, 'MAD DOG' HITMAN, and related stories used lines like, "one of the most dangerous fugitives alive," "the most wanted hitman in the country," and "the most dangerous man in America."

Eight FBI agents caught Joe by surprise on February 23, 1982, outside the Denonville Motel in Rochester. A rat had tipped his location. Paul Meyers, owner of the motel, witnessed the arrest:

"When they turned him around his face looked completely casual, like he was saying, 'So you got me, so what?'"

At Attica I couldn't shake bad vibes about my bust and resorted to desperate measures. I made elaborate plans to become the *second* inmate ever to escape from Attica.

Faking an illness, I got myself admitted to the prison hospital, behind which stood a guard tower that was left unmanned between midnight and 8:00 A.M. I told myself, *Get your ass out of the country. Go to Greece, just like Pete Diapoulos did. You speak the language. You'll be at home there.*

I arranged to obtain a pistol from an inmate, a needed accessory because die-hard officers patrolled the hospital, and a shank might not deter them. I figured I could round them up, secure them with sheets, lock them in a barred room and scale the unguarded wall. A call girl I knew had agreed to wait outside with a car.

At the key moment my gun supplier apparently got cold feet, stalled, and finally said he couldn't deliver the weapon for a week. Even that would have been okay, but then he ratted, and I needed to think of something else.

I saw doom approaching. I had never been so depressed. All my other arrests, even for the Richie Bilello murder, had carried sentences I found bearable. But if they nailed me for Clarence Jones, I would likely die in jail. I was forty-three years old, able to take care of myself, but the inmates were getting younger, more violent, more *crazily* violent, and the time would come when I'd get caught by surprise. Even before that happened, I'd have to kill a few of them, and my enthusiasm for prison battles had waned over the years.

I came up with another idea. I had watched others pull the bug act on numerous occasions, and decided to try it myself. At the least, I reasoned, it would postpone the upcoming trial while a battery of shrinks attempted to determine if I was faking. Maybe Gotti could buy off that witness for me. I mean it: she *could not* have identified me.

I scrounged a rope, tied it in a hangman's knot, and looped it over my head, wondering all the time if I really wanted to proceed with this charade. There I was, my feet flat on the floor, the rope not attached to anything except my neck, when a guard walked by. His eyes bulged, then he pressed the button on his walkie-talkie and shouted, "Suicide! We got a hang-up over here!" He meant "hanger."

I was still standing there, feet firmly planted on the floor, when the goon squad arrived. The guy in charge, a hack with experience, looked at me and shook his head, a can't-you-do-better-than-this expression on his face.

I consoled myself that at least John Gotti seemed concerned about my welfare. He kept my commissary account filled to the maximum, sent thrice-weekly messages that I "shouldn't worry," and then outdid even himself by dispatching an emissary: a gorgeous twenty-three-year-old Puerto Rican woman who said John wanted her to marry me so I could have regular conjugal visits. Also, she could deliver messages back and forth.

It was an offer worth mulling, but one I really couldn't accept. I remembered the looks on the faces of those cops, and the confident manner of Robert Neary, and I knew I was in a world of hurt.

Chapter 20

CONTRACT ON A U.S. ATTORNEY

THE ASSAULTS BEGAN ON JANUARY 13, 1983, IN THE Westchester County Jail bullpen an hour before our pretrial hearing got underway, when my codefendant Joe Kersch asked for an aspirin.

"You can't have one," the guard said.

"I've got a terrible headache," Kersch said. "I'm not going to court without an aspirin."

"Yeah, you are."

Whereupon half-a-dozen guards started clubbing *both of us*, knocking us to the floor, kicking us in the ribs. As they dragged us from the jail to the court, one of them said, "We got something real good for you when you get back."

I spent the first day of the trial wondering what had set off the guards. They might have been acting on behalf of associates of the murdered Jones (a major drug dealer), but more likely hacks being hacks, they simply knew our history, had worked themselves into a frenzy, and decided to take the first opportunity to prove we weren't so tough.

The "something real good" started at 9:00 P.M. that night. What happened was as described by my lawyer, Julia Heit, in her brief on appeal: the hacks entered my cell, slammed me against the wall, stripped me, and shackled me. Then one of them bent over me and bit a plug of flesh out of my cheek. One of his compadres took over and repeatedly smashed into my face with his fist. Another spat on me.

At the same time two other hacks were twisting my legs; I thought they would break the bones. Still another struck me with a metal object wrapped in a towel.

But the main tormentor, the one inflicting the most pain and getting the bulk of my attention, was the hack with the cigarettes. He would light one, frantically puff it to a red-hot glow, and grind it out on my exposed skin. Then he would light another, and another.

Naked and shackled, facedown on the bunk in my cell, I heard Kersch screaming from *his* cell; a similar treatment was being administered to him.

When the hacks were finally satisfied, they walked out with the promise that I could expect more of the same the next morning. I stayed chained all night, unable even to crawl to the toilet, with the cell window wide open to a freezing winter wind.

The next morning, January 14, the Westchester hacks cranked themselves into still another fury, swinging at me with their fists, each one taking his best shot.

In the courtroom the next morning Kersch and I looked like hell. Since they shackled us and made us wear other prisoners' clothing, the jurors had to wonder about what kind of animals they had been called upon to judge.

I sat there in a daze, barely conscious, as Kersch's lawyer registered a protest to the court about our treatment. After hearing the complaint, the judge granted a recess of several days for Kersch and me to "recover." The guards claimed they had beaten us as we had been trying to escape.

My appeal also documented the guards' next move: the beatings stopped, but the intimidation did not. The cell window was deliberately kept open to the January cold, and they removed the mattress from my bed. I was continuously shackled in place and deprived of anything to cover me. Worse, the guards destroyed my notes—names and telephone numbers of possible alibi witnesses—and wouldn't grant my request for pen and paper. After the beatings my mind was too disoriented to remember what I had previously written.

The evidence against me consisted of that eyewitness and an alert neighbor of the murdered Jones who had noticed a "strange" car in the apartment complex parking lot and written down the license number. The plates were traced to an acquaintance who had loaned me the vehicle.

The trial atmosphere resembled what one might encounter at a football game between two teams with loyal noisy fans. Our "supporters"—mostly a big contingent of middle-aged and older white women—filled one side of the courtroom. I had no idea what brought out the "Westchester County Knitting Society," as Kersch described them. In addition, a few of Gotti's beefy soldiers showed up each day, winking at me and glowering at the jurors. But if their purpose was to frighten, they didn't stay long enough or go far enough.

Sitting on the other side of the aisle were cops every bit as intimidating as Gotti's wiseguys. And these cops didn't pop in for a minute or two and then leave. They stayed, a battalion in blue, their very presence screaming *yes, we have jobs and homes, but right now making sure you nail these animals—which you'd better do—ranks more important.* Also on the other side were friends, relatives, and associates of Clarence Jones, a sea of black faces.

The judge gave me twenty-five-to-life, and I thought, immediately, *Oh, oh. This time it really is bye-bye Greek.*

What kind of trial did I get? My lawyer's appeal brief read, in part:

> Because the Correction Officers destroyed his clothing, the defendant was compelled to wear the clothing of another inmate, whose clothing did not fit. He thus appeared before the jury that was to determine his fate in a shabby and bruised state.

> In *Estelle v. Williams*, 425 U.S. 501, 505 (1976), the Supreme Court recognized that a defendant being tried while wearing prison garb created a "continuing influence" that could well "affect a juror's judgment by allowing impermissible factors [to come] into play." The Supreme Court stressed in *Taylor v. Kentucky*, 436 U.S. 478, 485 (1978) that "one accused of a crime is entitled to have his guilt or innocence determined solely on the basis of evidence introduced at trial, and not on grounds of . . . other circumstances not adduced as proof at trial."
>
> The fact that the defendant was subject to such severe torture immediately prior to and during his trial is shocking. It is no less shocking that his counsel (Heit replaced earlier counsel) did nothing to extricate him from this terrible ordeal and cavalierly had him proceed to trial under these horrendous circumstances. Counsel's silence on this record constituted nothing more than an implicit acquiescence to the barbarous treatment afforded his client by State officials. Accordingly, the defendant's conviction should now be set aside and a new trial ordered.

Thinking about that minimum twenty-five years I'd have to serve plunged my mind into depths of darkness, despair, and brooding thoughts of revenge. I can't even be considered for release until 2006. A good lawyer, I believed, could have beaten the Clarence Jones murder rap.

My friend Joe Kersch, who gave a partial confession (he never named me as his partner), received the same twenty-five-to-life. This tough guy—he was three times prison welterweight boxing champion—also absorbed a savage beating from those guards, who never would have dared fight him fairly.

After we were found guilty, they sent us to Sing Sing, where we filed a civil damage lawsuit for the injuries we suffered in Westchester County Jail. From Sing Sing I got transferred briefly to Attica, but the officials there didn't want me, saying that, like Kayo Konigsberg, I was too dangerous. They sent me to Auburn, and while there I learned Joe Sullivan had received a 100-year sentence. Without a legal miracle or, more likely, one of his patented escapes, Mad Dog would probably never get out.

I thought a lot about my friend of twenty years, and again realized there had never been anyone like him. Whenever possible—as an insurance policy—Joe insisted on cutting the throat of his victim. Behind his back, wiseguys gossiped that this "unnecessary" coup de grace confirmed a suspected deep streak of sadism, of blood lust. Maybe. But in the final analysis, if Mad Dog had stuck to his throat-slashing method—be it precaution or excess—he might not now be serving time for murder. After Joe had shot a man, his grisly work was interrupted by a noise upstairs. Leaving to investigate, he'd ordered his accomplice to finish the job. The guy with him hadn't had the stomach for it, which allowed the wounded man to survive and testify against Joe.

Joe Sullivan's life cried out for a movie to be made about it, and actor Jon Voight hung around Mad Dog when he was on the street, gleaning bits and pieces of his remarkable story. Joe was halfway serious when he confided selected details of his life. I wonder if Voight realized that *whatever* he told him ranked as understatement.

I found Sully just incredible. He joined the Fortune Society, a support group for convicts, helped a lot of people (who could deny that he knew of what he preached?), and became a sought-after speaker at prisons, colleges, and liberal gatherings. He employed humor to relax audiences, a few of whom knew they listened to perhaps the century's most merciless hands-on killer. After one speech he delivered for the Fortune Society, he headed straight out and fulfilled a murder contract.

The only person Joe had the slightest fear of was his wife Gail, a woman who rode him in ways that would have gotten Fat Tony Salerno killed twenty times over. Joe tried to respond, once, by threatening to whack her, but she just laughed. An icy broad. Gail didn't fear death, or him, and he knew it.

Joe Sullivan committed the vast majority of his murders between

1975 and 1981. He carried out hits for John Sullivan, Jimmy Coonan, Junior Persico, Carmine Tramunti, Fat Tony Salerno, and John Gotti, often traveling upstate or to other parts of the country on the jobs. The men he worked for were genuinely bad characters, much more dangerous than any of the old-time gangsters. Lucky Luciano and Frank Costello, for example, never had the balls of a John Gotti. Carlo Gambino and Albert Anastasia were diplomats with soft hands. The press dubbed Anastasia "Lord High Executioner," but the real tough guys were his hit men. Even Al Capone turned to mush in jail. I can't conceive of that happening to Gotti, Junior Persico, or Joe Sullivan. Mad Dog was a go-until-you're-dead street fighter whose favorite winning tactic was eye plucking. Quick as lightning, he could thrust his thumb deep into one inside corner of his opponent's eye, hook it slightly, and pop the eyeball out of socket. It's an aggression-stopper, taking *no* strength to execute; I think the technique should be taught in women's self-defense classes.

The modern gangsters who employed us were tougher than their predecessors. And much smarter—they had to be to outwit the cops. Meyer Lansky, "The Genius" of organized crime finance, wouldn't have lasted two weeks against the surveillance pressure, wiretaps, RICO statutes, computers, and the army of rats that bedevil godfathers today.

Regardless, the godfathers we knew also went down, and so did Joe and I. Now he has a lifetime to regret not going to Ireland, just as I regret not heading for Greece when I had the chance.

As mentioned, prison authorities viewed me as a menace, and I suppose I was, but the dangers to me were also very great. By any reckoning, I faced very long odds against surviving for twenty-five years on the inside. The state prisons were filling up fast with extraordinarily violent drug dealers—Latin Americans, Asians, young blacks with no respect for anything—and other punks who would gladly stick a shiv into a tough guy like me just so they could say they'd done it. This "new breed" of inmate featured a *non*functional brain fried by dope, an inability to read or write, and no fear whatsoever: with nothing to live for, why should he worry about dying?

In 1984 I was taken to MCC in Manhattan to give a deposition on our civil lawsuit. My cell partner at MCC was Junior Persico, boss of the Colombo family, a man I never saw smile. Persico had a paralyzed arm—the result of an attack by Larry Gallo—and a warrior's courage. He had taken over the reins of the Colombo family from Joseph Colombo himself, who was killed on June 28, 1971, at that Italian-American Unity Day rally in Columbus Circle by that black hit man working for Joey Gallo.

The Colombo family Persico headed dealt in hijacking, shylocking, cocaine, numbers, and extortion—a great deal of extortion. And the family dealt in murder. When Junior Persico marked someone to die, it happened—often from the Mafia don personally pulling the trigger. He would kill in a heartbeat, and didn't need a great deal of provocation.

Junior Persico controlled numerous nightclubs, some of which he shared with Fat Tony Salerno of the Genovese family. Members of the organization tended to be young, inexperienced, and trigger-happy, but their lack of sophistication was compensated for with boldness.

Junior Persico didn't rank as the only celebrity at MCC. There were a number of big-time Mafiosi, a gaggle of politicians, even a Soviet spy.

Everybody on our floor, believing the place was bugged, conversed in sign language. This was awkward, however, and code words were occasionally said aloud, or on some occasions people simply forgot and spoke.

I was popular among the Mafiosi who admired killers and thought it admirable that during a period when rats proliferated, I merely swallowed a twenty-five-year minimum. Sometimes I let myself feel pretty good about it, too, especially when someone like Junior Persico indicated approval. After all these years, I still craved acceptance.

It was in our cell that I first met Albanian drug lord Xhevedet

(Joe) Lika, known as the "three-legged man" because of his long cock, which he displayed proudly. He spent a lot of time strutting around naked, even played cards in the nude. Lika, 5'7", had an elongated torso, short stubby bow legs, and very white skin. He didn't like Italians, and they left him alone because he was so violent. Like Japanese kamikazes, his drugged-up suicide hitters would go after John Gotti, Paul Castellano, or even President Reagan, if Lika gave the word. There was no way to stop people like that, and Mafiosi knew it.

A few days after Junior Persico introduced us, Lika visited our cell while Persico was away. Usually he preferred speaking to me in Greek, but this day he talked in English, using a lot of "motherfuckers."

"You know motherfucking Mike Bici?" he asked.

"Yeah," I said. "He's at Auburn."

"The motherfucker. You hit that motherfucker for me? I pay you twenty thousand dollars."

Mike Bici was slated as the star witness in Lika's upcoming drug trial. Since I'd be returning to Auburn after my civil deposition, Lika figured I was his man. In need of more money for lawyers handling the appeal of my murder conviction (their meters never stopped running), I told him I'd try to take care of it.

But Lika wasn't finished. Two days later he called me into his cell and said, "I might want Bici's father killed."

"Why?"

"If you can't get that motherfuckin' Mike, then his father's gotta go. Can you help me with this?"

I said I could find someone.

"There's more," he said.

"Yeah?" Lika's mother? I wondered. This was a bloodthirsty little bastard.

He produced pictures of two men.

"This one, he's a motherfucking government lawyer. Alan Cohen. He thinks he can put me in jail and not pay. He dies for putting me in jail."

"How about the other guy?"

"Drug cop. Motherfucker arrested me. Broke into my home. He dies too."

"With the DEA?"

"That's it. D-whatthefuckyoucallit-EA."

It began to sink in. Lika wanted me to kill Mike Bici, and failing that, arrange a hit on Bici's father. He also wanted to whack an Assistant U.S. Attorney and the federal agent who busted him. I looked at the Albanian—he was buck naked—and saw a face twisted into hate.

"I hear you're good," Lika said. "Motherfuckers who work for me, they get caught. Then I get caught. You can help me, Greek?"

"Maybe. How much you willing to spend?"

"A half-million dollars. Something less, you understand, if your people can't get them and have to kill their wife and children instead."

And I believed him. One reason the Mafia gave Lika such a wide berth was because he would have an entire family blown away. He didn't give a shit about antiquated Cosa Nostra customs like "respect."

"Where did you get these pictures?" I asked, referring to the photos of Cohen and the DEA agent.

"Hey, there's nothing I can't get. They got shit about me, I got shit about them."

"Yeah," I said, neutrally.

"Who you gonna get?" he asked. "Joe Sullivan? He's your friend, I hear. I'd like that. The famous Joe Sullivan."

"Joe's in Comstock."

"Fat Tony Salerno?"

"I can't go to Fat Tony with shit like this."

Lika made me nervous. On what planet did he live? Everybody in organized crime knew Sully was locked away, and I suspected even schoolchildren understood that Fat Tony didn't hire himself out as a killer. I was talking with a loose cannon, nevertheless one offering half-a-million dollars. I didn't doubt he had the money, and twenty times that amount. Plus I had the perfect guy for him.

I called Jimmy Coonan. "Got something big for you," I said.

"The bigger the better," Coonan said.

"Come down to see me."

Coonan and his brother Jackie, each in a $1,500 suit, showed up in the visitor's room two days later. Coincidentally, Joe Lika was also in the big enclosure, talking with his wife and three kids.

"How's my man?" Coonan asked.

"I'm not doin' too good," I said, which elicited an inappropriate Richard Widmark cackle from him.

"What you got?" he asked, after palming several hundred-dollar bills into my hand.

I palmed them back. "These are too big for in here," I said. "Try to break 'em down next time you visit. Tens and twenties."

I told Coonan the deal: $300,000 for Cohen; $150,000 for the DEA agent; and $50,000 for Bici's old man, if I failed to take out his son Mike.

"The guy's crazy," Coonan said. "All them fuckin' Albanians are crazy."

"Yeah," I agreed.

Coonan sat thinking. His brother Jackie didn't say a word. I knew Coonan would go for it. Unlike Fat Tony, killing *was* a major part of his business.

"Tell him it's a deal," the Westies boss told me.

"Right," I said. "Take his money, do the job, and haul ass."

"It shouldn't be much of a problem," Coonan decided. He also decided he wanted $200,000 in advance.

"I don't see why not," I said.

Coonan got up to leave, and for just a moment he locked eyes with Joe Lika, who had been paying more attention to our conversation than to whatever his wife had been saying. Coonan gave him an almost imperceptible nod: it was a go.

Well, not quite. When Lika cornered me after the visits were over, he agreed to pay *$100,000* in front, more after the first killing took place. "Coonan won't turn down a hundred grand, right?" he said.

Wrong. Coonan got pissed off and threatened to forget the deal. He was a rich guy at this time, doing a lot of killing for the

Gambinos, and had established a solid friendship with John Gotti, heir apparent to Paul Castellano. "I don't need this shit," Coonan said to me. "Tell that crazy Albanian it's two hundred thousand or I'm out."

Lika said to offer him $150,000.

I did.

Coonan held out for $200,000.

Lika wanted the job done. "I *will* go that high," he said, "but try to get it for a little less."

Jesus Christ. Here I was relaying offers and counteroffers to my friend Jimmy Coonan from Joe Lika, a guy I didn't even like who expected me to negotiate *him* a better deal. *What the fuck are you doing, Greek?* I asked myself.

The question made me think about a lot of things. The simmering anger I felt about that twenty-five-to-life. Now I played messenger boy for Lika and Jimmy Coonan, and Lika hadn't offered me a dime over and above the $20,000 for Mike Bici, though I knew Coonan would cut up his share.

A dozen rationalizations flooded my mind, reinforcing, I suppose, an idea I had suppressed ever since the murder conviction: that I ought to start looking out for my own best interests, which didn't include a possible accessory-to-murder charge in the killings, for Christ's sake, of *federal government employees.*

I hated the idea of being a rat. I know everybody says that, but I believe my entire life points to this truth: the main satisfaction I obtained as a criminal came from being acknowledged as a tough guy, a hitter, an individual who knew the consequences and accepted them. Most important, the only friends I had were criminals; I wasn't comfortable with anyone else (I remembered the misery of my two tries at honest employment, pumping gas and selling pretzels), and if I went to the cops I'd become a pariah.

The thought wouldn't leave my head, though I tried to banish it, order it to go away. It made my stomach churn, and I cursed myself repeatedly, calling myself every name in the book. I became physically sick, retching in the toilet bowl, but the thought wouldn't go away. Hell, it won't hurt to think about it, I kidded myself, me who wouldn't rat on even a hated guard or some big son-of-a-bitch who was hurting young kids.

Maybe it could be done without anyone knowing, I began to think. A one-shot deal. No one would be hurt. Surely the Lika-Coonan information I possessed would register as a blockbuster with the feds, and I figured they likely would give me a quid pro quo, something for something. Specifically: reducing that fucking twenty-five-year sentence to fifteen, so maybe there'd be a few years left when I got out.

I honed the plan in my mind, waffling this way and that. I came up with a way to do it where nobody would suffer, but still I hesitated because *I* would know I'd been a rat.

What tipped me over the edge was a hack's joking aside that prisoners should watch what they said, "the walls have ears." I fantasized that listeners already knew the multiple murder plan, and I stood right in the middle of it. I convinced myself I could save everyone a lot of headaches, actually do them a favor, and help myself besides. I know now I was rationalizing, though some of it worked out pretty much as I planned.

A few days later I whispered in a guard's ear, "I want to talk to the U.S. Attorney."

Instead, when called out of my cell, I met Jim Nauwens, a criminal investigator for the U.S. Attorney, Southern District. We talked in his office, right next to MCC, in a building teeming with federal prosecutors.

Chapter 21

THE GREEK TURNS RAT

"I'VE GOT INFORMATION YOU'LL WANT," I SAID, NEVER BEING one to dance around the point. Still, I didn't like being here. No matter how I justified it to myself, it felt wrong.

"What is it?" Nauwens countered, also wasting no time. His manner was friendly enough, but he knew we came from opposite sides of the law. Both of us were wary.

I told him about my sentence. Obtain fifteen-to-life for me, I said, and I'll make you a hero for saving some important lives.

"I have to know what you've got."

The 5'10", soft-spoken, blond-haired Nauwens mimicked a New York wiseguy accent beautifully, and I judged him a straight shooter, a first impression that has been confirmed many times. I didn't kid myself that he was in my corner, but unlike other government men I later encountered, he never raised hopes only to shatter them after he got what he wanted. During this initial conference I believed him when he said he couldn't even suggest a deal to his superiors until he learned what I had to say.

I ran down the whole story about the contracts on Bici, Bici's father, Cohen, and the DEA agent. Nauwens took notes and asked questions, maintaining a poker face, but I knew the information rated top of the line.

"How about that fifteen-to-life?" I asked.

"What you've said needs to check out."

"I know that. It will. But no matter what you decide, *I'm not testifying against nobody*. I've given you the details you need to save some lives, but I'm not going further."

"Let me look into this," he said.

"Yeah. But do it carefully. I'm dead if word gets back to the inside."

Nauwens and others conducted their own discreet investigation and confirmed what I had told them.

A week later I found myself back in the investigator's office. I was asked whether I would be willing to enter the Federal Witness Protection Program.

"I don't think I'm interested," I replied. They'd want everything if I joined the Witness Protection Program, and I couldn't do that to the only friends I had.

I wanted to make *my own life better.* The feds hadn't given me anything yet, and I wondered if I'd made a mistake spilling my guts about Lika. I should have gotten something *before* telling them what I knew. I'd been a sucker, and now they ached for more. This crowd of investigators and prosecutors had a pretty good idea of the detailed, comprehensive information I could provide (twenty-five years doing business with godfathers and wiseguys, hearing their most intimate secrets). They didn't say it, but I don't think they ever intended to make a deal, even if I gave up everything.

The government wasted no time squashing Lika's murder plot. While elaborate precautions were taken to protect Cohen and the DEA agent, investigators made it clear—face-to-face—with Lika that they knew of his plans, and he'd be the sorriest son of a bitch in the world if they weren't dropped (it's hard to see how it could have been worse for him than it turned out: upon conviction for the drug charges, he was sent to Marion Prison, a horrible place, probably for the rest of his life.)

Federal agents began tracking Jimmy Coonan's every movement. He soon figured out what this meant, and although he had already abandoned the idea of whacking Cohen and the DEA agent, the pressure amounted to insurance against the deed ever being committed.

No one in MCC suspected I had provided the information that short-circuited the conspiracy. Lika and Coonan thought the feds had discerned the plot from tape recordings, which made sense: they weren't being prosecuted, so how could there be a live witness? It wasn't for lack of prosecutorial zeal that Coonan and Lika avoided finding themselves in the dock. Right from the start I was asked to wear a wire, record the whole story on tape. I refused.

So—no one had been hurt, though my position hadn't been improved a whit. It was worse, in fact. I knew I'd betrayed one of the few tenets sacred to me.

My civil deposition on the beatings in Westchester finally completed (Kersch and I ultimately received $180,000 in damages), I was returned to Auburn, where I became the rope in a tug-of-war between two powerful forces, the Mafia and the government. Although their goals were different—the former wanted my silence, the latter wanted to hear me sing—each employed a carrot approach. John Gotti, Junior Persico, Fat Tony Salerno, and John Sullivan all sent their regards, and promises of any assistance needed. The FBI stayed in touch, an agent several times dropping the word "protection."

It made me think. Did I need to be protected? Maybe yes. Might not some of the people who had hired me in the past decide that a dead Greek would put an end to their worries? I was no longer of use to them, and I knew scores of their secrets.

Correction officials transferred me to Comstock Prison in 1985 for what turned out to be a (probably) last reunion with Joe Sullivan. Locked near us was a heavyset punk—Joe called him a "garbage can"—named David Berkowitz, known to the world as Son of Sam.

"You're not too very well liked," I said to Berkowitz the first time I saw him. "Why did you shoot all those young girls?"

He was afraid, and should have been. "What can I say?" he answered. "That was my life."

I turned out to be wrong about his not being well liked. *Every* visiting day I saw women lined up to see him. Many of them had come to propose marriage.

Two events occurred in December that flopped me into the government camp: the murder of Gambino family godfather Paul Castellano, and a message I received from Gotti drug dealer Oreste "Ernie Boy" Abbamonte.

The powerful Castellano was gunned down, along with his underboss Tom Bilotti, on December 16, 1985, in front of Sparks Steak House on East 46th Street in Manhattan. I never doubted Gotti was behind the killing (he immediately became the new godfather), and I later learned from fellow rats I locked with that one of the shooters was John's brother Gene. Serving as a lookout was none other than Jimmy Coonan.

Now Gotti had even more to lose if I sang to the feds, but he was too smart to authorize what Ernie Boy Abbamonte did: send a message that said, "There's not a rock big enough for a rat like you to hide under."

No, John didn't approve that warning. I knew him too well to believe he'd alert his quarry. We had become friends at Dannemora, I'd met him three and four times a week during my brief 1981 flirtation with freedom, and he'd stayed in touch ever since. Ernie Boy acted on his own—maybe he had his reasons for hating me, though I never figured them out.

It took no genius to figure out *Gotti's* motives. I had been referred to as a "rat," and this meant the new godfather had learned about my role in the Lika case. Where could this information have come from except a source within the U.S. Attorney's office? Perhaps a Mafia mole? Or maybe some office flunkie not satisfied with the government pay scale? The feds have their own rats.

Rage at Gotti overwhelmed every other consideration. The

treacherous son of a bitch wanted me whacked. Well, maybe I'd be the one who did the burying.

I acted in unthinking haste, enraged that John Gotti had ordered my death. Well, I was no Willie Boy Johnson, willing to wait meekly for the assassins to show.

I called Jim Nauwens and said, "I want to talk to you."

"About the Program?" he asked.

"Yeah."

"You're gonna have to tell us everything."

"Yeah."

I had time for a talk with Sully. I told him straight away what I intended to do, believed he might kill me, and steeled myself not to offer a defense. Instead he waxed philosophical, talking about how remarkable it was that we had survived so long amid so much violence.

"I'll miss you, Greek," he said, "but I can't be seen with you no more, you understand."

I did understand. He couldn't hang around with a rat. He couldn't have anything to do with me again.

The feds transferred me to the Goshen, New York, County Jail, where a U.S. Attorney arranged for a polygraph test, which of course I passed. There were more debriefings by FBI agents and criminal investigators before I got sent back to MCC for the real show.

I mentioned earlier that I may hold the record for the number of prisons where I've been incarcerated. Herewith, starting with my arrest for the Clarence Jones murder, is the list: Westchester County Jail; Attica; Westchester County Jail (again); Attica (again); Auburn; MCC; Auburn; Comstock; Goshen County Jail; MCC; Otisville; MCC; Otisville; Attica; Oxford, Wisconsin; Springfield, Missouri; Washington, D.C.; La Tuna, Texas; El Reno, Oklahoma; Sandstone, Minnesota; Phoenix, Arizona; Attica; Maine State Prison; MCC; Ogden, Utah; San Diego, California; Texarkana, Texas; and, currently, Attica.

At MCC, where I passed another lie-detector test and was officially admitted into the Federal Witness Protection Program, they kept me in a special section reserved for rats. Ten and twelve hours a day, five days a week (and often on weekends), I sat in one or another U.S. Attorney's office and answered a barrage of questions. It was mass confusion. The feds talked to me, but so did state, county, and city investigators.

A detective might be allowed in to ask one question: "What happened to Tommy Trash?"

Boom! I'd tell him, and he'd hurry out to a library, morgue, or burial ground.

There were always guys coming and going, asking their questions, then jumping up to leave and check out my answers. They indicated I had a sort of blanket immunity, but I was so caught up in the celebrity that the exact details were never clear to me. I told them about murder after murder, my own and those of others, and whenever I gave them the location of bodies, they found them.

I was taken out to decent restaurants every day, for breakfast and lunch, and pizza was brought in at night. This was part of a keep-him-happy, keep-him-talking drill, but also part of the protection. Inmate cooks knew where their food went and liked nothing better than pissing in, or poisoning, the meals they sent to canaries.

Mickey Featherstone, one of the leaders of the Westies with Jimmy Coonan, was brought to the MCC tier housing the snitches and promptly began ratting on the rats. Fortunately, I knew not to trust him. He had gone around saying he was a Vietnam war hero, when in reality he had seen no action at all. Nevertheless, he had for years played the crazy on the streets of Hell's Kitchen and many people genuinely feared his little ferret face.

I wasn't one of them. During a 1970s fight in the Tombs with a gang of black guys, he'd deserted my crew and run to his cell. "Why the fuck did you disappear?" I asked him. But he was trembling so pitifully I just walked away. I knew all I had to know about Mickey Featherstone.

At this time he was ratting to the FBI about his boss Jimmy Coonan, and I later learned Coonan had reached out through the prisoner network for Joe Sullivan to arrange for Featherstone to be whacked. Joe agreed to try, and not just to help out his buddy Coonan. Sully feared the number of murders Featherstone could lay in his lap, and he also worried about Coonan turning snitch. That would be a disaster. Coonan could tie Sully to the Hoffa case—only Joe and I knew where the body was buried, and he didn't figure his best friend would talk.

Sully need not have worried about Coonan. Just as John Gotti wanted me whacked, Coonan yearned only for Featherstone's death, and although Mad Dog tried, his heart wasn't in it 100 percent. As an alternative to the role of snitch, he was planning an escape.

Still, he made an effort. But the feds had Featherstone tucked away, and Mad Dog, despite all his ingenuity and prison contacts, couldn't get the job done.

Featherstone fell for one of the oldest prison tricks, and that's how I learned he was ratting. When he'd ask about some people I knew, I'd lie to him, and sure enough a couple days later an investigator would say, "We know you're holding out on us, Frankos. What about this guy who killed Louie the Louse?"

"I'm telling you the fucking truth," I'd flare, "and I don't like your using that rat Featherstone to try to trip me up."

A few times, when my information wasn't *quite* sufficient to secure an indictment, an investigator would say, "Couldn't you be mistaken? Maybe what you witnessed happened this way," a way that would guarantee an indictment.

I always responded as follows: "I'm a rat, but I'm not going to be a *lying* rat."

After a few weeks the pats on the back began to lose their effect, and I started to ask what *they* were going to give *me*. "We're working on it," was the standard reply. "Right now we're more concerned with your safety."

I pointed out that I could be safe somewhere besides prison.

I know now it was all bullshit. The "protection" they intended was keeping me in prison, safe from other inmates. *But they never said this.* They let me *think* I might be released onto the street, as they'd done with Jimmy "the Weasel" Frattiano.

After seven months of intensive questioning, I was sent to Otisville. Now the "debriefings" centered on my upcoming grand-jury testimony. "When are you going to talk sentence reduction?" I asked, but it was always too early.

I appeared in front of a Manhattan grand jury for fourteen hours over a two-day period, telling the panel about Rocky Moro. They were particularly interested in how he shot that derelict for no reason in the early 1960s, and his involvement in the murders of Dominick LaMonica and Patsy Russo in the Worth Street warehouse.

Moro got indicted.

Next I testified for eight hours against John Gotti, Ernie Boy Abbamonte, Funzi Sisca, Arnold Squitieri, and Angelo Ruggiero. During this intensive session the grand jury wanted to know about Gambino drug operations, and I told them.

Gotti, Abbamonte, Sisca, Squitieri, and Ruggiero were indicted.

"What am I going to get in return?" I asked, but my handlers stalled for more time. There were scores of other criminals I could help them indict, and dozens of trials where they needed my testimony. "You can be bigger than Valachi," one investigator told me, but I wasn't interested in that shit. Guilt feelings assailed me. Thinking about what I was doing made me throw up, and nightmares—which I'd seldom had before—jarred me awake in the middle of the night.

There were screaming matches, and I finally shouted "Fuck you! I ain't testifying no more!" I said they could go after Moro, Gotti, and the others without my help.

Cooler heads tried to prevail, but they had nothing to offer me except "We're working to get you something." That wasn't enough. I said I wanted out of the Witness Protection Program and, after a great deal more haggling, they granted my wish. More accurately, they granted me a death sentence, and I knew it.

I got placed in the *general population* at Attica, and it didn't take long for a bunch of inmates to try to kill me. I was walking toward my cell in F Block when I sensed movement behind me: five guys, ten yards back, matching me step for step. Out of a cell up ahead appeared five more, who waited for me to come to them.

I did. Steadily advancing toward the cluster of tough punks less than half my age, refusing to alter my lifelong habits, I resorted to the pep talk: *Do the right thing by yourself, Greek. Fight the motherfuckers till you're dead. Go out like a man.*

"Fucking rat snitch!" one of them yelled, and cracked me with his pipe, literally caving in the left side of my face. I tried to swing at him, but they were on me front and back. Another punk laid his pipe across my nose, splitting it to the bone. A third club caught me on the right eye. I went down, my attackers on top of me, and one of them stuck a knife in my back. Each of them wanted a piece of the action, and the scene resembled a gigantic football pileup with both teams going for the fumble. The toughs were hitting one another in their zeal to pound me, and I was able to slither out from under them and launch a staggering run toward a group of guards sipping coffee at the end of the block. When I got there and collapsed at the guards' feet, one of them asked, "What happened to you?"

"You know what happened, you piece of shit," I gurgled through the blood in my throat.

"Oh. We got a tough guy here."

They took me to the prison hospital, where I was diagnosed too seriously injured to treat. Subsequently two hacks drove me the thirty-five or so miles to Buffalo Memorial Hospital.

The pain was terrific. My face had twisted into four separate parts, including the caved-in left side and a grapefruit-sized protuberance on the right. I had knots on the top of my head and a broken jaw. Making matters much worse was the conversation I had to listen to, between the hacks and an admissions nurse who didn't want to take me. As I slipped in and out of consciousness, I heard her complain about a lack of security, fear of someone finishing me off, and the danger of a lawsuit. "Drive him somewhere else," she said.

The hacks won, and a guard was posted outside my door until a week later when the FBI showed up.

But I still wouldn't testify. Not until the feds gave me something. What kind of fool would offer them everything (including in my case, his soul) and receive nothing in return? On the other hand, maybe they couldn't relent and offer a deal to such as me.

It's been this way for almost five years. Impasse. Occasionally someone comes by, in search of a lead into this or that crime, and I might assist, depending on my mood.

I reentered the Witness Protection Program, at the government's insistence, several months after my near-fatal beating at Attica, but I have refused to testify. I've had it with helping them. They move me often—"for your own protection"—and some prisons are better than others, but where I dream of being—on the outside, Greece, maybe—is perhaps forever out of reach.

Epilogue

A LETTER FROM MAD DOG

ON OCTOBER 10, 1990, MY MOTION FOR A NEW TRIAL IN THE Clarence Jones murder case was turned down. Westchester County Court Judge Anthony Scarpino, Jr., ruled that the beating I'd received in Westchester County Jail hadn't interfered with my ability to assist my defense counsel. Ironically, at the same time this ruling came down, a judge in another part of the country, in a case similar to mine, decided that the defendant *was* entitled to a new trial. The American court system is a crapshoot, and my last roll turned up snake eyes.

My lawyer at the time was the highly regarded Joel Aurnou (he represented Jean Harris in the Dr. Herman Tarnower killing). We did not have my case reviewed in the federal courts, which would have been a slow and expensive process. The money awarded me for those beatings in Westchester, and the considerable cache I'd accumulated before the Jones conviction, was all gone, mostly into the pockets of a variety of lawyers.

Around Christmas, 1990, I received a letter from Joe Sullivan, in answer to one that I'd written. Sully, using the lower-case "i," as many prisoners do, wrote from a prison cell in Fallsburg, New

York, saying that he couldn't feel anger or hatred for me because he loved me like a brother. Even though he said he understood my anger and disgust—it cost me to turn on our world and rat.

What this book is all about, I think, is relating a remarkable true story, certain to die with me if I don't tell it. The letter from Joe meant a lot to me. I'd wondered how he felt about my discussing his role in the Hoffa case, and hoped he knew they couldn't trace it to him—unless I testify, and I'd rather fade out like Willie Boy Johnson than do anything to hurt Joe.

In January 1991, I flew from San Diego to New York to testify for a friend of mine, Frank Sacco, who was on trial for murder. I knew this action wouldn't endear me to the government, which wanted me on the prosecution's side—not the defense—in criminal litigation. The fact that Sacco got convicted (he received twenty-five-to-life), despite being represented by F. Lee Bailey, didn't lessen the anger of the feds.

While awaiting my court appearance in the Sacco trial, I was lodged on the ninth floor of MCC, only a few cells away from John Gotti and his underboss, Salvatore (Sammy Bull) Gravano. Gravano, of course, would later provide the critical testimony that resulted in Gotti's conviction.

I didn't know Gotti was so near, but *he* knew I was there. He stood in front of my locked cell and stared at me, and at first I didn't recognize him. We hadn't seen each other since 1981.

"Tony the Greek," he said.

Recognition dawned. He seemed so different from the wiseguy I'd known. I remembered a backslapping, throw-his-arms-around-you hoodlum with an enormous ego and belief in himself. The godfather I now faced had aged and matured.

"I can't believe," Gotti said, "you turned and went to the feds." The younger Gotti's voice would have been loud, abusive, but *this* Gotti sounded almost hurt. "Everybody had the greatest respect for you, Greek, and look what you did to yourself. Look what *they* done to you. Them scumbags don't give a shit if you live or die. All they care about is what you can do for them, and when they're finished with you and the love affair is over, they send you to get killed."

A dozen thoughts raced through my mind, things I wanted to say to him, but there was no need. He was a criminal talking to another criminal, and he understood me very well.

"I know right now," he said, "I'm very embarrassed for you. I know you are going through hell right now, and you don't have to explain why you left me. I don't want to drive a nail in you while you're here, so nobody here will fuck with you. I give you my word."

I could tell he was almost finished. "You know the rules, Greek. Don't ever come back to this life. You know the rules."

Then he was gone. He'd said it twice, "you know the rules," and, I thought, yeah, I know them, and I knew, also, how much he'd gotten to me. The "rules" meant that the only friends I'd ever made were lost to me, and that my life would always be fair game.

After my testimony on Frank Sacco's behalf, I was returned to the federal prison in Texarkana, Texas, where I remained until March 2, 1992. Then the government decided it was time for me to move again. Possibilities mentioned were Florida, Minnesota, California, Utah, Wisconsin, Maine, New Jersey, Arizona, New York, and Michigan.

Michigan? Jesus Christ, I told my counselor, I wouldn't last one minute in Michigan, the home of Tony Jack and Jimmy Hoffa. I was so angry that they'd even consider sending me to Michigan that I forgot to say anything about New York, where the prisons are packed with inmates who would love to make a name for themselves with the Gambinos.

So in March 1992, I was sent to Attica and put in solitary confinement, where I remain as I write this in April. It's a miserable fucking environment. In the cell on one side of me is a guy dying painfully from AIDS. On the other side is a psycho whose only entertainment is throwing his feces at the guards. If they release me into the general population, however, my life expectancy could probably be tabulated in seconds.

Finally, this: just before I left Texarkana, my counselor did some computing and determined, as I had before, that I'd been in more prisons than any other American.

"What a beautiful fucking honor," I told him, "and thank you very much."

INDEX